The Lost Civilization Enigma

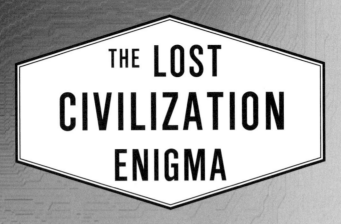

THE LOST CIVILIZATION ENIGMA

A New Inquiry Into the Existence of Ancient Cities, Cultures, and Peoples Who Pre-Date Recorded History

PHILIP COPPENS

best-selling author of
The Ancient Alien Question

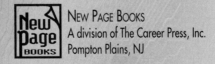

New Page Books
A division of The Career Press, Inc.
Pompton Plains, NJ

THE LOST CIVILIZATION ENIGMA
EDITED BY JODI BRANDON
TYPESET BY EILEEN MUNSON
Cover design by Howard Grossman/12E Design
Printed in the U.S.A.

To order this title, please call toll-free 1-800-CAREER-1 (NJ and Canada: 201-848-0310) to order using VISA or MasterCard, or for further information on books from Career Press.

The Career Press, Inc.
220 West Parkway, Unit 12
Pompton Plains, NJ 07444
www.careerpress.com
www.newpagebooks.com

Library of Congress Cataloging-in-Publication Data

Coppens, Philip.
        The lost civilization enigma : a new inquiry into the existence of ancient cities, cultures, and peoples who pre-date recorded history / by Philip Coppens.
                p. cm.
        Includes bibliographical references (p.   ) and index.
        ISBN 978-1-60163-232-6 -- ISBN 978-1-60163-582-2 (ebook) 1. Lost continents. 2. Geographical myths. 3. Civilization, Ancient. I. Title.
        GN751.C66 2013
        001.94--dc23
                                2012023292

Acknowledgments

When I was 10 years old, my history professor told us to do a small project on an Egyptian monument of our choice. I chose the Great Pyramid. I do not remember the grade I got—though it was good. I enjoyed Egypt so much that, for my own entertainment, I made the same report on the other two pyramids of the Giza Plateau. More than a decade later, I was asked to promote Marcel Mestdagh's studies on the Megalithic Civilization and make it available to a foreign—that is, non-Dutch—audience. I don't know when this seed was planted, but it was growing by the age of 10 and, in 1994, had reached maturity. Ever since, I have walked this path with the help of others, whom I have to thank.

Early on, in Belgium, the likes of Patrick Bernauw and especially Arnold Eloy were instrumental on my voyage of discovery. Since 1995, I have been helped by Herman Hegge, when together we created Frontier Sciences Foundation.

In my circle of friends, I would like to specifically thank: Theresa Byrne; Mary Parent; Patrick Ruffino; Paige Tucker; Jason Gossman; Sarah Symons; Marc Borms; Chris Norman; Duncan Roads; Cris Winter; Gerard Lohan; Eileen, Cathy, and Janeth Hall; Debbie Nicastro; Dawn Molkenbur; Stan Zaidinski; Fausto Callegarini; Tobi and Gerda Dobler; Marianne Wilson; Cynthia James and Carl Studna;

JoAnn Parks and MAX; Peter van Deursen and Anneke Koremans; Isobel Denham; Duncan and Linda Lunan; Laura Marini; Kelly Cole; Wendy Vincent and Peter Shoesmith; and Susan Marek. Apart from being the best friends anyone could desire, you make life beautiful. By default, I will have forgotten some, and I sincerely apologize for that!

I thank the research and devotion of the following authors and often friends: Robert Bauval; Graham Hancock; Greg Taylor; Wim Zitman and Hendrine; Hugh Newman; Sam Osmanagic and Sabina; Florence and Kenneth Wood; Robert and Olivia Temple; Howard Crowhurst; Hugh Newman; Andy Collins; David Hatcher Childress and Jennifer; Michael Cremo; Gary Evans; Ralph Ellis; John Ritchie; Gavin Menziens; Alice Gerard; and Marcus Allen.

This book would not have come about without the vision of Michael Pye at New Page Books. You and the team at New Page do formidable work, mostly behind the scenes, in delivering new and exciting information to the world.

I would like to thank the thousands of Facebook friends and followers, who allow me to have a great virtual banter on a daily basis! I would like to thank Nespresso, for allowing me to make delightful coffee in the morning, which is a true miracle when writing.

Each and every member of the Coppens, Sonck, Harkey, and Smith family, though I need to specifically mention my parents, my brother, Tom, and his wife, Kathleen, and my nephews, Daan and Arne, Papa and Mama, as well as Patrick, Conor, and Shane.

Finally, I thank Kathleen. Without her, I am no one. With her, I can do everything. A few weeks ago, we created a special drink—blanquette, a type of sparkling wine from the South of France, to which we added a caramel liqueur—and now, I toast this very drink to you, celebrating the completion of this book. Semper.

North Berwick,
April 12, 2012

Contents

Introduction

s history as the history books teach us? Or is civilization—when humanity began to cultivate plants, work metals, build monuments, and live in organized settlements—far more complex and older than we assume? As a 10-year-old child in school, my teacher taught that Greece was the cradle of civilization, even though in 1981, it was obvious that this was no longer the case: Egypt and Sumer were known to be far older civilizations, but somehow the textbooks used in Belgian schools had not caught up with "facts."

Thirty years later, the situation has somewhat changed, but the criticism leveled at "textbook historians" remains: There reigns a paradigm that even though we no longer believe that God created the world in 4004 BC, we still assume that civilization could not possibly have existed previously. Before 4000 BC, it is widely assumed, our ancestors were pretty much savages. That is simply not the case.

The latest archaeological findings have pushed the boundaries of civilization much further back, to 10,000 BC, with sites such as Jericho and, most recently, Göbekli Tepe in Turkey. The existence of Jericho and Çatal Höyük has been known for decades, and has been dated to 8,000 BC, but I challenge you to open your child's schoolbooks, or any popular book on archaeology, and find a reference to these cities in there. The few archaeological publications that do, treat these sites as stand-alone pockets of civilization, even though they are all situated within hundreds of miles of each other. The obvious answer seems to be that they were part of one culture, but no such argument is explored by scientists.

When it comes to truly "lost" civilizations, such as the lost civilization of Atlantis, historians even ridicule anyone considering making a scientific study of it. They argue that Plato created an idealized society, rather than report a historical account, for the historians "know" there was no such civilization in existence in 10,000 BC. It simply cannot be. What they fail to report is that Plato wrote about Atlantis in a book solely devoted to history, and that when skeptics in his own time went to Egypt to discredit him, they instead returned with verification that Egyptian columns indeed contained the story of Atlantis, as Plato had reported. It shows, at the very least, that the ancient Egyptians believed in a lost civilization of Atlantis. In short, it shows that the theory cherished by historians is simply wrong.

There is even evidence that signs of civilization—tools, objects, and legends—are tens of thousands—even millions—of years old. American author Michael Cremo cataloged hundreds of examples in a book he titled *Forbidden Archaeology*; it was his conclusion that such objects were deemed to be a "no go" zone by archaeologists, as it would upset everything we have assumed to be true about our history. But that legends were factual was proven in the 19th century, when Heinrich Schliemann showed that Troy was not just a fable invented by the ancient Greeks, but a veritable city. The myths had proven to be true!

In fact, there is good evidence that many of the reports of lost civilizations have always had a foundation in truth and reality. For many centuries, chroniclers doubted the existence of civilizations in the depths of the Amazon Rainforest. But today, Science is admitting its errors and acknowledges satellite imagery has revealed the traces of this lost civilization. Other claims of lost civilizations, such as Mu, remain outside of the reach of both archaeologists and explorers, but that doesn't mean they didn't exist! As the saying goes: The absence of available evidence doesn't mean it is evidence of its absence!

Apart from slowly rediscovering lost civilizations, new dimensions of known civilizations are discovered on an almost daily basis. Yet each time the boundaries of civilization are pushed back or expanded, the messengers of this new information are attacked. When the enigmatic Antikythera device was discovered off the coasts of Greece in 1900, it took many decades before it was recognized as an astronomical clock—a device that was able to graphically show the position of the sun, moon, planets, and certain stars. Dating to Ancient Greece, it is now heralded as the world's first computer, but most of the research into the device has been done by "rebel" archaeologists, who were often ferociously attacked by their colleagues for even considering this might be what it eventually turned out to be.

Most recently, this antagonism to expanding the scope of ancient civilizations has been most apparent in the controversy surrounding the so-called Bosnian Pyramids. The pyramid complex outside the town of Visoko, near the Bosnian capital of Sarajevo, would "merely" show that a civilization known as Old Europe, which blossomed between c. 5500 and 3000 BC, built pyramids. As Old Europe was in any other way on par with the Sumerian and Egyptian civilizations, why it would therefore not be able to build pyramids, is strange. But since the discovery of these pyramids in 2005, Science ferociously tries to maintain the existing paradigm, even threatening archaeologists not to partake in the excavations (otherwise they will never work at other archaeological sites ever again!). The historical time line, it seems, cannot be answered; historians seem to cherish the dawn date of 4000 BC far dearer than the Church ever did!

There is also evidence that at least in Bronze Age Europe (c. 3000 BC) there was contact between America and Europe. Whereas we like to believe that it took the dawn of the 21st century for the first global civilization and economy, at least these two continents were very much working economically together 5,000 years ago.

Our ancestors knew more than we give them credit for, and the Antikythera device is but one example of this. Florence and Kenneth Wood have identified a secret code that resides within Homer's *Iliad* and *Odyssey*. The Greek myths contain detailed stellar information, showing that the story has a layer that conveys quite advanced astronomical knowledge, including an understanding of the precession of the equinoxes, a discovery Science is not willing to credit our ancestors with that far back. Most recently, analysis of the construction of Göbekli Tepe has shown that it incorporates astronomical concepts (for example, depictions of some constellations). This shows that our ancestors, 12,000 years ago, had already mapped the stars and were aware of at least the most basic concepts of astronomy—but likely much more. This latter conclusion can be reached when we realize that the cave paintings in Lascaux, France, date back 20,000 years and also incorporate astronomical knowledge. Lascaux is not a cave where our ancestors drew some scenes of their daily hunting lifestyle, but was a religious sanctuary, containing the sacred knowledge of our times. The cave paintings have survived, but every other aspect of this civilization has disappeared—become lost to us.

Our history is far more interesting, far older, and more impressive than the standard textbooks and history books present us. A Neolithic tomb at Buthiers-Boulancourt, near Paris, contains the body of a man whose arm had been surgically and expertly amputated—5,900 years ago. Known civilizations, such as the Greeks, had objects that were able to visualize the orbits of the sun, the moon, and the planets. Known archaeological discoveries, like Jericho and Göbekli Tepe, show civilization is many thousands of years older than first thought. Adding lost civilizations such as Atlantis to this new image, is merely another chapter in the story of civilization. In the New World, too, what the Spanish Conquistadors found is far more complex and far more developed than we give the early inhabitants of America credit for.

The resulting picture is that civilization as we know it is not 6,000 years old, but at least 12,000 years old, and that our ancestors, tens of thousands of years ago, were already crafting tools and objects. It is definitely obvious that our civilization is not the first! What was there before? What has been lost and is waiting to be rediscovered?

Chapter 1

THE NEW INQUISITION

Many of us live with the idea that Science is about expanding the horizons of our knowledge—boldly thinking where no one has thought before. However, in truth, that is rarely the case. There are very few Indiana Joneses out there. Science has expressed no interest at all in the Ark of the Covenant or crystal skulls, even though the first object was the center of the Jewish religion and the latter at the heart of the Mayan religion. Instead, scientists have labeled crystal skulls modern fabrications, while they show no interest at all in recovering lost objects like the Ark.

When it comes to lost civilizations, all the evidence shows that Science is dogmatic and is unwilling to even listen to the arguments presented in favor of their existence. Those who claim to have found evidence are accused of being "unscientific"—whether they are amateur or professional scientists—and are told the discovery simply cannot be, as Science "knows" it is impossible. These days, Science has no problem proclaiming they are all-knowing when it comes to these subjects.

In the 1999 BBC documentary *Atlantis Uncovered,* Dr. Kenneth L. Feder, a professor of archaeology at Central Connecticut State University, stated:

When we come to something like the lost continent of Atlantis we are better off knowing that civilizations developed more or less independently just so nobody can say some people are better than others, some are smarter than others because we know what happens down the line when we believe that, so I'm not going to tell you that belief in Atlantis is necessarily the first step towards genocide, or Holocaust, but what I'm telling you is we are on a very slippery slope if we believe in fantasies and that those fantasies lead us down to places we really don't want to go.

Feder, in essence, argues that discussions about Atlantis, as well as discussions that civilizations traded and helped each other in their development is a "very slippery slope" and a "fantasy," and though he tells us not to immediately draw a comparison with genocide, he does draw that comparison. Seriously, Dr. Feder?

Science, it seems, is always more about preserving the status quo of what we already know than truly about expanding our boundaries of knowledge. Indeed, the evidence shows that the halls of academia are very much like the New Inquisition. They have not yet burned people at the stake, but they have thrown people in jail and destroyed the careers of those who tried to challenge the scientific dogma. The "heretics" are especially those who have tried to argue the case for the existence of lost civilizations or accidentally stumbled upon evidence that would upset the reigning paradigm. Such accidents often have had disastrous results for the innocent parties involved.

Archaeological Trench Warfare

The excavations near the French village of Glozel, a hamlet located 10 miles from the French spa town of Vichy, are among the most controversial of archaeological endeavors ever recorded. These excavations lasted between 1924 and 1938, but the vast majority of finds—more than 3,000 artifacts—were unearthed in the first two years. The artifacts were variously dated to Neolithic, Iron Age, and medieval times. That in itself was not controversial. It is how one eventually arrived at these dates that reveals a saga of archaeological feuding and fraud versus truth.

Glozel has been described as the "Dreyfus affair" of French archaeology, and the Dreyfus equivalent was Emile Fradin, a 17-year-old who, together with his grandfather Claude Fradin, stepped into history on March 1, 1924. Working in a farming field known as Duranthon, Emile was holding the handles of a plow when one of the cows pulling it stuck its foot in a cavity. Freeing the cow, the Fradins uncovered a cavity containing human bones and ceramic fragments. So far, this could have been just any usual archaeological discovery, of which some are made every week. That soon changed.

It is said that the first to arrive the following day to see what the farmers had unearthed were the neighbors. They not only found but also took some of the objects. From there, the news spread around the village. That same month, Adrienne Picandet, a local teacher, visited the Fradins' farm and decided to inform the Minister of Education. On July 9, Benoit Clément, another teacher, this time from the neighboring village and representing La Société d'Emulation du Bourbonnais, visited the site and later returned with a man called Viple. Clément and Viple used pickaxes to break down the remaining walls, which they took away with them. Some weeks later, Emile Fradin received a letter from Viple, in which the latter identified the site as dating from Gallo-Roman times—first to fourth centuries AD. He added that he felt that the site was of little interest. His advice was to recommence cultivation of the field—which is precisely what the Fradin family did. This might, therefore, have been the end of the saga, but not so.

Farmer Emile Fradin made an accidental discovery when plowing his field in Glozel. The artifacts he found were deemed to rewrite history and became the center of an archaeological circus that would see fraud, libel, and arrests. Today, many archaeologists continue to proclaim Fradin faked the stones, whereas the find is not known to be genuine.

Image copyright Agence Meurisse. Made available as part of Creative Commons License on Wikimedia.

The January 1925 *Bulletin de la Société d'Emulation du Bourbonnais* reported on the findings. It brought the story to the attention of Antonin Morlet, a Vichy physician and amateur archaeologist. Morlet visited Clément and was intrigued by the findings. Morlet was an "amateur specialist" in the Gallo-Roman period and believed that the objects from Glozel were older. He thought that some might even date from the Magdalenian period (12,000–9500 BC), which would make them extraordinarily old and one of the most important archaeological finds ever in France. Both Morlet and Clément visited the farm and the field on April 26, 1925, and Morlet offered the Fradins 200 francs per year to be allowed to complete the excavation. The family accepted.

Morlet began his excavations on May 24, 1925, discovering tablets, idols, bone and flint tools, and engraved stones. This material allowed him to identify the site as Neolithic. He published his "Nouvelle Station Néolithique" in September 1925, listing Emile Fradin as co-author. He argued that the site was, as the title of the article states, Neolithic in nature. Though Morlet dated it as Neolithic, he was not blind to see that the site contained objects from various epochs. He still upheld his belief that some artifacts appeared to be older, belonging to the Magdalenian period, but added that the techniques that had been used appeared to be Neolithic. As such, he identified Glozel as a transition site between both eras, even though it was known that the two eras were separated by several millennia.

Certain objects were indeed anachronistic: One stone showed a reindeer, accompanied by letters that appeared to be an alphabet. The reindeer vanished from that region around 10,000 BC, yet the earliest known form of writing at that time was believed to have been established around 3300 BC, and that was in the Middle East. The general consensus was that, for the Glozel region, one would have to wait a further three millennia before writing was introduced. Worse, the script appeared to be comparable with the Phoenician alphabet, dated to c. 1000 BC, or to the Iberian script, which was derived from it. But, of course, it was "known" that no Phoenician colony could have been located in Glozel, so rather than explain the site, it made the site even harder to understand. But what Morlet had shown was that rather than a site that seemed to have little or no importance, Glozel was a site that could upset the world of archaeology. Whereas he might have thought he was going to rewrite history and the story of how civilization evolved, it was, in truth, a time bomb, which would soon explode.

When news of the discovery reached them, it should not come as a wonder that French archaeological academics were dismissive of Dr. Morlet's report. After all, it was published by an amateur (a medical doctor) and a peasant boy (who perhaps could not even write properly). In their opinion, the amateurism dripped off their conclusion, for it challenged their carefully established and vociferously defended dogma on several levels. Prehistoric writing? A crossover between a Palaeolithic and a Neolithic civilization? Nonsense! And hence, the halls of academia began to attack the conclusions Morlet had reached, as they were simply impossible.

One person claimed that the artifacts had to be fakes, as some of the tablets were discovered at a depth of 5 inches. Indeed, if that were the case they would indeed be fakes, but the problem is that all the tablets were found at substantial depths. It is evidence of how the academics manipulated the facts, as the facts didn't fit the dogma. They were trying to explain Glozel away, rather than explain Glozel. It should be noted that the "5 inches" argument continues to be used by several skeptics to this day, who falsely continue to assume it is true.

Unfortunately for French academic circles, Morlet was not one to lie down easily, and today his ghost continues to hang—if not watch—over Glozel. Morlet invited a number of archaeologists to visit the site during 1926; they included Salomon Reinach, curator of the Musée d'Archéologie Nationale de Saint-Germain-en-Laye, who spent three days excavating. Reinach confirmed the authenticity of the site in a communication to the Académie des Inscriptions et Belles-Lettres. Even higher academic circles descended on the site: The famous archaeologist Abbé Breuil excavated with Morlet and was impressed with the site. In late 1926, he wrote two articles, in which Breuil stated that the authenticity of the Glozel site was incontestable. Breuil had also worked together with pre-historian André Vayson de Pradenne, who had visited the site under an assumed name and attempted to buy the artifacts from Fradin. When Fradin refused, Vayson de Pradenne became angry and threatened to destroy the site. Under his own name, he obtained permission to excavate from Dr. Morlet, but then claimed to have detected Fradin spreading salt in the excavation trench. Was Vayson de Pradenne keeping his promise that he would destroy the site? Morlet chose to attack, and he challenged Vayson de Pradenne to duplicate what Fradin had allegedly done. When he was unable to do so, or find where Fradin had supposedly salted the trench, Morlet felt he had successfully dealt with that imposter. He was wrong: Vayson de Pradenne's allegation made it into print and the heat of the Glozel affair intensified, despite several leading scientists found in favor of its authenticity.

At first, Breuil tried to remain neutral, but it would be a reindeer that soured the relationship between Breuil and Morlet, as Breuil had identified an engraved animal on a tablet as a cervid, neither reindeer nor elk. Morlet, however, had received confirmation from Professor August Brinkmann, director of the Zoology Department at Bergen Museum, Norway, and informed Breuil of his mistake. It was the moment when Breuil changed his attitude in the Glozel debate.

But rather than talk, which is what his attackers were doing, Morlet dug, unearthing throughout a period of two years, 3,000 objects, all of varied forms and shape, including 100 tablets carrying signs and approximately 15 tablets carrying the imprints of human hands. Other discoveries included two tombs, sexual idols, polished stones, dressed stones, ceramics, glass, bones, and so on. Surely these could not be fakes, as archaeologists were saying? Who would make thousands of artifacts? His attackers were straightforward in naming their suspect: Fradin.

Breuil was more open-minded than his colleagues, but it is apparent that he did not like to be proven wrong in the case of his cervid. So rather than admit his mistake, instead he drifted further and further in the ranks of those intent on discrediting Glozel, for no other reason than if Morlet's findings were true, the site would be thousands of years older than they thought it could be and—more importantly—than they had said in print. On August 2, 1927, Breuil reiterated that he wanted to stay away from the site. On October 2, he wrote that "everything is false except the stoneware pottery."[1] Just before that, at the meeting of the International Institute of Anthropology in Amsterdam, held in September 1927, the Glozel site was the subject of heated controversy, so much so that a commission was appointed to conduct further investigation. Its membership was largely comprised of people who had already decided the Glozel finds were fraudulent. Among the group was British archaeologist Dorothy Garrod, who had studied with Breuil.

The commissioners arrived at Glozel on November 5, 1927. During their excavations, several members found artifacts. But on the third day, Morlet saw commission members Dorothy Garrod, Abbé Favret, and Mr. Hamil-Nandrin slip under the barbed wire and set off toward the open trench before he had opened the gate of the excavation site. Morlet followed Garrod and saw that she stuck one of her fingers into the plaster pattern on the side of the trench, making a hole. He shouted out, reprimanding her for what she had just done. Caught in the act, she at first denied it, but in the presence of her two colleagues as well as the attorney, Mallat, and a scientific journalist, Tricot-Royer, she had to admit that she had made the hole.

This was clearly a smoking gun: A leading archaeologist had been caught trying to falsify an archaeological excavation. But what happened? It was agreed they would not speak about the incident, showing the gracious nature of all men involved toward Miss Garrod!

During the excavations of Glozel in 1927, Dr. Morlet caught Professor Dorothy Garrod red-handed as she and colleagues had entered the excavation site illegally, in what he considered to be clear efforts to contaminate the site, to claim there was nothing to the Glozel facts.

Image copyright Dr. Morlet (1927). From the personal collection of Alice Gerard.

However, Morlet did speak about it after the commission had published its unfavorable report. This might be seen as mudslinging, trying to get back at the commission, but, unfortunately for those willing to adhere to this theory, a photograph exists that attests to the incident having occurred. In it, Garrod is hiding behind the four men, who are in heated discussion about what she had just done. Most importantly, Tricot-Royer and Mallat also gave written testimony confirming Morlet's account.

What was Garrod trying to do? Some have claimed it was merely an accident, but it is remarkable that she was part of a posse that entered the site—in essence, they broke in—before the "official start" of the day and had "an accident" that could have been interpreted as evidence of someone interfering with the excavation. If others had found that the excavation had been tampered with, fingers would not have been pointed at Garrod but instead at Fradin—whom the archaeologists suspected of being the forger, burying artifacts in the ground only to have amateur archaeologists like Morlet, who did not know better, discover them. If this suggestion that Fradin had entered the site at night had been made, it would have resulted in a "case closed," and the Glozel artifacts would have been qualified as fraudulent. Fortunately, Garrod and company were caught in the act.

However, the incident did not cause any harm to Dorothy Garrod's career; she went on to teach a generation of British archaeologists at Cambridge. Perhaps unremarkably, she made sure to tell all of them that the Glozel artifacts were fakes. And several of her students echoed her "informed" opinion; the list included Glyn Daniel and Colin Renfrew, both fervent critics of the Glozel finds. We can only wonder whether the "finger incident" is known to these modern pillars of archaeology.

Decades later, when the skeptical archaeologists were challenged with evidence that thermoluminescence and carbon dating had shown that the Glozel artifacts could not be forgeries created by Fradin, Renfrew wrote in 1975: "The three papers, taken together, suggest strongly that the pottery and terracotta objects from Glozel, including the inscribed tablets, should be regarded as genuine, and with them, presumably, the remainder of the material.... I still find it beyond my powers of imagination to take Glozel entirely seriously."[2] So, let us get this right: Though all the archaeological evidence suggested the site was genuine, Renfrew's emotions and especially his "powers of imagination" prevented him from taking it seriously! That is, of course, not science, but simply evidence of the fact that Renfrew is a bad scientist; he cannot accept hard, scientific facts! It is precisely this attitude that has prevented archaeologists from addressing the issue of lost civilizations.

But back to the past. Morlet sent a letter to *Mercure de France* (published on November 15, 1927), still upset with Breuil's qualification of the site as a fake and having spotted one of his students sticking an unwanted finger into an archaeological trench:

> From the time your article appeared I declared to anyone who wanted to listen, especially to your friends so that you would hear about it, that I would not allow you to present a site already studied at length as a discovery which had not been described before you wrote about it. I know that in a note you quoted the titles of our articles; that you thank me for having led you to Glozel; and that finally you give thanks to our "kindness" in having allowed you to examine our collections. You acknowledge that I am a good chauffeur. I have perceived, a little, that I have also been a dupe. Your report on Glozel is conceived as if you were the first to study the site, so much so that several foreign scholars are misinformed about it. Your first master, Dr Capitan, suggested to me forthrightly that we republish our leaflet with the engravings at the end and his name before mine. With you, the system has evolved: you take no more than the ideas.[3]

Morlet was highlighting one of the main goals of the archaeologists: to have their name on top of a report and be identified as the discoverer of Glozel. It is standard practice in Science, in which amateurs specifically are supposed to stand aside and let the "professionals" deal with it—and thus take the credit for the discovery. Again, Morlet did not want to have any of it.

The archaeological commission's report of December 1927 declared that everything found at the Glozel site, with the exception of a few pieces of flint axes and stoneware, was fake. It meant that the accepted view of history remained standing, for nothing at Glozel was genuine.

Still, members of the commission, such as Professor Mendes Corra, argued that the conclusions were incorrect and misrepresentative. In fact, he argued that the results of his analyses, when completed, would be the opposite of what had been claimed by Count Bégouen, the principal author of the report. Indeed, Bégouen later had to confess that he had made up an alleged dispatch from Mendes Corra! So the first evidence of fraud came from the likes of Garrod and Bégouen, *not* Fradin! It shows the power of Science and how it is able to mold opinions, for a century later, the standard line is that Garrod and Bégouen are pillars of Science and Fradin a fraud!

The need to condemn Glozel is further illustrated by René Dussaud, curator at the Louvre and a famous epigrapher. Dussaud had written a dissertation that argued that our alphabet is of Phoenician origin. If Morlet was correct, Dussaud's life's work would be discredited. Dussaud made sure that would not happen, and thus he told everyone that Fradin was a forger and even sent an anonymous letter about Fradin to one of the Parisian newspapers. When similar finds to those at Glozel were unearthed in Alvo in Portugal, Dussaud stated that they, too, had to be fraudulent—even though the artifacts were discovered beneath a dolmen, leaving little doubt they were of Neolithic origin. When similar artifacts were found in the immediate vicinity of Glozel, at two sites at Chez Guerrier and Puyravel, Dussaud wrote: "If, as they claim, the stones discovered in the Mercier field and in the cave of Puyravel bear the writing of Glozel, there can be no doubt the engravings on the stones are false."[4] Deny, deny, deny, for otherwise, it would show Dussaud's thesis was wrong.

Faced with such attacks, what could a little-educated farmer like Fradin do? In a move that seems to have been a few decades ahead of his time, on January 10, 1928, Fradin filed suit for defamation against Dussaud. Indeed: A peasant boy of 20 was suing the curator of the Louvre for defamation!

Dussaud had no intention of appearing in court and must have realized that, if he did, he could lose the case. He needed help, fast, for the first hearing was set for February 28, 1928, and Fradin had already received the free assistance of a lawyer who was greatly intrigued by a case of "peasant boy versus Louvre curator." Dussaud therefore engineered the help of the president of the Société Préhistorique Francaise, Dr. Félix Régnault, who visited Glozel on February 24, 1928, and, after the briefest of visits to the small museum, filed a complaint against "X," as if Régnault did not know who was operating the museum. That the entire incident was engineered is obvious, as Régnault had come with his attorney, Maurice Garcon, who immediately traveled from Glozel to Moulins to file the complaint. The accusation was that the admission charge of four francs was excessive to see objects which, in his opinion, were fakes. The police, of course, quickly identified X as Emile Fradin. The next day, the police searched the museum, destroyed glass display cases, and confiscated three cases of artifacts. Emile was beaten when he protested against the taking of his little brother's schoolbooks as evidence. Saucepans filled with dirt by his little brother were assumed to be artifacts in the making. But despite all of this, the raid produced no evidence whatsoever of forgery.

However, Dussaud had played this card to perfection: Fradin's suit for defamation could not proceed because a criminal investigation was underway. It meant that the defamation hearing set for February 28, 1928, would not happen for as long as the criminal investigation continued. Dussaud, it seemed, had won. Meanwhile, a new group of neutral archaeologists, the Committee of Studies, was appointed by scholars who, since the November conference in Amsterdam and specifically since the report's publication in December, were uncomfortable with how the archaeological world was handling Glozel. They excavated from April 12 to 14, 1928, and continued to find more artifacts. Their report spoke out for the authenticity of the site, which they identified as Neolithic. It seemed that Morlet had been vindicated.

Meanwhile, the excavations and controversy surrounding Glozel made it a destination for tourists. This so enraged the archaeologists that they organized a raid on the museum, destroying most of the display cabinets and injuring some of Fradin's family members. Any vindication was soon outdone when Gaston-Edmond Bayle, chief of the Criminal Records Office in Paris, analyzed the artifacts seized in the raid and in May 1929 identified them as recent forgeries. Originally, Bayle had said that it would take only eight or nine days to prepare a report, but a year passed without anything being set down on paper. This, of course, was excellent news for Dussaud, as it delayed his defamation hearing. To pave the way for the report's release, on October 5, 1928, information was leaked to the papers, who played their part by faithfully stating that the report would conclude that the Glozel artifacts were forgeries. In May 1929, Bayle completed a 500-page report, just in time to postpone once again the Dussaud case, which was scheduled for hearing on June 5, 1929.

Bayle argued that he could detect fragments of what might have been grass and an apple stem in some of the Glozel clay tablets. As grass obviously could not have been preserved for thousands of years, it was obviously a recent forgery, he reasoned. The argument is very unconvincing, for the excavations were obviously not handled as a forensic crime scene would be treated. Most likely, the vast majority of these artifacts were placed on grass or elsewhere after they were dug up from the pit—a practice that continues on most of today's archaeological excavations; archaeology, at this level, was and is not a forensic science. Later, it would even emerge that some of the objects had also been placed in an oven to dry them—which would later interfere with carbon-dating efforts on the artifacts. But that heating up an artifact in an oven would one day interfere with dating the artifact was unknown in the 1920s, when carbon dating didn't even exist.

Bizarrely, in September 1930, Bayle was assassinated in an un-related event—but not unfamiliar charges: His assassin accused him of having made a fraudulent report that had placed him in jail! After his death, it was found that Bayle had lived an extravagant lifestyle that was inconsistent with his salary. Most damagingly, Bayle was close to Vayson de Pradennes, who was the son-in-law of his former supe-rior at the Criminal Records Office. It seems the Breuil–Vayson de Pradennes–Dussaud axis was not only powerful in archaeological cir-cles; it could also dictate to the wheels of the law. The court accepted Bayle's findings, and on June 4, 1929, Fradin was formally indicted for fraud. For the following few months, Fradin was interrogated every week in Moulins. Eventually, the verdict was overturned by an appeal court in April 1931.

For three years, Dussaud had been able to terrorize Fradin for his "insolence" in filing a suit against him. Unfortunately, though the wheels of the law had largely played to the advantage of the "axis of ar-chaeology," in the final analysis, righteousness had won. The defama-tion charge against Dussaud came to trial in March 1932, and Dussaud was found guilty of defamation, with all costs of the trial to be paid by him. But eight years after the first discovery, the leading archaeologists continued to claim that the Glozel artifacts were fraudulent, though all the evidence—including a lengthy legal cause—had shown that was absolutely not the case. But why bother with facts when there are pet theories and reputations to be defended?

Morlet ended his excavations in 1938, and after 1942 a new law outlawed private excavations—a perfect law, of course, for archaeolo-gists, who ever since have been solely in charge of excavations sites and can therefore conclude whatever they want without any oversight or external verification. Indeed, the law has given archaeologists free reign, in the—clearly wrong—assumption that all they are after is the truth!

Meanwhile, the Glozel site remained untouched until the Ministry of Culture re-opened excavations in 1983. A full report was never published, but a 13-page summary did appear in 1995. This "official report" infuriated many, for the authors suggested that the site was medieval, possibly containing some Iron Age objects, but was likely to have been enriched by forgeries. It therefore reinforced the earlier position of the leading French archaeologists. But on June 16, 1990, Emile Fradin received the Ordre des Palmes Académiques, suggesting that the French academic circles had accepted him for making a legitimate discovery—and that he was not a forger. The Glozel excavation site, however, continues to be seen as a giant hoax. Emile Fradin was equally honored that the British Museum requested some of his artifacts to go on display in 1990 in this "holy of holies" of archaeology. What he did not know (because of a language barrier) was that the exhibit was highlighting some of the greatest archaeological hoaxes and forgeries in history.

What Glozel teaches us is that when amateur archaeologists make extraordinary discoveries, they better wet their chests, for the halls of academia will do everything to take over and, if unsuccessful, to mock the findings, going to any lengths necessary to protect their reputation. And the final verdict is that despite no evidence whatsoever of fraud, but with evidence that the archaeologists were committing fraud and defamation, Science continues to see Glozel as a hoax. In the final analysis, Glozel is unlikely to have been evidence of a lost civilization. But when it was discovered, it was believed to have been evidence that would completely rewrite the history books and push back the discovery of writing many thousands of years. It could still be, if only archaeologists would revisit the case with open minds and retest the artifacts involved.

Confirming Chinese Pyramids

Though pyramids are large, and the Great Pyramid just outside of Egypt's capital Cairo is very large, they dwarf in comparison to the Great Wall of China, humanity's largest building project so far. The Wall stretches over a formidable 6,352 kilometers (3,948 miles); if it were reassembled at the equator, it would girdle the globe with a wall 8 feet high and 3 feet thick. Despite the controversy whether or not we can see the Great Wall from space (apparently, you can't), in 1920, in *The Travels of Marco Polo*, historian Henri Cordier wrote: "China's ancient past is denied both to us and its population. Its grand past is slowly unveiled, similar to how Egypt's was revealed. Later on, one learned of buildings, standing stones and other monuments that were not mentioned by the Chinese historians (as part of their history)."[5] The largest country in the world was, and is still, largely there to be discovered. And for a period of time, the people of China were presented a history of their country that was known not to be true. China, of course, is not unique in this, but it will be the example we use.

Though accepted as a great civilization, its ancient treasures were barely known to the Western world a century ago, and in the vast rural areas of China, much remains to be explored. Turn back the clock a few decades, and we were confronted with rumors of pyramids in China. Twenty years ago, there was no real proof—outside of China—that these pyramids were real; now, less than two decades later, everyone can visit them, showing how quickly paradigms can change, if we allow them to change!

The Chinese pyramids were largely only known through travelers' accounts of their voyages through that country. In 1912, Fred Meyer Schroder and Oscar Maman traveled to Shensi (or Shaanxi, as it is now more commonly written), in the province of Xi'an. They dealt in tobacco and candles, but also supplied the Mongolians with weapons. Their guide along the Chinese–Mongolian border was a monk, Bogdo ("the holy one"), who told them they would soon stumble upon some ancient pyramids. Though he himself had never seen them, he knew some could be found around the old town of Sian-Fu (Xi'an). Bogdo knew that seven pyramids had been discovered.

When he finally saw them, Schroder estimated that the tallest structure measured 300 meters high and its sides 500 meters long. This would mean that this pyramid was the largest in the world, twice as large as the Great Pyramid of Egypt; the volume was 20 times as large as the Great Pyramid! Though we should expect that the people who built the Great Wall would be able to build the greatest pyramid, history was about to be rewritten. Schroder noted that it was aligned north-south/west-east, like the Great Pyramid, continuing that "in the past, they were apparently partly covered with stones, but those have disappeared. A few stones lie at the bottom. It is an earthen pyramid, with giant gullies on its sides. They were the reason why the stones loosened and fell down. Its sides are now partially covered with trees and shrubs. It almost looks like a natural hill. We rode around the pyramid, but did not discover any stairways or doors."[6] When questioned about its age, Bogdo believed that it was at least 5,000 years old—and therefore as old or older than the Great Pyramid. He stated that Chinese ancient records claimed that even then the pyramids were deemed to be "old"—and thus seemed to predate anything that we knew about Chinese history. Evidence of a lost civilization?

Schroder's account of the pyramids is detailed, but was not the first. In 1908, Arthur de Carle Sowerby and Robert Sterling Clark saw the pyramids during their expedition and wrote about them in their 1912 account, *Through Shên-Kan*:

> The visitor to Hsi-an [Xi'an], as he travels over the rolling plain from no matter what direction, cannot fail to notice numerous mounds of unusual shape dotted about everywhere like immense molehills, often

attaining a height of at least 100 feet, and standing on bases of very considerable area. So remarkable are they that he will instinctively seek information concerning them, and will learn that they are the tombs of kings and emperors, and their wives, and of scholars and sages notable in their day. But few indeed have anything in the way of tombstone or epitaph to tell who sleeps beneath the tones of yellow earth; though, concerning some, fantastic legends still linger in the minds of the people.[7]

A third early report originated from the Segalen mission, a tour of China that French doctor, ethnographer, archaeologist, writer, and poet Victor Segalen made in 1909–1914 and 1917. In 1913, he measured the pyramid's height at 48 meters, encompassing five terraces. One side measured 350 meters in length, a stunning 120 meters longer than the side of Great Pyramid at Giza. The Segalen mission also revealed the existence of more pyramids and tombs along the River Wei, the largest tributary of the Yellow River that flows past Xi'an. He also dated the structures to the Han period, following that of Emperor Qin Shi Huang (259–210 BC), the man who had built the first Great Wall, bringing the entire story into the folds of known Chinese history. But though the pyramids were no longer evidence of a lost civilization, they were clearly adding a great dimension to a known civilization.

The Cold War largely placed China off-limits to Western visitors. Throughout these turbulent decades, the stories of the early explorers and their reports of pyramids in China fed the imagination of Western pyramidophiles. New Zealand author Bruce Cathie became interested in the Chinese pyramids and wrote on the subject in *The Bridge to Infinity,* published in 1983. Cathie reported that a member of the Chinese Embassy had officially informed him there were no such things as pyramids in the Shensi province: "There are a few tumuli (burial hills), but no pyramids."[8] Cathie saw this as a straightforward denial of the Chinese that no such structures existed; the Chinese quickly clarified their statement: a letter from Chinese authorities, dated November 1, 1978, addressed to Cathie, stated that the scientists had learned that the so-called "pyramids" were burial tombs of emperors of the Western Han dynasty: "Records give a different version of the emperors' lives. As the graves have not been scientifically analyzed and no markings were seen on the ground, it is difficult to formulate conclusions."[9] So there were pyramids, but these were tombs, not pyramids—though they were pyramidal in shape! Confused?

Rules and regulations for travelers were somewhat eased following the death of Chairman Mao Zedong in 1976, but real change was slow. American historical travel writer David Hatcher-Childress wrote about Chinese pyramids in 1985, but was unable to visit them. The major breakthrough came only in 1994, after the collapse of the Iron Curtain, when German tour operator Hartwig Hausdorf was allowed to enter former "no go" areas and came away with fresh knowledge of the Chinese pyramids. So, in 1994, Hartwig Hausdorf and his company of fellow travelers landed at the new Xi'an airport, near the neighboring town of Xianyang, and, driving to the city and their hotel, saw one pyramid that stood along the road. It had been "discovered" a few years earlier, when Xi'an's airport was relocated and a road to the city was built. In 1995, he told me:

> It's a small miracle I received the go-ahead to enter some "no go" areas. I was, in fact, the only one who was granted such favors. I assume there are two reasons for this. I regularly visit China with a group of tourists. In 1993, I became acquainted with Chen Jianli, an avid researcher of his country's past. He assured me that he would try and open a few doors inside the Chinese Ministry of Tourism. In fact, in March 1994, I was able to visit some former "no go" areas in the Shaanxi province. I passed around some copies of my German book, *Die Weisse Pyramide (The White Pyramid)*, to

the right people. I talked to archaeologists who at first denied any pyramids existed, but finally recognized that they did exist. I was most pleased when the same people gave me further permission to enter other "no go" zones when I returned in October 1994. I never expected any of this would happen to me. But it seems it had to happen eventually. Following decades of rumor, someone had to clear the picture.[10]

And thus it was a tour operator and amateur archaeologist, not a professional archaeologist, who confirmed the existence of Chinese pyramids.

In March 1994, Hausdorf climbed a pyramid and saw a few more from its top. In October 1994, he climbed the same pyramid again and was able to count 20 more pyramids, all in the immediate vicinity. It confirmed what had been seen from a U.S. Air Force map of the area around the city of Xi'an, made with the use of satellite photographs, which showed at least 16 pyramids. But old Chinese— or is that scientific?—habits died hard, it seemed. In March 1994, Hausdorf also met Professor Feng Haozhang, a prominent member of Beijing's academic circle, his assistant, Xie Duan Yu, and three colleagues. At first, they denied the existence of the pyramids. But when Hausdorf showed them three photos of three different pyramids, they caved. Hausdorf described this encounter: "It was as if I had entered a hive. The photographs I took in both March and October 1994 are the proof that squelched five decades of rumor. Most scientists denied the existence of pyramids in China. If any scientist still clings to that, show him my photographs."[11]

Less than two decades later, anyone traveling to Xi'an will come face to face with the pyramids and is free to explore them. What was once denied, the subject of rumor and speculation, is now in plain view and accepted by all.

In 1945, this enigmatic photograph taken over China revealed the existence of pyramids in China. But until the early 1990s, their existence remained unconfirmed and often denied by Chinese authorities. Today we know they are real.

Image copyright Hartwig Hausdorf. Used with permission.

But even though we know of the pyramids' existence, we know little else about them. They have still not been excavated by Chinese archaeologists. One of the pyramids—burial mounds—is that of Emperor Qin Shi Huang himself, the man who built the first Great Wall, the first Emperor, but also the man of the famous so-called Terracotta Army, which is one of the main tourist attractions in Xi'an. His "pyramid" sits just 1 mile from where the army was buried. It is believed that Qin Shi Huang's mausoleum once stood almost 330 feet in height, though today it measures to just 150 feet. Its sides measure between 1,600 and 1,700 feet, giving the structure a volume that also exceeds that of the Great Pyramid. One story goes that automatic crossbows and arrows designed to fire are installed inside if the tomb is entered. It may seem a tall claim, but could be true! In *Records of the Historian: Biography of Qin Shi Huang,* Han historian Sima Qian describes the automatic crossbows and a burial chamber containing miniature palaces and pavilions with flowing rivers and surging oceans of mercury lying beneath a ceiling decorated in jewels depicting the sun, moon, and stars. There could be truth in the latter statement, as the ceilings in some of the excavated satellite tombs did indeed contain depictions of stars. Recent scientific work at the site has also shown high levels of mercury in the soil of Mount Li, tentatively indicating that Sima Qian may have provided an accurate description of the contents of the pyramids. A magnetic scan of the site has also revealed that a large number of coins are lying in the unopened tomb. A preliminary, month-long excavation was done in 1986 and revealed extensive damage, probably by Tang and Song robbers, which has led some archaeologists to conclude that the interior structure, despite Sima Qian's wonderful description, may be found largely void.

As it turns out, Emperor Qin Shi Huang was greatly intrigued by mythology and lost civilizations. He died while on a tour to Eastern China, searching for the legendary Islands of the Immortals (off the coast of Eastern China) and for the secret of eternal life, which he did not find. Reportedly, he died of swallowing mercury pills, which were made by his court scientists and doctors, but which erroneously contained too much mercury. Equally ironic was that these pills were thought to make him immortal. Qin Shi Huang was buried in his mausoleum, together with the famous Terracotta Army nearby.

That famous Terracotta Army of China is one of the greatest archaeological findings in recent history. It was made in March 1974 by local farmers drilling a well to the east of Qin Shi Huang's pyramid. The figures were found in three separate pits, with an empty fourth pit also having been discovered. In all, 8,099 figures have thus far been unearthed at the site; they include infantry, archers, and officers, and are manufactured in a crouching or standing pose. Each figure was given a real weapon, such as bronze spears, halberds or swords, or wooden crossbows with bronze fittings. It is believed that these weapons date to as early as 228 BC and may have been used in actual warfare—perhaps the unification of China. This was only discovered because of an accidental discovery in 1974. It is impossible to estimate how much of our history is still waiting to be discovered, but both Glozel and the Terracotta Army make it clear that great discoveries are often completely accidental.

But what the story of the Chinese pyramids also reveals is that the rumors were true and that once there was some form of open-mindedness on the debate, major discoveries and confirmations were made. The main reason why archaeologists embraced the Chinese pyramids and the Terracotta Army is because they were principally in charge of the excavations and revelations, and—most importantly—that the discoveries were substantiation of what archaeology already "knew": They were major discoveries, but not controversial or destroying the reigning paradigm. The same fate, however, did not befall the Bosnian Pyramids!

Discovering Bosnian Pyramids

Bosnia may soon lay claim to having the world's oldest pyramids—which shouldn't come as a surprise, seeing the area has the oldest European civilization as well, which archaeologists have unimaginatively named "Old Europe," though it is also referred to as the Vinca culture, named after a prominent archaeological site that revealed evidence of this civilization. The term was coined in the 1980s by archaeologist Marija Gimbutas to describe a relatively homogeneous pre-Indo-European Neolithic culture in the Balkans. Though Gimbutas's work is accepted within the field of archaeology, that field has done little to incorporate her findings in textbooks. For example, statues found in Old Europe are identical to statues of the so-called Ubaid Period of Sumer, suggesting that the civilization of Old Europe influenced the ancient Sumerian civilization. That is a possibility rarely discussed. Nor is it wildly known that there was this civilization in the Balkan, as early as 6500 BC and therefore thousands of years older than the Egyptian or Sumerian civilization. As recently as November 2007, archaeologists excavating a settlement in southern Serbia, believed to be at least 7,000 years old, announced that this civilization had great expertise in creating bronze artifacts—a discovery that required a radical re-dating of the Bronze Age!

Though Gimbutas put Old Europe on the map, little has been done on the subject since her death in 1994. There are several reasons why. First, Old Europe is an inconvenient civilization that forces people to rewrite the traditional textbook perspective, which says that civilization began to flourish in Egypt and Sumer in the fourth millennium BC. Wrong: Old Europe shows civilization flourished in the Balkan in the seventh millennium BC. Equally, Gimbutas's perspective on Old Europe was that this was a matriarchal society, in which both genders were equal, and that this was supplanted with a patriarchal society in the Bronze Age. This interpretation has resulted in endless series of attacks, for, as a whole, Science does not like it when evidence is interpreted from a matriarchal rather than a patriarchal society. Finally, it was the personal crusade of Australian-born archaeologist Vere Gordon Childe (1892–1957), who was responsible for the fact that Old Europe is not recognized for what it was: the oldest civilization in Europe. Gordon Childe instead forced the Vinca culture to be seen as an outlying cultural entity influenced by more "civilized" forces. Childe's dogmatic stance and clout meant that the Vinca culture received only scant attention and today remains largely unknown.

However much these debates continue to reign in the halls of academia, today, the Balkan is on archaeological fire because of something far more imaginative: the potential discovery of the largest and oldest pyramid!

In the past decade, the old paradigm that pyramids could only be found in Egypt and Central America has been substituted by a new perspective, which is that pyramids are a global phenomenon and have been built by numerous civilizations in several ages. The Pyramid of Cholula in Mexico is now regarded as the largest, though not the tallest, and the pyramid complex at Caral in Peru is the oldest, conservatively dated to 3100 BC. Most of these findings have received little to no media attention, and even many historians are unaware of these new facts. When I spoke to a gathering of 20-plus leading Egyptologists in August 2008, including the deans of archaeology of Ein-Shams and Cairo University, one of whom would go on to become the Egyptian Minister of Antiquities, they expressed utter surprise to learn that there were pyramids in Peru and that these were so old!

If all indications are correct, all of these pyramids fail in comparison, both in age and size, with the largest pyramids in the world, located just outside of the Bosnian capital of Sarajevo, in a normally quiet, rural town of Visoko, the very heartland of Old Europe.

The story of the Bosnian pyramids began in 2005, when Bosnian-born entrepreneur Semir "Sam" Osmanagic was shown the enigmatic Visocica hill that rises above Visoko. Could this be a pyramid, a local amateur archaeologist asked him. It could be.

Osmanagic decided to invest in a preliminary geological survey, which concluded that further exploration of the structure was recommended. Furthermore, when his own book on the Mayan pyramids fell open on a page showing a photograph of the Pyramid of the Sun in Teotihuacán, Mexico, Osmanagic thought the resemblance to be so similar that he decided to call the hill of Visocica "Pyramid of the Sun"—the name has stuck. With this, the otherwise-tranquil Visoko has become one of the most controversial archaeological sites in the world—controversial because just about everyone involved in pyramid research has given an opinion on the subject.

Dr. Zahi Hawass, then Secretary General of the Egyptian Supreme Council of Antiquities and seen as one of the leading scholars on pyramids, felt he had to give his opinion on the structure, committing a number of faux pas along the way. For example, when Dr. Hawass was asked by Osmanagic to provide the name of an expert, he offered Dr. Ali Barakat. A geologist, Dr. Barakat meticulously investigated the structures for 42 days in 2006 and concluded that they were man-made. However, Dr. Hawass pretended afterward that he'd had nothing to do with the Bosnian saga, even though he had!

Since, Dr. Barakat is not alone in speaking in favor of the man-made nature of Visocica and other apparent pyramids nearby. Archaeologist Dr. Nabil Mohamed Swelim, holder of three PhDs and the discoverer of four pyramids in Egypt, visited the structures in September 2007, and he, too, concluded that they are man-made "pyramid hills," distinct from pyramids. (A pyramid hill is a natural hill that is artificially enhanced to conform to the pyramid structure, whereas a pyramid is built from the bottom up.)

Fortunately, there is a growing and impressive list of scientists—mostly from Egypt, Eastern Europe, and Russia—who conclude that these structures are man-made. But their voices, specifically in the

Western media, have gone unheard. Indeed, the First International Scientific Conference, Bosnian Valley of the Pyramids (ICBP), held August 25–30, 2008, received minimal exposure in the Western press, despite the participation of the likes of Dr. Alaa Shaheen, archaeologist and dean of the faculty of archaeology at Cairo University; Dr. Hassan El-Saady, historian and vice dean of the faculty of arts at Alexandria University; Dr. Mostafa El-Abbadi, founder of the modern library in Alexandria (the Bibliotheca Alexandrina); and Dr. Mohamed Ibrahim Aly, Egyptologist and archaeologist in the faculty of arts at Ein-Shams University, Cairo, and future Minister of Antiquities; and many others. Instead, the few reports in the western media focused on the critics, who labeled the conference pseudo-scientific. What equally went unreported is that invitations from Dr. Swelim to the critics to attend were ignored by those critics.

The most avowed critic of the Bosnian pyramids in the Western world is archaeology professor Anthony Harding, of the University of Exeter, UK, who at the time was also president of the European Association of Archaeologists. He voiced his opinion on the matter as early as April 2006, and drove around the town of Visoko for a few minutes in June that year, afterward labeling the Visocica pyramid a natural formation. He practiced "science by taxi ride."

Immediately after the ICBP in August 2008, Professor Harding approached some of those who made the official conclusion/recommendation (which is that the site requires and warrants continued excavation), stating that the archaeological establishment had condemned the Bosnian pyramids as a fraud. Harding has never put any hard, scientific facts on any table to support such a serious allegation. In the program for the European Association of Archaeologists September 2008 Malta conference, he summed up the discovery as the "Bosnian pyramid fiasco," which "has drawn attention to the way in which the creation of fictitious pasts can be used for political and nationalist ends."[12] On a number of occasions, I contacted Professor Harding for comments, but he never replied. In other interviews, however, he made it clear that he had an opinion about these pyramids before going to Visoko, and that opinion was that they were not man-made structures.

Harding, as the president of the European Association of Archaeologists, sees himself as the leader of a scientific crusade against so-called "pseudo-archaeology"—the Bosnian pyramids project being one of the few crusades he is able to wage, with Osmanagic as the sinner who goes against God's commands. Indeed, there are unconfirmed reports that Harding threatened archaeologists who adhered to his organization that if they worked on the Bosnian Pyramid project, he would make sure they never worked again anywhere else!

So why all of this controversy? As with any discovery, and especially the resultant publicity, exaggerated claims are made—or fabricated—by the media. Indeed, in this case, early media reports claimed that the structures were 12,000 years old, whereupon the skeptics immediately tried to argue that this claim had been made by Osmanagic himself. Some observers even argued that the pyramids are extraterrestrial in origin. Such statements seem to have shocked Professor Harding the most, and he holds Osmanagic responsible for them all. As with Fradin, the messenger is always the first and easiest target.

In a blog of April 23, 2008, titled "Aliens to Science," American historian Merima Bojic wrote especially in regard to the Western scientific media's handling of the pyramids issue:

> [Colin] Woodard referred to Visoko as a nationalistic enclave of the Bosnian Muslims and seemingly tried to connect Mr Osmanagic to such a nationalistic movement as well. He falsely claimed that Dr Barakat and Dr Schoch measured the pyramids and concluded that they fail to perfectly align with the cardinal points....

[John] Bohannon, who writes for the prominent *Science* magazine, was also an author of false articles that were so bizarre they do not even merit mention.[13]

Bojic refers here to Vuc Bacanovic, who, in the Bosnian gossip magazine *Dani,* called Dr. Swelim "senile" and "a fool"—terms that are seldom used in scientific debates, but that were used in the case of the Bosnian pyramid controversy—and which were later used by Bohannon for his article in *Science*!

In short, one group of people has decided to quickly rule out the possibility that these structures are man-made. These people then went to extremes in trying to preserve their names, reputations, and beliefs, when evidence flooded in that these pyramids are indeed man-made. Dr. Swelim discovered pyramids in Egypt and his opinion on the Bosnian pyramids should not be put aside. But they do just that. They pretend this is not happening and they hope it will go away.

Amid all of this controversy, Osmanagic has continued to find archaeologists who are willing to lead the excavation. In fact, in 2010, the Bosnian pyramid site was the largest archaeological site in the world—an indication hopefully that times are changing!

After several years of archaeological research, a most interesting picture is emerging that shows that these Bosnian pyramids might not be evidence of a lost civilization, as some initially thought, but evidence of a lost dimension of a known civilization (that is, Old Europe).

A New Dimension to a Forgotten Civilization

Visoko is within the catchment area of Old Europe. Vinca artifacts have been found in the town of Visoko, showing Old Europe was present here. The evidence unearthed as part of the Bosnian pyramid project strongly suggest that Old Europe may have been a pyramid-building culture. This conclusion might seem surprising and novel, but in essence it shouldn't be too controversial, though it is.

So, what is the Bosnian Valley of the Pyramids? What is at the heart of this controversy? The Pyramid of the Sun, which dominates the skyline over Visoko, has been the main focus of investigations. The structure does not merely look man-made, but with a height of 720 feet, it is much higher than the Great Pyramid of Giza (480 feet), and thus would be the tallest pyramid in the world. As is the case with the Great Pyramid, each side of the Visocica Pyramid of the Sun is perfectly aligned with the cardinal points. Indeed, as one approaches Visoko, it is hard to believe that it took until 2005 before someone seriously pondered the notion that the hill could be a pyramid. In fact, it has since been discovered that, in 1984, one local author, Pavao Andelic, referred to Visocica as a "town pyramid," but nothing further was done to investigate the claim.

The bottom of the Visocica Pyramid has been built upon, and the streets of Visoko are extremely steep, as they are on the slope of a pyramid. Most interestingly, Osmanagic was told early on in his research that several homeowners in these areas of Visoko had wanted to build cellars, but could not because of a cement-like layer hidden approximately 1 meter below the surface. During the civil war of the 1990s, it was reported that the hill resonated when hit by artillery fire. Whereas artillery impact normally produced a sound that lasted one to two seconds, when it hit the hill it created a type of echo that lasted five to six seconds. It was clear that the hill had something unusual about it.

The most visited excavation site on the Pyramid of the Sun, about one-third of the way up the hill, has revealed the presence of large blocks of conglomerate between 50 and 100 centimeters below the surface. Similar excavations have been conducted on the other sides of the pyramid; in each case, a layer of this conglomerate has been found just below the surface. It has been suggested that the entire hill once had a 6-meter-thick covering of conglomerate. Just next to the main "tourist" site, however, the surface layer, comprising approximately 40–80 cm of sand, has been removed over a much bigger area to reveal a uniform, cement-like (conglomerate) coating. This coating leaves little doubt in the eyes of the visitor that it is indeed man-made. However, none of the skeptics have ever referred to this section; instead, they've focused on the much smaller and less interesting site nearby.

The sides of the Pyramid of the Sun are coated with a layer of conglomerate, which research has shown was a type of prehistoric cement. For the true surface of the pyramid to be revealed, the archaeologists merely have to remove a thin layer of top soil.

Image copyright the author.

As mentioned, Egyptian geologist Dr. Ali Barakat, too, has concluded that these blocks are man-made. Moreover, laboratory analysis results from the Civil Engineering Institute of Tuzla, made public by geophysicist Dr. Enes Ramovic in September 2006, have determined that the cement comprising these blocks had been poured in situ. In addition, a biology expert has maintained that the experiment of planting trees on the hill 40 years ago should be deemed a failure, as the tree roots have not been able to penetrate the conglomerate layer. He argued that this suggests the layer is man-made, as tree roots normally have no problem penetrating a natural surface. In November 2008, Osmanagic gave samples of this conglomerate to Joseph Davidovits. Davidovits is an expert in geopolymers, rocks that have been created in laboratory conditions. He confirmed that the rocks of the pyramid were not natural, but indeed man-made, further evidence that the Pyramid of the Sun had an artificial coating.

In my opinion, the best visual evidence for the artificiality of the pyramid can be found on the western side of the pyramid, which was partially excavated by the Pyramid Foundation in 2006. Here, too, the team found large rectangular slabs just under the surface, as well as man-made stone structures on the slope of the plateau. The overall impression is of a paved access plateau to the pyramid—a plateau that measures no less than 420 meters in length.

Work of a different nature on Visocica has been carried out by Russian scientist Oleg Khavroshkin, of the Schmidt Institute of Earth Physics at the Russian Academy of Sciences in Moscow. He performed a geophysical analysis between July 20 and August 4, 2007. These scans suggested "the existence of hollow cavities below the ground. These inhomogeneities were registered at Vratnice, Pljesivica [Pyramid of the Moon] and the tunnels. In the vicinity of the well shaft at the Pyramid of the Moon, clusters of frequencies were observed, resulting probably from such nonhomogenous cavities."[14] In short, potential chambers.

Dr. Muris Osmanagic, one of Bosnia's most eminent mining engineers and professors (as well as the father of Sam Osmanagic), has concluded in his book, *About the Cultural Layer of the Bosnian Pyramid Builders,* that

> the only possible and rational solution is that the great Pyramid of the Sun was a natural hill (composed of clay marl), modified into a pyramid. In such a case, the coating layer of concrete blocks make[s] up 6.28 per cent of the body of the pyramid, composed of clay marl, or 2,6 mln m3 [2.6 million cubic meters], [on a par with] the volume of the Khufu Pyramid stone blocks. This was already within the realm of the possible for this then highly developed civilization.[15]

But all of these scientific reports have not stopped the skeptics from claiming there is nothing to these structures. Once a scientist has made up his mind and has gone on record, whatever the amount of evidence to the contrary, he cannot be swayed to change his opinion. Historian Dubravko Lovrenovic, who heads the Bosnia–Herzegovina Commission for the Preservation of National Monuments, stated on Bosnian federal public television that he would burn himself alive on top of Visocica if it turned out to be a pyramid! Later, he denied he'd ever said this, but with the help of Gavrilo Grahovac, the Federal Minister of Culture and Sports, he stopped all excavation on the Pyramid of the Sun.

Despite such opposition (though Osmanagic also has supporters within the various levels of Bosnian government), since 2005, a total of seven potential pyramids have been identified, though only two have been archaeologically explored so far. "Only" 190 meters high—which would still make it higher than the Great Pyramid—and situated lower in the valley is the Pyramid of the Moon, the foot of this pyramid has become a second showcase of the Pyramid Foundation's work. Here, excavations show a type of floor lying on sandstone, followed by a second layer in approximately 1-meter-high steps. Nearby, the team probed the location where two faces of the pyramid meet and found a freestanding stone structure. It is but one fortuitous discovery in a series of enigmatic findings. Extensive excavations on the top of the Pyramid of the Moon have revealed the same type of "flooring." Archaeologists uncovered a layer of topsoil with natural layers of sandstone below, but separating both is a thin layer of rectangular stone blocks that look similar in size to modern paving slabs. In substance, they look as if they were poured and laid side by side. Interestingly, some are broken, but these fractures are always random; their original shape is always rectangular. Whether they are natural or man-made remains a subject of intense debate, but, if natural, this is one of the oddest geological formations on Earth, say leading geologists.

The Pyramid Foundation team has identified other potential sites of interest in the valley. One is the Pyramid of the Dragon, which together with the pyramids of the Moon and the Sun makes a perfect equilateral triangle when lines are drawn connecting the apexes of each pyramid, each side having a length of 2,173 meters. No work has been carried out on this third potential pyramid due to the presence of land mines on its slopes, but nature rarely creates such perfect triangles—especially not when the structures consist of three-dimensional triangles: pyramids, each of which orientated toward the cardinal points.

Furthermore, observations by engineer Goran Cakic have revealed that there is also a solar show occurring between the pyramids of the Sun and the Moon. On June 21, 2008, the summer solstice, he observed that the shadow of the Pyramid of the Sun at noon formed a "parallel pyramid" of the same height next to the Pyramid of the Moon. Even more interesting is that on August 20, 2008, between 6:30 and 7:30 p.m., the Pyramid of the Sun's shadow touched the entire Pyramid of the Moon. Coincidence, perhaps, but more likely design—perhaps part of a sacred light show that typifies many ancient cultures. A similar phenomenon can be seen on the slope of the main pyramid in the Mayan complex of Chichen Itza, where on the equinoxes, the sun creates a light and shadow effect along the slopes of the pyramid, which makes it appear as if the stone serpent becomes alive.

The so-called Bosnia KTK tunnels—after the name of the factory on whose grounds they were found—are part of the underground complex of tunnels that leads from various parts of VIsoko toward the Pyramid if the Sun. The tunnel complex fell in decay in c. 1200 BC.

Image copyright the author.

The best evidence for the artificiality of these structures, however, is the nearby tunnels. The town elders tell everyone who wants to hear that they used to enter various tunnels in and around Visoko as kids, walking through them from one side of the town to the other. When a factory was constructed near the river, large cavities had to be filled in with cement so that the premises could be built. Another known tunnel is the Topuzovo Polje tunnel, which starts near the River Bosna, but has been filled in with debris. But, according to historical accounts, this tunnel once led to the Pyramid of the Sun. So far, two tunnel complexes have been properly explored. About 2 kilometers from the Pyramid of the Sun is Ravne, a tunnel system where the main tunnel has various offshoots, running at 45- or 90-degree angles. In the past, these side tunnels were blocked off with carefully positioned dry stone walls. Along the main passageway, several large, enigmatic stones have been discovered; their purpose remains a mystery. These stones contain a number of inscriptions suggestive of a language. When stalagmites were discovered in one side tunnel, Italian geologists Dr. Dario Andretti and Dr. Luciano Leoni were able to conclude that these would have taken 2,600 to 2,900 years to form, which means the tunnel can be dated to at least 1000 BC—and most likely is older. This date is of interest, for Dr. Barakat's research indicates that approximately 3,000 years ago—that is, in c. 1000 BC—an earthquake damaged at least one face of the Pyramid of the Sun. Further evidence of such an earthquake is visible on the Pyramid of the Moon, where the stone "pavement" on the top shows obvious signs of folding. Circa 1000 BC, something happened that partially destroyed these structures, and this may explain why the Ravne tunnel complex has been filled in with sand and why other tunnels have collapsed.

Even Bosnian pyramid skeptic Katherine Reece has argued on the Internet that these tunnels are man-made: "ancient mining tunnels dating from as long ago as 3500 BC when the area was being mined for copper."[16] It underlines that she accepts that there was human activity here at that time, though she is totally unwilling to entertain the notion that there is a pyramid nearby. However, mining experts from Zenica, Banovici, and Kakanj have shown that there are no traces of minerals in these tunnels and that, hence, the tunnels could never have been copper mines.

Another opponent who has come around on the tunnels issue is historian and archaeology professor Dr. Enver Imamovic, from the University of Sarajevo, who at first claimed that the tunnels were natural caves, even denying that there are side tunnels at 45 degrees—which he said was a lie perpetrated by Osmanagic—but he also stated that he had not visited them at the time he made the claim. In short, he was accusing someone of lying, though he had not verified anything whatsoever! Since, he has accepted that these tunnels are not natural caves. Instead, it is suggested by the pyramid proponents that these tunnels were used to enter the interior of the Pyramid of the Sun, where, it is speculated, kings of Old Europe may once have been buried. Though no evidence has been found for this conclusion, it is completely logical.

Meanwhile, in September 2007, a team from the National Museum of Bosnia and Herzegovina excavated the nearby site of Okoliste and concluded that, c. 4700–4500 BC, around 3,000 people lived in the settlement—one of the largest ever found in Bosnia. This shouldn't be surprising, seeing that Visoko is known to have been one of Bosnia's most fertile lands and hence a cherished location for settlers. From the development of civilizations elsewhere, we know that such settlements often had a surplus workforce, which, like elsewhere, might easily have been used to start a building project—the Bosnian pyramids, perhaps?

Furthermore, pyramid-like objects have been found within Old Europe. Dr. Gimbutas wrote in *The Goddesses and Gods of Old Europe* (1974) about how the

> richly incised decoration on the Tisza altar from Kökénydomd [in southeastern Hungary] may relate to cosmogonical myths. Its triangular front is covered by meanders and divided into two levels by a horizontal band of meandering lines. In the center of the lower register two eyes and a nose are set in a triangle.... Groups of parallel lines, arranged in three, form panels along each side of the altar. The decorative organization suggests several levels of cosmic waters.[17]

In Egypt, the Giza Plateau has been portrayed symbolically as the primeval hill, which rose from the Waters of Chaos. Considering that the Tisza altar displays triangles (the two-dimensional rendering of the three-dimensional pyramid), this at the very least shows that Old Europe worked with the same cosmogonical material in its myths as the other pyramid-building cultures.

There is therefore a substantial body of evidence from which one can conclude that these hills have been artificially enhanced, and that there were "civilized people" present at the right time, in the right place, to have created these pyramids. However, it is equally clear that a smoking gun, which would convince anyone, remains to be found—but, equally, it might be just a spade's turn away. All false perceptions and ego trips aside, the Bosnian Valley of the Pyramids has much validity and will rock the old pyramid paradigm in years to come. But the research project will continue to be controversial for some time longer. In time, the Bosnian pyramids will not only be added to the new paradigm of pyramid structures that appear across the world, but they will also reveal a new dimension to the Vinca culture and show that the pyramids are, as an idea, far older, than the ancient Egyptians. Either way, a new page is being added in the development of civilization, and Science is slowly coming around to the idea that there might be something to these pyramids.

On August 29, 2008, the first International Conference on the Bosnian Pyramids, attended by leading Egyptologists and archaeologists from many countries, including Dr. Nabil Swelim, Egyptologist and archaeologist; Dr. Oleg Khavroshkin; Dr. Alaa Shaheen, archaeologist, dean of the faculty of archaeology at the Cairo University; Dr. Hassan El-Saady, historian, vice dean of the faculty of arts at the Alexandria University; Dr. Anna Pazdur, physician, Radiocarbon Laboratory, Silesian University, Gliwice, Poland; Dr. Mona Haggag, archaeologist, secretary of the Archaeological Society of Alexandria, Egypt; Dr. Mostafa El-Abbadi, historian, founder of the modern library in Alexandria (Bibliotheca Alexandrina), Egypt; and Dr. Mohamed Ibrahim Aly, Egyptologist and archaeologist, faculty of art at the University Ein-Shams, Cairo. Dr. Mohamed Ibrahim Aly concluded:

> Work at the archaeological location "Bosnian Valley of the Pyramids" in Visoko, Bosnia and Herzegovina, is an important geo-archaeological and epigraphical research that requires further multidisciplinary scientific research which should answer the origin of the Bosnian pyramidal hills and the extensive underground tunnel network as well as other archaeological sites in the vicinity.[18]

When these findings were announced at the subsequent press conference—I was drafted to make the above announcement in English—it was clear that this was a hard—if not devastating—blow for the ardent skeptics, who see this as nothing more than a delusion, if not a "folie à un," namely Sam Osmanagic's. But the skeptics were not going to give up easily. During that press conference tabloid journalist Vuk Bacanovic, the avowed critic of the project, made his presence felt by holding a 10-minute monologue. Bacanovic had not attended a single minute of the conference, yet spewed out certain old and new allegations, none of which made any sense to begin with. (For example, he seemed to want to have an individual roll-call of all conference attendees that they supported the findings, though it was made very clear that all participants supported the conclusions and everyone was present in that auditorium. If Bacanovic had been present during the conference, he would have realized this, but of course, he did not want to know.)

Before the conference, Swelim had invited some of the most vociferous critics of the project, including Anthony Harding, Mark Rose, and some selected others, to attend. Of all critics, only Dr. Blagoje Govedarica responded, though in a less-than-straightforward manner. He, however, refused to attend. The conference showed the tremendous divisions within archaeology, in which entire sections simply want nothing to do with this project, for a number of reasons, none of them to do with science, but all to do with ego and preconceived notions or dogma. Indeed, Harding went as far as to announce that members of his organization were "forbidden"—and hence, one could argue, the Bosnian pyramids are part of a field of study that one man has labeled "forbidden archaeology": archaeological discoveries scientists refuse to look at, however scientifically sound they are.

Forbidden Archaeology

In 1993, Michael Cremo and Richard L. Thompson wrote *Forbidden Archaeology: The Hidden History of the Human Race*. At 914 pages, it is the thickest book in my library. Its size forebodes that there are many topics to be covered that archaeologists consider to be "no go" zones. The book tackles bones and artifacts that show that people like us existed on Earth millions of years ago. However, they show that for the past two centuries, the scientific establishment has ignored these remarkable facts because they contradicted the dominant views of human origins and antiquity. Indeed, Italian scientist G. Sergi in 1884 wrote: "By means of a despotic scientific prejudice, call it what you will, every discovery of human remains in the Pliocene has been discredited."[19] The Pliocene stretched from c. five to two million years ago.

Cremo and Thompson list dozens of examples of evidence that have been removed from the archaeological record because it did not fit—and hence it became forbidden archaeology. Their end conclusion is that the total evidence "including fossil bones and artifacts, is most consistent with the view that anatomically modern humans have coexisted with other primates for tens of millions of years."[20]

When the book came out, the world of archaeology—unsurprisingly—did not like it, and as there was little to take away from the evidence presented by the authors, went after the authors. And the color of the dust jacket! Cyprian Broodbank described it in *Antiquity*'s book section like this: "All the reasons and evidence why modern humans are not rather recent but most ancient, a very large, very odd compilation of every anomaly in a very pink jacket."[21]

By and largely, *Forbidden Archaeology* was treated as non-existent, for Cremo and Thompson were not one of "them," but outsiders. The Church of Science can easily pretend these heretics do not exist and if they do somehow attain notoriety or media attention, they are quickly identified and ridiculed as heretics and burned at the scientific stake, whether that is the popular press or scientific publications. If, as with Fradin, they still refuse to go away, then forecasts of financial ruin or legal cases are employed in attacking the heretic.

However, in June 2011, *Antiquity* editor Simon Stoddard and deputy editor Caroline Malone finally did herald a major problem with archaeology, namely the non-publication of fieldwork. There can be several years, even decades, before the findings of archaeological excavations are published, and in the meantime the artifacts that were dug up don't exist. In 2001, it was reported that 89 percent of all Italian archaeological material had not been published. But Stoddard and Malone went on to speak of "another dimension of archeological iconoclasm...that of falsification.[...] We personally remember meeting a brilliant colleague who over-extended the distribution of Mycenaean sherds in Tuscany by creative re-use of sherds from a museum store."[22] They argued that this cheating would not have been detected by studying his published work.

In October 2000, Japanese archaeologist Shinichi Fujimara was videotaped planting artifacts at a site in Japan, and photographs from the tape were published on the front page of a leading national newspaper, *Manichi Shimbun*. Fujimara, deputy director of the Tohoku Palaeolithic Institute, admitted planting 61 of 65 artifacts found at the Kamitakamori site and all 29 artifacts found at the Soshinfudozaka site. Archaeologist Paul Bahn expanded on this, writing in *Antiquity*:

> In archaeology as a whole the above types of dishonesty have flourished for the simple reason that nobody is willing or able to expose the culprits publicly, although there are frequent mutterings in conference corridors or behind closed doors. Even here, I am unable to name names, since it would expose both me and this journal to litigation [...] no one, least of all the media, checks the facts; or simply because most people find it hard to believe that scholars could lie and cheat so brazenly."[23]

But it is obvious that when it comes to outsiders—amateur archaeologists—archaeologists and their publications have no problem whatsoever in going after someone. They just don't go after their own.

Cremo himself has experience of how scientists have tried to boycott television programs in which his book was going to be discussed:

When working with producer Bill Cote on the NBC television special *The Mysterious Origins of Man,* I found we were blocked from seeing the anomalous artifacts from the California gold mines, which were being kept out of sight in the storage rooms of a museum controlled by the University of California at Berkeley. We also found that orthodox scientists, led by UC Berkeley paleontologist Jere Lipps, engaged in an organized effort to stop NBC from broadcasting the program. When that failed, another paleontologist, Allison R. Palmer of the Institute for Cambrian Studies, tried to get the Federal Communications Commission to punish NBC for having shown this program, which directly contradicted the sacrosanct Darwinian account of human origins."[24]

Cremo is not preaching against evolution, but is arguing that Darwinist archaeologists have shoehorned the archaeological evidence in a too-narrow time frame.

In 1973, Virginia Steen-McIntyre was part of the investigate team of the site of Hueyatlaco in Mexico, where stone tools of a type made only by anatomically modern humans were uncovered by archaeologists had been found and were dated to about 250,000 years. However, the reigning paradigm states that modern man is only 100,000 years old and that we reached the Americas only 25,000 years ago, so the archaeological establishment rejected these findings as they "knew" they "had" to be wrong. Though her colleagues were wary to publish these results, Steen-McIntyre wasn't. Indeed, the initial team leader, Cynthia Irwin-Williams, never published a final report on the site, confirming the criticism identified by Michael Cremo, as well as Stoddard and Malone.

Cremo argues that the basic problem of archaeology is knowledge filtration, the process whereby evidence that supports the preconceptions and theories is accepted, whereas other evidence that does not, is rejected. If the discoveries happened in the past, modern archae-ologists will only be aware of the attitude of their colleagues, but not of the original source material. Renfrew's point of view on Glozel was shaped by Garrod, and other modern archaeologists have taken their lead from him. Few, if any, will ever have studied the controversy of Glozel based on original source material. It is precisely this mindset that has stopped archaeologists from expanding our view of history. It is why they rebelled about the Bosnian pyramids. It is why they do not want to touch the topic of Atlantis at all.

One might be lenient toward archaeologists and say that they do not know any better—that they are merely misinformed by genera-tions of archaeologists. But this is a too-lenient approach. The vitriol and extent to which they go to, as shown in the cases of Glozel and the Bosnian pyramids, reveals that they act as a modern Inquisition, intent on hunting down and destroying the new heretics that dare to speak out and say that history is not as we know it, and that there is evidence for lost civilizations. Quite literally, archaeology condemns those to burn; in the case of Emile Fradin, they literally threw him in jail and charged him with fraud. And if they could have had him burned at the stake, they would have.

Chapter 2

LOST CIVILIZATIONS OF THE OLD WORLD

IN SEARCH OF TROY

The *Iliad*, recounting the final 51 days of the 10th and final year of the Trojan War, and the *Odyssey*, detailing Ulysses' voyage home, are the oldest, and perhaps still the grandest, epic poems of Western literature. When Homer wrote these accounts remains the subject of speculation. Herodotus claimed he lived 400 years before him, which would place him c. 850 BC, though others argue he lived in 1200 BC. Ever since, for millennia, the story of the legendary battle and voyage has been told to millions of children and adults. Through time, fewer adults believed that these battles and voyages had truly taken place and more started to believe that Troy was "just" a myth.

Heinrich Schliemann was born in 1822. For Christmas in 1829, his father gave him a copy of Ludwig Jerrer's *Illustrated History of the World*. He would later say he was 8 years old when he claimed that he would excavate the city of Troy. In his memoirs and books, Schliemann wrote that when he was 8, his father took him on his knee and told him the story of the *Iliad*, the forbidden love between Helen, the wife of the king of Sparta, and Paris, son of Priam of Troy, and how their elopement resulted in a war that destroyed a civilization. That story, said Schliemann, awoke in him a hunger to search for the archaeological proof of the existence of Troy and Tiryns and Mycenae. In fact, he was so hungry that he went into business to make his fortune so he could afford the search.

In the 19th century, Heinrich Schliemann was convinced that Troy was not a mythical city, but could be found. Excavations of the town of Hissarlik in Turkey were, for Schliemann, evidence that it was the site of Troy. Today the real nature of Troy is no longer disputed by archaeologists, though others are not at all convinced that Hissarlik is the correct location of Troy.

Schliemann searched for Troy in many places. When Schliemann began his quest, the consensus was that there had never been a real Troy. Of the few who did accept its historical nature, most pointed to a hill named Bunarbashi, in Turkey. Schliemann visited the location, but as the *Iliad* mentioned that Mount Ida was visible from the walls of Troy and no mountain could be seen from Bunarbashi, he ruled the location out.

Using geographic clues from the *Iliad,* Schliemann located another hill near the village of Hissarlik that seemed to fit Homer's descriptions. Furthermore, in 1822, Charles Maclaren had published a book claiming Hissarlik was Troy. In 1868, Frank Calvert published *Ithaka, der Peloponnesus und Troja,* in which he claimed that Hissarlik, Turkey, was Troy. Apparently, Schliemann was at first skeptical, but Calvert persuaded him. As his family owned the eastern half of the site, he invited Schliemann to join the excavations, which began in 1871.

Homeric Troy was thought to be in the lowest levels of the site, so everyone dug through the upper levels, reaching fortifications that were identified as the very walls of the mythical Troy. In 1872, however, Calvert published an article, stating that the Trojan War period was missing from Hissarlik, which infuriated Schliemann. In May 1873, a cache of gold was found and was quickly labeled "Priam's Treasure." In the following years, he began digging at the Greek archaeological site of Mycenae, as well as sites in Ithaca, which he believed were linked with the *Odyssey.* By 1878, he was back at Hissarlik.

Later archaeologists condemned his methodology, with Kenneth W. Harl in the "Teaching Company's Great Ancient Civilizations of Asia Minor" lecture series, even claiming that Schliemann did to Troy what the Greeks couldn't do in their times, which was destroying and leveling down the entire city walls to the ground. But Schliemann did something and is remembered for something, which is convincing the world that Troy was real. Before Schliemann, Troy was largely seen as mythical—an invention by Homer. But when Heinrich Schliemann discovered Troy, he made a powerful statement that civilizations that were deemed to be fictional, were actually historical fact.

After Schliemann's death in 1890, excavation in Hissarlik continued. More than a century later, there is ever-growing dissent that Hissarlik is Troy, with various authorities vociferously arguing Hissarlik cannot be Troy. To quote Sir Moses Finley: "the more we know the worse off we are"[1]—so much so that it is now, despite what most people believe, deemed unlikely that Hissarlik is Troy. We should have known, for even the Roman geographer Strabo had this to say when he was shown Hissarlik: "this is not the site of the ancient Ilium."[2] Henceforth, the quest for Troy is back on. The question is: Where is it?

There is a well-known statement that "Homer is not a geographer." This is because of one simple problem: When Homer describes a location, this often does not conform to reality. For example, Strabo wondered why in the *Odyssey* the island of Pharos, situated just outside of the Egyptian city of Alexandria, was said to be a day's sail from Egypt. In reality, it wouldn't take five minutes. Places like Rhodes were never described as an island by Homer, though you would think he would. The location of Homer's Ithaca does not conform to reality, either. Dulichium, the long island, has never been identified, for where it is supposed to be, there is nothing. Professor John Chadwick thus concluded: "[T]here is a complete lack of contact between Mycenaean geography as now known from the tablets and from archaeology on the one hand, and Homer's accounts on the other."[3]

Most observers have hence claimed that Homer never visited the locations, made the landscape up, and so forth. But some recognize that if Troy was not Hissarlik, Homer's Pharos may not have been near Alexandria—and that would mean that the entire *Iliad* and *Odyssey* may not have occurred in those locations in and around the Mediterranean Sea that have become associated with them. Hence, we need to ask the question of whether these two ancient heroic accounts are indeed fabricated after all.

One important clue comes from Plutarch, who wrote that the island of Ogygia, mentioned in the *Odyssey*, was situated "five days sail from Britain, towards the west."[4] Indeed, such a location would make sense of Homer's description of the site: A large number of seabirds is said to fly around Calypso's Cave on Ogygia and the North Sea, and its islands are far better known for their large number of seabirds than the rather tranquil coasts of the Mediterranean Sea. Elsewhere, Homer refers to the wild or singing swan, which is found in Siberia and Scandinavia, whereas Mediterranean countries only know the silent swan, which only make a sound when they are about to die. Furthermore, the movement of the tides is often evoked by the bard, in both literal and figurative senses. The tides are notoriously un-dramatic in the Mediterranean Sea, but all the more impressive along the shores of the North Sea.

This would place Homer's epic in northern Europe, which may seem startling at first, but not to such well-respected authorities as Stuart Piggott: "The nobility of the [Homeric] hexameters should not deceive us into thinking that the Iliad and the Odyssey are other than the poems of a largely barbarian Bronze Age or Early Iron Age Europe."[5]

So Europe, rather than the Mediterranean, but where in Europe? For Felice Vinci in *The Baltic Origins of Homer's Epic Tales,* the answer is the Baltic States, along the coastlines of Denmark, Sweden, Norway, Finland, Poland, and so forth. As to the location of Ogygia, for Vinci it should be identified with the Faroe Islands, specifically the island Kalsoy.

Vinci is not the first to argue for a Scandinavian setting. It was also offered by Swedish historian Martin P. Nilsson. Others, such as British philosopher and historian Bertrand Russell, stated that the Mycenaean civilization originated with fair-haired Northern invaders of Greece. One obvious question is why a northern European story would become the backbone of the Mycenaean—Greek—civilization in southern Europe. For Vinci, the answer is simple: When the climate of Northern Europe became colder, these people were forced to migrate south. One tribe, the Achaeans, reached the Peloponnese and founded the Mycenaean civilization. The migrants had brought their legends with them, but the geography of the north did not transpose on the south—hence the discrepancy.

That Ogygia is not situated in the Mediterranean Sea seems clear. Its vegetation does not conform to the Mediterranean climate. And in Homer's epics, there are frequent references to fog and even snow, and to how the sun does not seem to set but instead lingers just beyond the horizon, a phenomenon that is typical for summer in the northern regions. In the *Odyssey,* we read: "Here we can perceive neither where darkness is nor where dawn is / nor where the Sun shining on men goes down underground / nor where it rises."[6]

Furthermore, the sea is never described as being bright, but gray and misty. The characters wear tunics and thick, heavy cloaks, which they never remove, not even during banquets. The sun and its warmth are seldom mentioned in the book, yet are what would immediately come to mind in a Mediterranean setting. Indeed, there is nothing in this geographical description that hints at a Mediterranean setting; even if Homer was not a geographer, he should at least have known what a typical Mediterranean landscape looked like, as he is believed to have lived there. Instead, it seems he lived elsewhere.

So where precisely does Vinci locate these battles? The *Iliad* is placed along the Gulf of Finland, and the *Odyssey* in and around Denmark. Troy itself is Toija in Finland; Thebes is Täby in Sweden; the Peloponnese was Zeeland, in Denmark. Vinci's argumentation is linguistic, showing similarities in place-names, but hence suffers from a potentially fatal flaw, as most of these names cannot be traced back to before c. AD 800. This means that a gap of two to three millennia exists; as mentioned by Vinci himself, these people left their homeland in 1000 BC, so how can we be certain where what was, as there was no continuous tradition present?

Even though we can therefore not fully identify the Baltic States as the home of Troy, Vinci's research has underlined another problem that historians do not like to deal with: the fact that various civilizations actively exchanged information and materials. Vinci's research shows that there is some connection between northern and southern Europe, for there was an active trade between these Baltic States and Mycenea, as revealed by the large quantity of Baltic amber that was found in the most ancient Mycenaean tombs in Greece.

Though Vinci may be right, Piggott is most definitely right: The Achaean warriors used chariots to move across the battlefield, a method of fighting that was unknown in Greece. But similar chariot fighting was described by Julius Caesar when he invaded Britain; what our Roman warlord witnessed seemed to be taken word-for-word from Homer's accounts. Furthermore, the "great walls" of Troy (never said to be made out of stone) could be identical with the palisades around various megalithic tumuli and Celtic settings. The sweet wine the warriors drink may seem typically Mediterranean at first, but we now know that wine was grown in northern Europe but that honey was added to it, making the wine sweet. Such an addition was not required for Mediterranean wines, and once again, it seems Homer's heroes were thus fighting elsewhere. Finally, in Homer's account, everyone drinks from bronze chalices, which is typical of Celtic customs—and largely absent from Mediterranean cultures.

A Celtic setting therefore works, but the question does remain: Where in northern Europe? In *Where Troy Once Stood,* Dutch-born author Iman Wilkens argues that the Trojan War was a major conflict between the European continent and the British Isles for free access to a raw material that was found nearly exclusively in Cornwall and that was essential in the Bronze Age as crude oil is at present. This raw material was tin for the production of bronze.

The Cornish tin mines were exhausted in 1200 BC. Without tin, there was no bronze and, as a consequence, Europe returned to more primitive living conditions. Until the emergence of the Greek and Roman civilizations, Europe had a recession that lasted four centuries. In c. 1400 BC, Bronze Age Europe knew tin was a diminishing resource and that export to continental Europe might end soon, in favor of keeping the tin in Britain. How could continental Europe attain tin? There were only two possibilities: trade or war.

The trade option was unrealistic, as the continent had nothing to offer in return. Hence, war was the only option. That, for Wilkens, is the true stage of the Trojan War: the struggle of the European continent to continue its way of life, resulting in an attack on Britain.

Interestingly, in the Middle Ages, there was a widespread belief in the Trojan origins of many western European people. The Romans claimed they descended from Aeneas; the British and the Franks claimed Trojan stock. The British were never precise, claiming that Brutus the Trojan had founded "New Troy," which they identified with London. In 1879, in the wake of Schliemann's discovery, French-born Belgian lawyer Théophile Caillieux argued that Troy was situated in England's East Anglia, where he discovered two huge war-dikes (ditches) between Cambridge and the Wash.

Wilkens was too focused on the frequent mention of dikes in Homer's account, suggesting that the war involved low-lying lands—which is perhaps one of the few uncontested issues of Homer's geography. The Fleam Dyke and the Devil's Dyke of East Anglia are indeed enigmas. The Devil's Dyke is the largest monument of its kind in Britain. The Fleam Dyke is a ditch and rampart 85 feet wide and up to 11 feet high, running for 3 miles from Fulbourn across the dry chalklands to Balsham.

The Fleam Dyke near Cambridge is, together with the Devil's Dyke, a long dike whose purposes are officially unknown. According to Iman Wilkens, Cambridge was the site of the original Troy and the dikes featured in the War of Troy, which was not fought in Turkey, but in England.

Image copyright the author.

They obviously served a military purpose and formed a barrier. It is known that the wide plain had already been cleared around 1500 BC and that the barriers were likely erected to stop horse-drawn war chariots. Officially, though, they are said to be only 1,200 years old (that is, dated to AD 800) and constructed by the Saxons. Still, the problem is that no one knows what battles were fought here. Caillieux and Wilkens hence put two problems together, concluding that the barriers were there to stop the Achaeans in their path to attack Troy. For them, Troy was located on the heights just above Cambridge, the Gog

Magog hills; the acropolis of Troy (known as Pergamus) was identified with the Wandlebury Ring. This hill fort once had concentric ditches and earthen walls, which were kept in place by wooden palisades. All that remains of this structure is the ditch—the Ring—which is still 16 feet deep in places.

Wilkens identifies Argos with France and Mycenea with the modern French town of Troyes, whose name is indeed taken from Troy. Ithaca is placed in Cadiz, in southern Spain, making the battle stage for the *Iliad* a truly Europe-wide war. All of these locations have strong Celtic, megalithic connections, and a war between Britain and the continent over tin is logical, given the knowledge that the metal was extremely precious. The work of Barry Cunliffe, a former professor of European archaeology at the University of Oxford, also underlines that this ocean-facing megalithic civilization had experienced sailors, conforming to the strong sailing tradition that runs through Homer's epics.

As for the *Odyssey,* Wilkens transforms this into a transoceanic voyage, with our hero reaching the New World, as well as places like Senegal, the Cape Verde Islands, the Dutch Antilles, and Cuba, before arriving back home in Ithaca (Cadiz). As for Ogygia, to Wilkens this is the island of St. Miguel, in the Azores.

For the past century, Homer's epic poems have largely been decoded in efforts to find the physical stage of its events. Before, epic poems were all about a symbolic nature, and this has largely been pushed since Schliemann put Troy on a map. But it would be foolhardy to forget the symbolism of this tale. Ulysses' voyage in the *Odyssey* is often seen as being a description of a man's initiation into a mystery cult; some of the battles have an archetypal nature. For Edna Leigh, as recounted in *Homer's Secret Iliad* by Florence and Kenneth Wood, the *Iliad* was indeed not a historical, but an astronomical text. In fact, she felt it was the world's oldest substantial astronomical text. She believed that the Iliad was created to preserve the ancient knowledge of the heavens. The battles were not to be found on planet Earth, but in the stars—not an alien star wars, but astronomical events and information presented as a story.

There are several star names listed in the *Iliad,* so at the very least, the text definitely has some astronomical connection. Furthermore, sailing instructions in the *Odyssey* are given with such confidence that they must reflect the learning of a man who could use the night's skies for practical purposes. But Leigh went much further than these basic astronomical observations. Eventually, she would identify no less than 650 stars and 45 constellations in the *Iliad.*

Her strongest point is the Catalogue of Ships, which is believed to have been the oldest part of the *Iliad.* Equally, it is the most boring; it is literally a catalog of ships that participate in the attack on Troy—a very boring part of an otherwise-great epic—so boring that it might be an index, or catalog, of stars?

Leigh detected an underlying theme in the epic. She realized that the main warriors of the *Iliad* were stars; the brighter the star, the more powerful the warrior was. Their victims were always the less bright stars. When seen as such, the Greek and Trojan regiments represented 45 constellations; the commanders and leaders were the 73 brightest stars in the constellations, such as Aeneas (Spica), Agamemnon (Regulus), Menelaus (Antares), Aias (Canopus), Patroclus (Procyon), Paris (Betelgeuse), and of course Odysseus (Arcturus).

For Leigh, Troy is the universe, as we see it: the night's sky. The scheming and battles were the futile efforts to halt the precession of the equinoxes, specifically the decline of Thuban in Draco as the pole star, and the return of Sirius, the brightest star, to the skies of Greece—for that is indeed the location where she places it. Sirius was identified with the hero Achilles, the greatest warrior at Troy. Hence also why Achilles is known to chase Hector—Orion.

This battle in the sky between these various stars was visible from roughly 2800 BC to c. 1800 BC. Still, as the return of Sirius to our skies occurred in the ninth millennium BC, she argues that the entire story began then, with the return of Achilles to the field of battle (c. 8900 BC), the story ending in c. 2200 BC, shortly before the arrival of the new pole star.

Achilles' return to the battlefield, to which Homer devotes several books, is indeed a moment of astronomical importance. It is one of the most elaborate descriptions, with the smith-god Hephaestus creating a new shield for Achilles: "He wrought the Earth, the heavens, and the sea, the Moon also at her full and the untiring Sun, with all the signs that glorify the face of Heaven—the Pleiades, the Hyades, huge Orion, and the Bear, which man also call the Wain and which turns round forever in one place, facing Orion and alone never dips into the stream Oceanus."[7] These particular constellations mark the area of the night sky in which Sirius and its constellation, Canis Major, reappeared. And for Leigh, *that* is the importance of Homer's message.

In the end, we are left to wonder who is right. Schliemann? Vinci? Wilkens? Leigh? The only conclusion we can draw is that the quest for Troy is still open. Leigh's "star code" does not need to be exclusive to the possibility that Troy was a real city. A real battle could have been the inspiration to add an extra layer of star lore to it. In modern times, certain historical details are often changed to tell a better story; why would Homer be any different? What the quest for Troy has taught us is that what was once thought to be fictional is definitely not without true value, creating insight into our forefathers. And what the research of Vinci and Wilkens has shown is that European history is far more complex and interesting than commonly known.

Sailing to Hyperborea

2000 BC. The edge of the world. That describes the Outer Hebrides, off the western coast of the northernmost part of Scotland. These islands are remote times two, even by modern standards. Still, there is something here that attracted, thousands of years ago, a large enough population to build the Callanish Stones, one of the most spectacular and grandest megalithic monuments anywhere. In fact, it has earned the nickname "Stonehenge of the North."

For a megalithic site, Callanish is also quite unique, for unlike the tried and tested settings of most megalithic monuments, Callanish is laid out as a circle consisting of 13 stones, is 13 meters in diameter, and toward the outside has further megalithic stones in the shape of a Celtic cross. It is therefore not grand in size, but in appearance. The average height of the stones is nevertheless an impressive 4 meters, though the range varies from 1 to 5 meters; all stones are local Lewisian gneiss, which, at three billion years old, is the oldest type of stone of Britain. It makes one wonder whether our ancestors knew how special this stone was and whether it was for this quality that they used it in this circle. The stones might have come from a cliff at Na Dromannan, a mile inland from Callanish, where there are some visible remains of a destroyed stone circle.

Callanish sits on the main Isle of Lewis, diagonally across from Stornoway, the present "capital" of the islands—though it only has a population of 6,000. Callanish (in Gaelic, Calanais) sits near Loch Roag, on a peninsula, on a ridge, which means there are good views over the surrounding area, though the very top of the natural outcrop called Cnoc an Tursa, upon which the stone circle sits, obscures views toward the south. Indeed, there are some "platform rocks" just next to the entrance gate that allows one to look down upon the construction. It's an interesting question to ask whether it was once used as such in ancient times, too. Some archaeologists speculate that the natural outcrop was indeed part and parcel of the structure, and note that the southern avenue is actually aligned toward it.

Archaeologists state that construction on the site began c. 2900 BC, with the stone circle itself created c. 2200 BC. Gerald and Margaret Ponting think that the central, 4.7-meter-high, 7-ton stone was put up first. If so, the site would have begun as one gigantic standing stone. It might thus have been on par with another gigantic standing stone—bigger than the Callanish one—on the northern shore of the island. The Clach an Trushal at Balanthrushal is 6 meters tall and 2 meters wide; it is the largest single monolith in Scotland and remains very impressive, despite today being cramped in by modern structures.

Other stone circles, such as Stonehenge, also have avenues leading up to it. But Callanish is quite unique as lines of stones lead toward it from all cardinal points, though the northern avenue is by far the longest and the only one that is a double row. This avenue is 83.2 meters long and once counted 39 stones, of which now only 19 remain. The terminal stones are set high and at right angles, as if they are blocking stones. The width of the avenue goes from 6.7 to 6 meters.

The southern avenue is precisely orientated north-south and measures 27.2 meters. The eastern avenue has only five stones left, and is 23.3 meters long. The western one is 13 meters long, and has a mere four stones. The boundary stone of this western avenue has a subliminal image in it: a head, with a defined eye and nose, which looks inward, toward the stone circle. Does it tell us this was a vantage point, and does it invite us to look toward the center of the circle?

What was Callanish's purpose? As with Stonehenge, people have tried to decode Callanish's astronomical clock. The adventure began with Sir Norman Lockyer, who argued that the northern avenue was aligned to Capella, but this would have occurred only c. 1800–1790 BC, a full half millennium, if not more, after Callanish was supposedly created. More recently, Aubrey Burl has proposed that the eastern row was aligned to the rising of the Pleiades, but he noted this would only work c. 1550 BC, again very late in the site's existence. In his turn, Professor Alexander Thom suggested that the alignment of the northern avenue (when looking southward) pointed to the setting of the midsummer full moon behind Mt. Clisham, a hill that delineates the horizon. There is another alignment at Callanish that is seldom mentioned: Looking from the main site to the east, another site, Callanish XIV, which is a single standing stone, becomes a good marker for the equinoctial sunrise.

But Callanish's importance is not so much to the sun and the stars, but to the moon. It is primarily linked with the extreme southern setting position of the major standstill of the moon. In fact, three stone circles near Callanish are also orientated to this event, and other monuments on the island suggest the same orientation.

This lunar phenomenon occurs every 18.5 years, and, when seen from Callanish, the moon would alternate between skirting the top and bottom of the undulating horizon of Mt. Clisham, or the so-called Sleeping Beauty. She is outlined in the shape of the hills south of Callanish. The locals refer to it as Cailleach na Mointeach, the "Old Woman of the Moors." However, the Cailleach was also the creator deity, and often said to have married the sun god. An association with the moon would therefore have neatly fitted in with the astronomical mythology.

The moon rises at the level of her breasts—twin peaks. The moon then passes through the Callanish stones two to five hours later. As this happens, if a person stands on the hillock at the higher south end of the site—the natural outcrop—the moon is "reborn" with a person silhouetted within it. It suggests that the hillock was definitely part of the complex, even though it now stands outside of the site's boundary wall.

Apart from the Sleeping Beauty, the outline of the hills has also given her a pillow to rest her head on: a conical hill, Roineval, 281 meters high. Conical hills were very important to our ancestors—some such as Silbury Hill were man-made additions to a sacred megalithic landscape. The hill's incorporation in this sacred landscape might suggest it was held sacred by the builders of Callanish and might have been seen as a hill of creation, or a place of emergence—if not the residence of the Cailleach herself.

Callanish was part of an intricate complex, carefully planned and worked out by our ancestors—ancestors, however, about whom we know very little. It was only in 1857 that Sir James Matheson, who owned Lewis, told his chamberlain, Donald Munro, to have the stones cleared of peat. The average depth of the moss was recorded as 5 feet, and it meant that the circle was buried in peat for nearly 3,000 years. Like so many other stone circles in Europe, it was therefore abandoned in the period of c. 1000 BC, when the "megalithic era" all over Europe ended. There is therefore a 3,000-year gap separating us from the last user. Could legends and folklore therefore reveal some historical truth?

In the 17th century, these stones were called "Fir Bhrèige"—false men—and around 1680, John Morisone wrote that "It is left by tradition that these were a sort of men converted into stone by ane Inchanter: others affirme that they were sett up in places for devotione."[8] Another legend is that when the giants that lived on the island refused to convert to Christianity, St. Kieran turned them to stone—and voila, the Callanish Stones were born. The latter legend can be found at various megalithic sites, but is unlikely to contain any interesting clues.

Martin Martin visited in 1695 and observed that "it was a Place appointed for Worship in the time of Heathenism, and that the Chief Druid or Priest stood near the big Stone in the centre, from when he address'd himself to the People that surrounded him."[9] Another local belief says that at sunrise on midsummer morning, the "shining one" walked along the stone avenue, "his arrival heralded by the cuckoo's call."[10]

The most interesting explanation for Callanish was nevertheless an insight arrived at by Aubrey Burl, who would be able to marry hard scientific observations of the stone circle with Greek legends. He remembered the Greek legend of Hyperborea, which describes a temple on a faraway, northern island:

> They say also that the moon, as viewed from this island, appears to be but a little distance from the earth and to have upon it prominences, like those of the earth, which are visible to the eye. The account is also given that the god visits the island every nineteen years, the period in which the return of the stars to the same place in the heavens is accomplished, and for this reason the nineteen-year period is called by the Greeks the "year of Meton."[11]

The reference comes from the first century BC Greek writer Diodorus Siculus, who stated that at this temple, there was a "spherical temple" where Apollo "skimmed the earth at a very low height."[12] Most commentators assume that, if anything, this could be a reference to Stonehenge and that Hyperborea as such was Britain. However, Burl realized that Stonehenge is 500 miles too far south to have the correct lunar latitude to provide for a display as described by Diodorus. The correct latitude for this phenomenon is around the Isle of Lewis. And noting that at Callanish, the observation of a lunar phenomenon that occurs every 19 years was indeed a key incorporation into the site's layout, Callanish is definitely the best candidate for the Hyperborean temple. It is, in fact, at this moment in time, the only candidate.

Interestingly, the account of Hyperborea states that the island was the birthplace of Leto, the mother of Apollo. Could this be a reference to the Sleeping Beauty, the Cailleach? The "Old Woman of the Moors"? Even more interesting is the observation that this means that the Greeks saw the birthplace of their deities in places that were almost 2,000 miles from their homeland.

Diodorus Siculus further relates that the island's inhabitants were looked upon as priests of Apollo. Apart from the temple, there was also a city that was sacred to this god, and the majority of its inhabitants were players on the cithara, a type of lyre. Coincidentally or not, historians have identified that Scotland knew this type of instrument.

There are more "coincidences." The Celtic deity Mac nOg is the equivalent of the Greek Apollo. He was the son of Bu-vinda, or the White Cow, who gave her name to the Irish Boyne Valley, the site of that other impressive megalithic complex, Newgrange. Interestingly, there is a legend of a Gaelic-speaking white cow, which emerged from the sea during a famine. The cow told the people to come to the Callanish stones and she would give them each a bucket of milk. Are such legends further evidence that perhaps some of the more obscure legends, such as how the locals still call the hills on the Southern horizon "Sleeping Beauty," did survive the millennia, handing down knowledge about the site's original use?

Siculus said that Hyperborea was an island whose size was comparable to Sicily; this fits the Hebrides. Equally, he states that "at the rising of the Pleiades, the sun is seen to set at the equinox,"[13] a phenomenon that also applies to Callanish, though, as mentioned, it did not occur at the time of its construction—but did occur later, when the temple was still in use. Furthermore, the western row points to the equinoctial sunset, so Diodorus's description not only fits individual elements of Callanish, but fits it as a whole. In fact, Burl had previously speculated whether short stone rows, such as the eastern-western rows at Callanish, were erected about 1800–1500 BC, which is the time frame when the Pleiades are rising at Callanish and when these rows might therefore have been added to the structure.

That Callanish was recorded in Greek stories should not come as a major surprise. Diodorus took his information from Hecateaeus of Abdera, who in turn relied on the lost writings of fourth-century BC Greek explorer Pytheas of Massilia (modern Marseilles). Pytheas sailed to northwestern Europe in c. 325 BC. He traveled around and visited a considerable part of Great Britain, and is credited as the first person to describe the Midnight Sun and polar ice, though, of course, we have seen that Homer equally spoke of this Midnight Sun.

The question is: Was Pytheas the first foreign visitor to arrive at Callanish? Another legend linked with Callanish states that the stones were brought in ships under the leadership of a high priest and erected by black men. Some have speculated whether these were dark-haired Irishmen from the south (and porcellanite axes from County Antrim have shown links between the north of Ireland and the Outer Hebrides), but "black men" could—more likely?—refer to skin color, rather than the color of their hair. And we have that other legend of Princess Scota, a refugee of Pharaonic Egypt, coming to Ireland and Scotland. In fact, she is said to have given her name to Scotland—the land of Scota.

Still, we know that the stones for this circle came from Lewis themselves, and hence as part of this particular legend is unlikely to be true, we should not put too much emphasis on the "black men" just yet. Still, nothing should be excluded. The stones on the east side of the avenue are consistently about three-quarters as high as the stones on west side. As uninteresting as this observation might appear to be at first, it is a feature that is nevertheless characteristic of northern Irish avenues and double rows, and of those on the Crozon peninsula in western Brittany. It highlights that whoever built Callanish, was perfectly aware of similar developments elsewhere in Europe, and followed the same architectural "trends." That other regions of Europe were therefore aware of Callanish and came to visit, should not surprise anyone.

THE FIRST EUROPEAN UNION

Since the 14th century, English monarchs have been crowned on the Stone of Scone, also known as the Stone of Destiny, which was placed underneath the Coronation Chair. The Stone ended up in Westminster Abbey (though since 1996, the stone resides in Edinburgh Castle) after Edward I took it from Scone. From the time of Kenneth MacAlpin, who created the Kingdom of Scone in the ninth century, all the kings of Scots had been crowned upon the Moot Hill, seated upon the Stone of Scone. But even after the Stone's removal by King Edward I in 1296, the Moot Hill continued to be the crowning place of the Scottish Kings.

Though the Stone is seen as typically Scottish, its origins—and especially its mythical origins—do not seem to be Scottish at all. Around the time the Stone

The Moot Hill in front of Scone Palace in Scotland was the site of the coronation of Scottish kings. Just in front of the chapel was the Stone of Destiny—now a replica stone—which, according to tradition, came from Egypt and was brought to Scotland by Scota, the Egyptian princess.

Image copyright the author.

was taken to England, Robert of Gloucester (1240–1300) wrote that the first Irish immigrants brought the stone with them into Scotland, stating it was a "whyte marble ston."[14] So rather than sandstone, or black basalt, the stone is then said to be white marble. As Robert of Gloucester wrote at a time when an official stone was still in residence in Scone, his account of the nature of the stone carries much weight—and would indeed indicate that the stone currently on display is a fake.

The Stone of Destiny, on which Scottish kings were crowned and which was once said to have been Jacob's Pillar, before being brought to Scotland by Egyptian Princess Scota, originally rested in Scone, until it was taken from there to Westminster in the late 13th century.

Image copyright the author.

The history of the Stone goes further back in time than Ireland, though. Hector Boece wrote in *Scotorum Historiae,* in 1537, that Gaythelus, a Greek, the son either of the Athenian Cecrops or the Argive Neolus, went to Egypt at the time of the Exodus, where he married Scota, the daughter of Pharaoh, and after the destruction of the Egyptian army in the Red Sea, fled with her by the Mediterranean until he arrived in Portingall, where he landed and founded a kingdom at Brigantium, now Santiago de Compostella, on the northwestern coast of Spain. Here he reigned in the marble chair, which was the lapis fatalis cathedrae instar, or "fatal stone-like chair," and wherever it was located, portended kingdom to the Scots—those who had followed Scota in exile.

Simon Breck, a descendant of Gaythelus, brought the chair from Spain to Ireland, and was crowned in it as King of Ireland. Later, Fergus, son of Ferchard, was the first king of the Scots in Scotland. He brought the chair from Ireland to Argyll, and was crowned in it. He built a town in Argyll called Beregonium, in which he placed the Stone. The 12th king, Evenus, built a town near Beregonium, called after his name Evonium, now called Dunstaffnage, to which the stone was taken. Dunstaffnage is near Oban, on the western coast of Scotland, and the same legend states that Fergus Mac Erc built a church on the island of Iona and commanded it to be the sepulcher of the future kings. Iona was indeed a sacred island, in the West, of pagan religious importance, for it became one of the key objectives of early Christianity to have as a powerbase. As funerals of kings and coronation ceremonies go hand in hand, the stone's location in Dunstaffnage would make great sense, because of its proximity to Iona.

There are several ancient accounts that speak of the foreign origins of this stone. Though not all accounts are identical, they largely do overlap. The *Scalacronica,* compiled in 1355, states that Simon Breck, the youngest son of the king of Spain, brought the stone from

Spain, where it was used for coronations. Breck "placed it in the most sovereign beautiful place in Ireland, called to this day the Royal Place (Tara), and Fergus, son of Ferchar, brought the royal stone before received, and placed it where is now the Abbey of Scone."[15] In this account, there is no stopover in Dunstaffnage, but the story does identify the Stone of Scone with the Lia Fail, "the speaking stone," which named the king who would be chosen to rule. Its residence was the coronation place of Ireland, Tara, near modern Dublin.

The Stone of Destiny at Tara was the coronation site for Irish kings. It was also the very center of Ireland, a division that had been carefully created and that reveals that the people of ancient Ireland had mapped their island with extreme precision.

Image copyright the author.

A similar account can be found in the *Scotichronicon,* compiled in 1386, which repeats that Gaythelus married Scota and led those that survived the disaster to Spain. Simon Breck then went to Ireland, setting up the stone in Tara, before Fergus took it to Scotland.

Legend or a memory of a real odyssey? Donald Watt, the translator of *Scotichronicon,* wrote that "It scarcely needs saying that none of this is history in the proper sense."[16] If real, we see how Europe was far less isolated in those distant times than history pretends. Historians are quick to argue there is no validity to these legends of the Stone of

Scone, but perhaps we should not be so quick. Herodotus stated that the enigmatic Etruscans that lived near Rome originally migrated in Italy from the Near East, an "opinion" archaeologists largely disregarded and denigrated at the time. Herodotus stated that they emigrated from Lydia, a region on the eastern coast of ancient Turkey. After an 18-year-long famine in Lydia, Herodotus reports, the king dispatched half of the population to look for a better life elsewhere. The emigrating Lydians built ships, loaded all the things they needed, and sailed from Smyrna (Izmir) until they reached Umbria, Italy. For millennia, the mythical origins of the Etruscans were seen as most unlikely. But recently, geneticists have shown that the Etruscans—and their cattle—*did* migrate to Italy from the Near East, vindicating Herodotus. As there is a logical reason why these Egyptians would have fled their country, dismissing the possibility that the legend of the Stone of Destiny is a factual account may come to haunt those who do so too vociferously.

What stories like Scota's highlight is that, whereas most are told that European history still largely begins with the Greek and Roman civilizations, in the eighth century BC, Europe was far more interesting than that. There was an active, cross-continental trade of goods—including tin—thousands of years before Julius Caesar wrote about the Celtic tribes. One archaeologist who has not shunned away from this is Barry Cunliffe, who argues that the so-called Atlantic Zone—which incorporates Iceland, Britain, the Atlantic shores of France, Spain, and Morocco—in megalithic times once had an intense trading culture. In fact, he and others argue that the megalithic civilization (Stonehenge, the stone rows of Carnac, Callanish, and so many other thousands of sites) were all constructed by this ocean-facing civilization.

One man who sailed in the footsteps of these megalithic sailors is Peter Marshall, who recounts his voyage in *Europe's Lost Civilization: Uncovering the Mysteries of the Megaliths.* His boat was *Celtic Gold,* "a 7-metre sloop that traveled at about 4 knots—the same length and speed of the ancient hide-sewn boats which probably once plied the waters along the Western Atlantic seaboard and into the Mediterranean."[17] This was not a holiday: "My intention was to follow in the wake of ancient mariners from Scotland to Malta [...] By travelling in a boat similar to theirs in size and speed, I hoped to demonstrate that the megalithic builders were capable of such long-distance navigation."[18] Marshall demonstrated just that.

Whereas I've labeled this section of the book "The First European Union," Marshall's final chapter is titled "The Golden Age," as he demonstrates that the Megalithic Era, which lasted for several thousands of years in Europe, is truly a lost civilization—a Golden Age of this continent. Though thousands of megaliths dot the landscape of France, Britain, and other western European countries, there is a general reluctance to see these as evidence of a lost, pan-European civilization that once flourished here. And it makes for the interesting observation that megaliths truly are everywhere, but archaeology has hardly done anything with them. We call the civilization the "megalithic civilization"—literally the civilization of big stones. For apart from the fact that this civilization erected "big stones"—sometimes freestanding, sometimes in specific configurations (such as at Stonehenge, Avebury, Carnac, or Callanish)—we know little about this civilization. It truly is a lost civilization, yet is visible underneath our noses whenever we travel through Western Europe.

Cunliffe pushes the start of this civilization back to 8000 BC, when Britain was still part of the European mainland. The last Ice Age ended in c. 10,500 BC and, whereas many might think that the ice disappeared quickly, it took thousands of years before the sea levels reached their present levels. Unsurprisingly, therefore, along the shores of Western Europe, there are rumors of lost civilizations, like Lyonesse off the coast of English Cornwall, Hy-Brasil off the Coast of Ireland, and the lost civilization of the Dogger Bank, an area of the North Sea currently submerged, but that once was above sea level.

The Dogger Bank is a large sandbank in a shallow area of the North Sea about 60 miles off the east coast of England. Depths range from 50 to 120 feet. The Dogger Bank is a vast area of 6,800 square miles, about 160 miles long and up to 60 miles wide. "Doggerland" survived until c. 6200 BC. Doggerland was more of an archaeological discovery than a legendary civilization—though some have, of course, linked it with Atlantis since. Interest began in 1931, when a commercial trawler dragged up an antler point. Later vessels brought back mammoth and lion remains, as well small numbers of prehistoric tools and weapons, showing that the land was inhabited. When Doggerland finally submerged in c. 6200 BC, only two scenarios could have happened: Its inhabitants drowned, or they escaped and resettled. One scenario could therefore lead to ancient legends of a vast island disappearing into the sea, killing its inhabitants, or stories of "foreigners" coming from elsewhere, settling in what in this scenario would be most likely Great Britain or maybe the Netherlands.

Doggerland is not the only island that disappeared around the British coast. Far more famous is Lyonesse, located between Cornwall and the Scilly Isles. Lyonesse's fame came from its inclusion in the Arthurian legends, in the story of Tristan and Isolde, as the home of Tristan, whose father was king of Lyonesse. There is the island of Ys, a mythical city on the coast of Brittany that was swallowed by the sea. Ys is often placed in the Douarnenez Bay, a bay in Finistère, the far western tip of France's Brittany peninsula. Finally, there is Hy-Brasil, off the western coast of Ireland. The island appeared on several maps; the last sighting of the island occurred as recent as 1872. Some have suggested this is none other than the Porcupine Bank, an area of the Irish shelf 120 miles west of Ireland. This raised area may once have risen above the waters of the ocean, becoming the legendary Hy-Brasil.

What all of these stories show are that there is good archaeological evidence that parts of what is now the North Sea and the Atlantic were once—thousands of years ago—above water, and that some of this land, and later islands, were inhabited. Hence stories of sunken civilizations should not be treated as suspect, but accounts of these lost lands. Whereas the fame of these civilizations has become embellished through time, their very existence should not be doubted.

The legends of these lost civilizations also show that there was far more mobility across Europe than most historians would like to see. Indeed, if anything, modern history is typified by its isolationist stance, which is that most if not all civilizations developed independently from each other. The fact of the matter is that most civilizations developed together and the lines drawn between various civilizations by historians are largely illusionary.

The biggest division remains between the European civilizations and those of the Mediterranean Sea. Stories like Scota's show that there was a far more homogenous exchange of goods and people across this continent than currently accepted. We have already seen how the civilization of Old Europe exchanged with the earliest era of the Sumerian civilization. But the origins of one civilization are the subject of intense debates between historians and "pseudo-scientists": Ancient Egypt. Historians claim Ancient Egypt developed locally, whereas others say that the culture of Ancient Egypt came from elsewhere—often identified as Atlantis. Who is right?

Into Egypt, From Where?

In January 2003, I made inquiries to visit the Hoggar Mountains and the Tassili n'Ajjer, one of the most enchanting mountain ranges on this planet. The two geographically close but nevertheless quite separate landscapes are located in the Sahara Desert in southeast Algeria. I was told that if I could pack my bags immediately (literally), I could join the three weeks' trip. Unfortunately, I could not, but planned to go on the January 2004 trek.

A few weeks later, Dutch and German tourists were kidnapped in the area (though the English group I would have joined experienced no such problems). Some of the tourists were held captive for several months before German and Dutch troops were sent in to free the hostages from their rebel captors. The kidnappings have since stopped most if not all tourists from traveling toward the magical rock paintings of the Tassili, as insurance brokers are unwilling to provide coverage. At a time when the world was beginning to wake up to the magical reality of the Tassili paintings, international political tension has placed the prehistoric rock paintings off-limits.

Despite the fact that the rock paintings of the Tassili can be visited, the few people who have written about these rock paintings in popular accounts have largely relied on the pioneering work of Henri Lhote and his team. Lhote stated that the Tassilli was the richest storehouse of prehistoric art in the whole world. He wrote a series of books, the best known of which is *The Search for the Tassili Frescoes: The Rock paintings of the Sahara* published in 1959. It is a popular account of the hardships he encountered in trying to discover and make drawings of the rock paintings that were scattered on the rock faces in the various corners of the Tassili.

Lhote built on the work of Lieutenant Brenans, who was one of the first to venture deep into the canyons of the Tassili during a police operation in the 1930s. As the first European to enter that area, he noticed strange figures that were drawn on the cliffs. He saw elephants walking along with their trunks raised, rhinoceros with ugly-looking horns on their snouts, giraffes with necks stretched out as if they were eating at the tops of the bushes. Today, the area is a desolate desert. What these paintings depicted was an era long gone, when the Sahara was a fertile savannah, teeming with wildlife and humans—in short, a lost civilization.

The conditions of the Tassili are very otherworldly. One could argue it is an otherworldly landscape. Some have actually described it as a lunar landscape. Otherworldly is also a fitting description of the paintings. Lhote described some of them as "Martian faces" in *The Search for the Tassili Frescoes: The Rock paintings of the Sahara*; he used the term as they resembled the alien faces that he had seen on television sci-fi documentaries. The term would later be used by the likes of Erich von Däniken to speculate whether some of the figures were indeed depictions of extraterrestrial visitors. The Martians were what Lhote more scientifically would label round-headed people, though they do indeed look otherworldly.

Other researchers, notably Dutch author Willem Zitman, have identified an astronomic connotation to the various figures. He specifically focuses his attention on the so-called swimmer, depicted at Ti-n-Tazarift, and argues that this is in fact the depiction of a constellation. He also argues for a connection between the rock paintings of the Tassili and the origin of the Egyptian civilization, wondering whether the shamans of the Tassili might not have been the Followers of Horus, the group of demigods that the Ancient Egyptians credited with the dawn of their civilization and who were said to have come from the West—the very direction in which the Tassili is located. Lhote identified an Egyptian dimension, though he was at pains to draw a clear outline of how Egypt would slot into the Tassili rock paintings.

In his book, he showed two paintings that had an unmistakable ancient Egyptian character. Furthermore, they were out-of-place art and did not fit in with the other paintings that he had found. His discovery caused commotion in scholarly circles, as it seemed irrefutable proof of contact between the Tassili and Ancient Egypt. The question was how. Eventually, it emerged that the paintings were done by one member of Lhote's team, who played a successful prank on Lhote. The pictures were reproduced up to the early 1970s in editions of his book before being removed from successive reprints. Today, the paintings have been discretely erased from Jabbaren and Aurenghet, and the Touareg guides shake their head if the photos are shown, having never seen them. As a result, archaeologists will speak down on the possibility of a connection between the Tassili and Ancient Egypt. Others, of course, might argue that this is part of an archaeological cover-up, whereby one member of his team was forced to lie, whereby the establishment later removed the paintings from the cliffs to remove this Egyptian connection.

"If at one stage Egyptian (and maybe also Mycenaean) influence can be observed, the most archaic of the Tassili pictures belong to a school unknown up to now and one that apparently was of local origin"[19] Lhote concluded. Lhote's team found several urban settlements, where the artists responsible for the paintings lived. He found small concentrations of human activity around Tan-Zoumiatak in the Tin Abou Teka massif. It was a little rocky citadel that dominated the gorge below. The citadel was cut through with a number of narrow alleys. Lhote described the art he found here: "There were life-size figures painted in red ochre, archers with muscular arms and legs, enormous 'cats,' many scenes with cattle, war-chariots and so forth. Up to this time I had never seen figures of this sort in the Tassili and the mass of paintings that I managed to view that day quite put into the shade all those I had seen up to then."[20]

It was a highlight so far, but more impressive sites were to follow. At Jabbaren, he found a city with alleys, crossroads, and squares. The walls were covered with hundreds of paintings. Jabbaren is a Tuareg word meaning "giants" and the name refers to the paintings found inside the city, some of which depict human figures that are indeed gigantic in size. One of them measured up to 18 feet high. Several of these paintings depicted Martians, and for Lhote, it was the first time he discovered paintings of hundreds of oxen. Jabbaren was soon labeled one of the oldest sites of the Tassili, with some of the rock paintings now dated to 9000 BC.

Ti-n-Tazarift was another city. Its center was marked by a huge amphitheater with a diameter of more than 500 yards. It had an immense public square with houses grouped around it. Given off from it were avenues, streets, passages, and even blind alleys. The city stretched for a mile and a quarter. The true marvel in the crown of the Tassili, however, was Sefar. Little is written about the city. Lhote does not provide many details, except a map, showing its extent, as well as the presence of several streets and avenues, tumuli, tombs, and something that he calls the "esplanade of the Great Fishing God."[21] Lhote named the character as such as he seemed to be carrying fish. But a closer inspection of the photograph that successive expeditions have taken, suggests what Zitman had always felt could be the truth: Rather than a fishing god, was this character not depicted in a pose that the ancient Egyptians knew as smiting the enemy? It was a pose that was used by the Pharaohs to display their mastery over the forces of chaos—the so-called "Striking the Enemy" pose? In this scenario, the links between the Tassili and Ancient Egypt become very interesting and once again suggest that the ancient legends', rather than modern academic, opinion is correct.

The Great Fishing God of Sefar is thus potential evidence that there is indeed a link between Egypt and the Tassili. Some of the rock paintings also show boats, such as at Sefar and Aouanrhet. These depictions are very similar if not identical to what was discovered by the likes of archaeologist Toby Wilkinson in similar sites and similar rock paintings in the region between the Nile and the Red Sea. He dated these paintings to the fifth millennium BC, which overlaps with several of the paintings of the Tassili. Like the Tassili, the desert area where Wilkinson uncovered these paintings was then verdant grassland. Like the Tassili, these Egyptian paintings are a complex mixture of motifs, depicting crocodiles, hippos, and boats from the Nile along-side ostriches and giraffes from the savannah, and suffused with cattle imagery and the religious symbolism that would characterize classical Egyptian art. This should by now sound familiar....

For Wilkinson, these rock paintings show that pre-Pharaonic Egyptians were not settled flood-plain farmers, but semi-nomadic herders who drove their cattle in between the lush riverbanks and the drier grasslands. He also identified that several of these paintings were located around ancient trade routes. For a semi-nomadic people, it is by no means a long stretch of the imagination to argue that they trekked throughout the savannah, from east to west and backward. And thus, in pre-dynastic Egypt, Egypt and the Tassili were more than likely one—or at least far more closely connected and exchanging than the standard model of history prefers.

Both Wilkinson and Zitman argue for a radical reinterpretation of the origins of Ancient Egypt. For Wilkinson, the rock paintings in southern Egypt provide proof that it is there that we should look for the "Genesis of the Pharaohs" (also the title of his book). For Zitman, the origin of Ancient Egypt can be found in a culture and area that stretches into the Tassili, where there is the pose painted on a cliff face in Sefar that would later adorn the front walls of several Egyptian temples. That cannot be a coincidence. Furthermore, it also coincides with what Lhote wrote: "The most common profile suggested that of Ethiopians, and it was almost certainly from the east that these great waves of pastoralist immigrants came who invaded not only the Tassili but much of the Sahara."[22]

The Tassili has thus added a new chapter to African history—but it is a new chapter at the beginning of the book. It is the history of what is known as the Neolithic wet period, which lasted from 9000 to 2500 BC, when much of the Sahara was habitable for humans and when the dunes were covered with grassland, supporting hippos, lions, crocodiles, zebras, giraffes, and so forth. By 7000 BC, there were hunters, dancers, bakers, and even sailors. There were shamans, leaving rock paintings on the cliff faces. The earliest examples of Saharan rock art are invariably engravings, sometimes on a very large scale, representing the ancient and partially extinct wildlife. That they were at this time nomadic hunters is inferred from a lack of representations of domestic animals. One of the most prominent and common representations is the Bubalus Antiqus, the ancestor of modern domesticated cattle, resembling the modern east African buffalo, but with much larger horns. As it became extinct around 5000 BC, it has allowed archaeologists to date the Tassili rock paintings.

Lhote then identified the round-headed people as the next phase. This peculiar style is apparently limited to the Tassili, but there are similarities with the large cave at Wadi Sora in the Gilf Kebir and paintings in the Ennedi, showing that these people got very close to Egypt.

However, the consensus among Egyptologists is that the Egyptians did not penetrate the desert any further than the area around Djedefre's Water Mountain, a sandstone hill about 50 miles southwest of the Dakhla Oasis. The discovery of hieroglyphic inscriptions in this oasis in 2003 by German explorer Carlo Bergmann caused a sensation in Egyptological circles, as it forced them to extend the activities of the Pharaonic administrations an unprecedented 50 miles further out into the unknown and waterless Western Desert!

Now, however, that dogma has been shattered by the discoveries made by Mark Borda and Mahmoud Marai, from Malta and Egypt, respectively, when surveying a field of boulders on the flanks of a hill deep in the Libyan desert, more than 400 miles west of the Nile Valley. Borda and Marai have stated that they discovered engravings on a large rock consisting of hieroglyphic writing, a Pharaonic cartouche, an image of the king, and other Pharaonic iconography. The short text yielded astonishing revelations. In the annals of Egyptian history there are references to far-off lands that the Pharaohs had traded with, but none of these have ever been positively located. Borda states that the decipherment revealed that the region of their find is none other than the fabled land of Yam, one of the most famous and mysterious nations that the Egyptians had traded with in Old Kingdom times, a source of precious tropical woods and ivory: "Its location has been debated by Egyptologists for over 150 years but it was never imagined it could be 700 kilometers west of the Nile in the middle of the Sahara desert."[23] With the dogma that the Egyptians never went anywhere now shattered, the field is laid wide open for further explorations. But making a step into the Tassili and adding it to the history of Ancient Egypt might be harder than making a small step on the Moon. Indeed, it would not be a big step for Mankind, but it would be big step for archaeology if ever or whenever it is taken.

CIVILIZATION ONE?

Civilization is far older than we assume. Europe did not begin with the Greeks or Romans in the eighth century BC, but at least in 9000 BC, as underlined by the work of Barry Cunliffe. In the Sahara, we can push back civilization to that same period, 9000 BC. But in the Middle East, the sites of Göbekli Tepe and Çatal Höyük show that civilization, capable of building extraordinary towns, manufacturing tools and jewelry, already existed in 10,000 BC!

Five millennia separate us from the birth of ancient Egypt in c. 3100 BC. Add another five millennia and we are in 8100 BC. Add another millennium and a half, and we have the date when Göbekli Tepe, in the highlands of Turkey near the Iraqi and Syrian borders, was constructed. Archaeologically categorized as a site of the Pre–Pottery Neolithic A period (c. 9600–7300 BC), the world's oldest temple sits in the early part of that era and so far has been carbon-dated to 9500 BC.

It is the time frame when Plato's Atlantis civilization is said to have disappeared. And it was built an incredible 5,000 years before the rise of what many consider to be the oldest civilization, Sumer, not too far south of Göbekli Tepe as one goes down the River Euphrates and leaves the highlands of the Taurus Mountains in Turkey.

Göbekli Tepe is an incredible site. David Lewis-Williams, professor of archaeology at Witwatersrand University in Johannesburg, says that "Göbekli Tepe is the most important archaeological site in the world."[24] It is a small hill on the horizon, 15 kilometers northwest of the town of Sanliurfa, more commonly known as Urfa, which has been linked with the biblical Abraham (some claim that Urfa was the town of Ur mentioned in the Bible) and which once hosted the Holy Mandylion, linked with Christ's Passion. Once also known as Edessa, Urfa is on the edge of the rainy area of the Taurus Mountains, source of the river that runs through the town and joins the Euphrates. Urfa was (and still is) an oasis, which could explain why Göbekli Tepe was built nearby. A life-sized statue of limestone that was found in Urfa, at the pond known as Balikli Göl, has been carbon dated to 10,000–9000 BC, making it the earliest-known stone sculpture ever found. Its eyes are made of obsidian.

Göbekli Tepe was another accidental discovery. An old Kurdish shepherd, Savak Yildiz, discovered the site in October 1994 when, spotting something, he brushed away the dust to expose a large, oblong stone. A survey of the site had been carried out by American archaeologist Peter Benedict in 1963, but he identified the area as a Byzantine cemetery. When German archaeologist Harald Hauptmann, and Adnan Misir and Eyüp Bucak of the Museum of Urfa began excavations in 1995, they soon learned that the site was so much more.

Göbekli Tepe is a series of mainly circular and oval structures set in the slopes of a hill, known as Göbekli Tepe Ziyaret. Ziyaret means "visit," but this is often left out of the name. Though some translate

Göbekli Tepe as "Navel of the World," and Gobek does mean "navel" or "belly," and Tepe means "hill," the most correct translation of the site's name should be "bulged-out hill."

The more sensationalist media have made attempts to link Göbekli Tepe with the biblical Garden of Eden. Göbekli Tepe is indeed old, but it is not unique; nor was it a garden. However, throughout the past 50 years, the time frame for the beginning of civilization has been pushed back from the rise of the Sumerian civilization in the fifth millennium BC to the construction of Göbekli Tepe, 5,000 years before. Alas, it has been a voyage that has not received the attention it should have had.

The discovery of the biblical town of Jericho and its stone walls, dated to c. 8000 BC, was the first to push back the date of the birth of civilization. 'Ain Ghazal is often seen as a sister site of Jericho and, with its 15-hectare area, is the largest Neolithic site in the Middle East and four times as big as Jericho. American Gary O. Rollefson, its principal archaeologist, was able to date the town to 7250 BC, and there is evidence of agriculture in the area dating back to c. 6000 BC—later than the establishment of the town itself. In its heyday, 2,000 people lived at 'Ain Ghazal. However, by 5000 BC the town was completely deserted. Thirty statues have been found there, measuring between 35 and 90 centimeters; they are human in appearance but may represent deities or the spirits of ancestors. Jericho's discovery added weight to the argument that the Bible is history, not myth. But when it was next learned that there are even older sites than Jericho, unfortunately not located in Palestine but further north in Anatolia, southeast Turkey, media interest in these new discoveries seemed to wane.

The most famous of these sites is Çatal Höyük. It was discovered in 1958 by British archaeologist James Mellaart, who began excavations in 1961 and eventually dated the site to 7500–5700 BC. It is the largest and best-preserved Neolithic site found to date. Mellaart described it as a Neolithic Rome, and it is indeed worthy of the name town. Its constructions show obvious signs that its inhabitants possessed a religion—labeled by some to be a Mother Goddess cult, although this theory has been the subject of much controversy. What is known is that the dead were buried beneath the floors of the buildings and that several of these structures contain depictions of bulls. Some people have gone so far as to suggest that there is likely a common origin between Çatal Höyük and the Minoan civilization of the Greek island of Crete, despite the fact that 3,000 years separate the two.

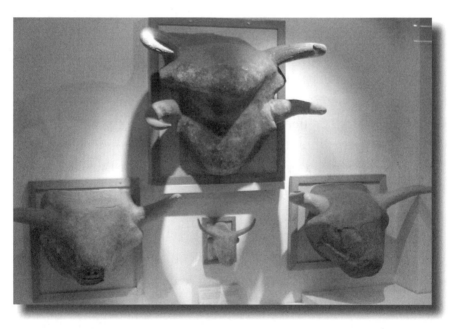

Çatal Höyük is one of the earliest human settlements and for decades was considered to be one of the earliest examples of civilization. The discovery of Göbekli Tepe has pushed back the birth of civilization a further 3,000 years, now dated to the eighth millennium BC. Çatal Höyük shows clearly the accomplishments of our ancestors and a specific preference for the bull.

Image copyright Stipich Béla. Made available as part of Creative Commons License on Wikimedia.

Çatal Höyük was the first of several discoveries to slowly unveil the Turkish region's ancient history. Göbekli Tepe is therefore but one of several extremely old sites, but is the oldest discovered so far. However, the existence of these sites has only been reported within the specialized press, although each site has a wow factor.

The site of Çayönü, located about 96 kilometers from Göbekli Tepe, conforms to a design that is known as a grill plan, as it looks like a grill. This reveals that careful planning went into its construction. Americans Linda and Robert Braidwood, together with Turkish archaeologist Halet Çambel, began to excavate Çayönü in 1964 and found that the floors of the buildings were made of terrazzo (burned crushed lime and clay), although at the time of the discovery it was thought that this had first been used by the Romans. The site also revealed the use of metals and the earliest evidence of the smelting of copper, though some nevertheless argue that the copper was originally cold-hammered rather than smelted. The use of copper should not come as a total surprise, as the site is within range of copper ore deposits (as well as obsidian) at Ergani in nearby Diyarbakir Province. All of this in a site dated to 7500–6600 BC. Çayönü is often seen as the site that began the epoch that would culminate in Çatal Höyük.

Çayönü presented evidence of the first farmyard pigs, but it also revealed a hoard of human skulls, one found under an altar-like slab and stained with human blood. Some have concluded that this is an indication of human sacrifice; others have been unwilling to go that far based on a single type of artifact. Other archaeological evidence suggests that some people were killed in huge death pits, and children were buried alive in jars or roasted in large bronze bowls. Çayönü is therefore civilization, but perhaps not as we like to know it.

Another important site is Nevali Çori, in the Hilvan Province between Diyarbakir and Sanliurfa. Here, Harald Hauptmann began excavations in 1979 and was able to uncover large limestone statues. In 1991, the site was submerged with the construction of Lake Atatürk Dam. It shares many parallels with Göbekli Tepe and is dated to 8400–8000 BC. All the artifacts retrieved are now in museums, including a life-sized egg-like head with crude ears and a carved ponytail, found in a niche at the center of a northwestern wall. Interestingly, the ponytail is actually a curling serpent that ends in a mushroom-like cap. Whatever being the figure is meant to represent, German archaeologist Klaus Schmidt believes it was worshipped as a deity.

Nevali Çori set the stage for Göbekli Tepe: Shortly after its disappearance under the waters, Göbekli Tepe emerged from the sands. Many people highlight the T-shaped pillars of Göbekli Tepe as the "signature" of the site. However, such T-shaped pillars were also found in Nevali Çori. Site-wise, Nevali Çori is more square than circular in design, although a square precinct has been found at Göbekli Tepe, too. Although there are several parallels between the two sites, Nevali Çori's pillars are nevertheless smaller, and its shrine is located inside a village.

In comparison, the site of Göbekli Tepe is small. British author Andrew Collins has compared its size to that of three tennis courts. The site's principal excavators are Klaus Schmidt and Harald Hauptmann of the German Archaeological Institute in Istanbul. All of the complexes in Göbekli Tepe that they have unearthed so far are typified by structures containing the site's typical T-pillars.

These pillars were used as drawing boards, and many depict animals, with an apparent preference for boars, foxes, reptiles, lions, crocodiles, and birds, as well as insects and spiders. Most of these were carved out of the flat surfaces of the pillars. However, some are three-dimensional sculptures, including one find, made during the 2006 excavation season, of a reptilian creature descending on the side of a

T-pillar, demonstrating that whoever created this had mastered the art of stone carving—on a par with much of what we would see thousands of years later in Sumer and Egypt.

So far, four circular/oval complexes have been excavated. The walls are made of un-worked dry stone and the floors of terrazzo. The interior of the walls usually have several T-pillars set along them in a radiating pattern, the depth of the pillar normally against or near the wall so that the two main surfaces of the pillar could be carved and seen by whoever was inside the complex. A low bench runs along the entire exterior wall of each complex.

The structures are situated on the southern slope of the hill, orientated roughly north-south with their entrances to the south. All the T-pillars were excavated from a stone quarry on the lower south-western slope of the hill. One pillar remains in situ in the quarry; it is 7 meters long and 3 meters wide, and if fully excavated would have weighed about 50 tons, underlining that building with stones that weigh tons did not begin in Egypt or in England with Stonehenge.

Complex A, the first circular structure to be excavated, is nick-named "the snake column building," because depictions of the snake somewhat dominate the carvings on the T-pillars. One is of a net containing snakes. Another pillar, however, depicts a triad of bull, fox, and crane, positioned one above the other. Some pillars only feature a bull, others only a fox, and so on.

Complex B measures 9 meters in diameter when measured from east to west, and 10 to 15 meters north to south (part of it is still to be excavated). It is nevertheless the only complex dug to floor level, revealing the terrazzo floor surface. Two central pillars have a large fox depicted on them. One central pillar, no. 9, is 3.4 meters high; pillar no. 10 is 3.6 meters high; their weights are 7.1 and 7.2 tons, respectively. The complex was built to house these monolithic pillars, which proves how well-versed our ancestors were in working with gigantic stones, not merely in quarrying them, but in shaping and decorating them as well. Archaeologists believe that 200 T-pillars originally stood at Göbekli Tepe. If each weighed "only" 5 tons, it would still mean that 1,000 tons of pillars were excavated and decorated, and it highlights the importance of the site and the effort that went into creating it, anno 10,000 BC.

Complex C is nicknamed "the circle of the boar," as it depicts various wild pigs. There remain nine pillars around the wall, but several were removed at some point in the past. One pillar shows a net of birds. As later cultures are known to have caught migratory cranes in nets, could this be a custom that was practiced much earlier than assumed? Complex C is also of interest because a U-shaped stone has been found there that is deemed to have been the access stone. This stone has a central passage of 70 centimeters in width, and one side of the U is topped with a depiction of a boar; the other side unfortunately is missing. Again, the U shape and the boar underline the craftsmen's technical expertise in carving, which is shown even more so on pillar no. 27, featuring the earlier-mentioned three-dimensional reptilian creature. This intricate sculpture could be regarded as being on a par with Michelangelo's statue of David.

Complex D is nicknamed "the Stone Age zoo." Pillar no. 43 has scorpions, and some pillars are indeed so profusely decorated—much more intensively than in the other complexes—that "zoo" is quite an apt description. Once again, there are two central pillars (nos. 18 and 31), though other pillars reveal symbols, such as one in the shape of the letter H, as well as one with an H turned 90 degrees. The site has revealed other symbols, specifically a cross, a resting half-moon, and horizontal bars—evidence that the origin of writing is likely to be much older than is currently assumed. Pillar no. 33 is the star of the complex. Schmidt states that the shapes on this pillar come close to the Egyptian hieroglyphs. Hence he posits the existence of a pictographic language in the 10th millennium BC.

Combined, these four complexes—and others, still unexcavated—are a series of ovals and resemble the layout of the oval-shaped Stone Age complexes found on Malta. This is all the more remarkable, as Malta's oval shapes were considered unique, though some of the megaliths on Sardinia also display some oval-like tendencies, but not as profoundly as at Göbekli Tepe.

A rock temple lower down on the slope is equally oval in shape and has an opening to the burial chamber. Whereas at other sites these openings are so narrow that a human could not navigate to the interior, here it is wide enough to enter.

Elsewhere on the site, on the northern slope of the hill, there is a rectangular complex named "the lion column building." Its four pillars have depictions of leonine creatures, which could also be tigers or leopards. One pillar has a 30-centimeters-high graffito of a squatting woman who appears to be giving birth.

Excavations at Göbekli Tepe are still ongoing; only a quarter of the suspected 200 T-pillars have been discovered so far, and not all the structures have been unearthed. In short, further surprises may be in store. It is early to draw major conclusions, but what could it all mean? The site definitely demonstrates that things that we thought were much more recent are far older and all present in one site, sitting in a region that shows that a civilization worthy of that name existed there in the 10th millennium BC, millennia before anyone would have dared to guess a few decades ago.

Klaus Schmidt has labeled Göbekli Tepe "the first temple" and "a sanctuary of the Stone Age hunter."[25] He sees the site as part of a death cult, not specifically linked with a sedentary group, but a type of central sanctuary for several of the tribes living in the region. The carved animals are believed to have been there to protect the dead. At Çayönü, as previously described, one structure has a cellar that was found to contain human skulls and bones. So far, though, Göbekli Tepe has no evidence of habitation, and therefore appears to have been purely a religious center.

Once again it appears that, just as the ancient Egyptians did, the civilization that constructed Göbekli Tepe had far greater regard for their religious buildings than for any structures of a practical or more materialistic nature. Still, with only Complex B excavated to floor level, no tombs or graves have been found to date.

Some have voiced criticism as to whether hunter-gatherers could have created such a structure as Göbekli Tepe. The many flint arrowheads (and the lack of construction tools) found around the site would seem to support this criticism, and one could even see these artifacts as part of sacred hunts rather than as part of the daily activities to put food on the table—if indeed tables even existed then.

Schmidt maintains that the hunter-gatherers convened at the site at certain times of the year. Whether these meetings were determined by solar or lunar cycles is anyone's guess, but it is nevertheless an interesting question to ponder. Equally, one could logically conclude that those who constructed the site lived there and were a dedicated resource supported by others who sustained them in dietary and housing needs. Archaeologists have estimated that up to 500 persons would have been required to extract the 10- to 20-ton pillars and move them from the quarry to their destination, a distance ranging from 100 to 500 meters. However, Schmidt actually believes that maintaining the community of builders was the real reason behind why our ancestors "invented" agriculture: They began to cultivate the wild grasses on the hills to sustain this sedentary population. In short, he believes that religion motivated people to take up farming.

As well as appearing to have ritual significance, Göbekli Tepe, with its large and exquisitely decorated stone blocks, reveals that its creators had an extraordinary ability and familiarity with stone masonry and carving. That our ancestors in 10,000 BC were so skilled is an archaeological discovery that is wiping out long-cherished beliefs about the origin of civilization.

As for the carvings, why were some and not other animals chosen? Why do the depictions seem to have no apparent organization but appear to be a rather random collection? The truth is, we don't know. In later civilizations, all of these animals were given divine attributes. Some cultures chose to depict snakes because these animals shed their skin, which they saw as a symbol of rebirth. Others opted for the same animal for different reasons. So far, there is no way of knowing what beliefs the creators and users of Göbekli Tepe held.

Some observers have pointed out that some of the cranes are depicted with human-like knees and have suggested that a form of shamanism was practiced inside this temple. Sister sites have revealed sculptures of a mixture of animal and human, specifically that of the body of a bird with a human head. As it happened, thousands of years later the ancient Egyptians used this symbol as a hieroglyph to depict the ba, the human soul freed from the body at death or during shamanic flight.

Andrew Collins has specifically underlined the shamanic potential of these sites in modern-day Turkey. The image of the previously mentioned naked woman depicts her hair in the shape of a hemispherical mushroom cap. The side of one pillar at Göbekli Tepe features a series of serpents with mushroom-shaped heads, four winding their way downward and a fifth one climbing up to meet them; the other side shows several interwoven serpents wearing mushroom-like caps, eight emerging at the top and nine at the bottom. Is this evidence of a ritual involving hallucinogenic mushrooms or similar mind-altering substances? If so, Göbekli Tepe might have much in common with the rock paintings of the Tassili, where similar scenes were found, suggesting that our ancestors used hallucinogenic substances to explore other dimensions. It is likely that the origins of belief in an afterlife and the existence of superior intelligences could be derived from the practitioners of Göbekli Tepe and the Tassili—or maybe we need to travel even further back in time.

The bones of vultures have been found at Nevali Çori, Göbekli Tepe, and Jerf el-Ahmar (in Syria). A communal cave site, Shanidar, in the Upper Zagros Mountains of northern Iraq, contained a series of severed birds' wings covered with red ochre. The remains have been dated to c. 8870 BC. The wings are believed to have been used in some ceremony, but precisely in what manner remains unknown. However, it is known that, in the distant past, the people of this region placed the bodies of the dead on high constructions and let vultures eat the flesh of the dead. Depictions of such a Neolithic excarnation tower have been found on a mural in Çatal Höyük. Interestingly, human bones have recently been found in the soil that once filled the niches behind the megaliths at Göbekli Tepe. Schmidt argues: "[T]he ancient hunters brought the corpses of relatives here, and installed them in the open niches by the stones. The corpses were then excarnated."[26] Not just vultures but wild animals seem to have taken part in this ritual. This may explain why so many animals are depicted on the T-pillars: Perhaps the people who constructed these sites felt that "something" of the dead lived on in these animals.

What is known is that Göbekli Tepe and its sister sites have pushed back the age of monolithic building much further in time. Previously, we looked to the likes of Stonehenge and the Egyptian pyramids, but now we find that our ancestors were hauling massive stones to build their constructions around 12,000 years ago. Even if a structure such as the Sphinx were suddenly found to be 10,000 years old, the immediate reaction might now perhaps be: "So what? It is not that unique." Furthermore, if the dates for some of these sites in Turkey pre-date the assumed time frame for such events as the disappearance of Atlantis or the Great Flood, it means that these ancient ancestors cannot be neatly placed as survivors from a deluge.

Our ancient history has grown much more interesting and complex. The cultures that followed the establishment of Göbekli Tepe had domesticated pigs, sheep, cattle, and goats, and they cultivated wheat species such as einkorn. Indeed, recent analysis has shown that the first cultivation of domesticated wheat occurred at Karacadag, a mountain 32 kilometers from Göbekli Tepe. Other domesticated cereals such as rye and oats also originated here. According to Schmidt, this adventure began in c. 8000 BC, many thousands years sooner than recently believed.

It is easy and tempting to label this region as the cradle of civilization, but the fact of the matter is that it has already been proven that corn (maize) was engineered in Mexico at the same time, only underlining how the frontiers of "civilization" are being pushed back on both continents. In fact, there is evidence of Barbary sheep being cultivated by our ancestors in North Africa as early as 18,000 BC. Furthermore, several grains of emmer wheat have been found at the Palestinian site of Nahal Oren, suggesting cultivation of this crop occurred there as early as 14,000 BC.

Most importantly, Göbekli Tepe is not alone. Another site, Karahan Tepe, 63 kilometers east of Urfa in the Tektek Mountains, deserves equal attention. Discovered in 1997 and investigated by archaeologist Bahattin Çelik of the Turkish Historical Society, it has been dated to c. 9500–9000 BC. It has a number of T-pillars, as well as high reliefs of a winding snake and other carvings similar to those at Göbekli Tepe. Covering an area of 325,000 square meters, Karahan Tepe is much bigger than Göbekli Tepe. The stone pillars are spaced 1.5 to 2 meters apart and protrude above ground level, waiting for an archaeologist to expose them fully. Other carved stones include a battered torso of a naked man and polished rock with forms of goats, gazelles, and rabbits.

It is too early to draw any extraordinary conclusions from these sites, apart from the fact that our history is no longer as we know it. Just as Jericho proved in part that the Bible contains historical facts, though, these sites may yet substantiate some of the Sumerian myths that claimed that agriculture, animal husbandry, and weaving was brought to mankind from the sacred mountain Du-Ku, which was inhabited by the Anunna deities. Though it's unlikely that this mountain was Göbekli Tepe, we are probably in the correct general vicinity here at the frontier of the Taurus Mountains.

Around 8000 BC, descendants of the creators of Göbekli Tepe turned on their forefathers' achievements and entombed their temple under thousands of tons of earth, creating the artificial hill—a "belly"— that we see today. Why they did this is unknown, though it was a decision that preserved the monument for posterity, but also involved an extraordinary amount of time and effort on their part. Schmidt argues that the local landscape began to change around that time: As the trees were chopped down, the soil began to lose its fertility; the area became arid and bare, and the people were forced to move elsewhere. Could it be that they began to make their descent and, millennia later, established what is known as the Sumerian civilization? Such a scenario is just one possibility.

Even in ancient Egypt, religious constructions were often abandoned if not dismantled after a while, because they belonged to a particular astronomical cycle of time that had since passed. If that were the case with Göbekli Tepe, it would mean that knowledge of astronomy is older by millennia. The past five decades have so radically reshaped our understanding of the period 10,000–4000 BC, specifically the level of "civilization" our ancestors had achieved in those days, that this shouldn't at all come as a surprise. It seems that it's a given that, somewhere, even older towns are waiting to be uncovered.

However, entering into the mindset of these hunter-gatherers—how they saw these animals and what they believed happened to the dead—is a difficult subject that will require years of study. Alas, it is an area where few archaeologists dare to tread, and in all likelihood they will hop from one site to the next, as they've done for several decades, and will only uncover the fact—in some cases, reluctantly—that civilization is much older than we've assumed. Already, other sites are vying for Göbekli Tepe's fame. The previously mentioned site of Jerf el-Ahmar, located along the Euphrates in Syria, has been dated to 9600–8500 BC. Other sites will certainly soon submit their applications. It's likely they will all reveal that they are part of our history, but not as we know it.

Chapter 3

Lost Civilizations of the New World

Copper Trade Inc., 3000 BC

Prehistoric cultural exchange is an ideological enemy of most historians. But it is a matter of fact that tin was traded throughout Europe in the Bronze Age, for otherwise there would not have been a Bronze Age. But the issue of the Bronze Age and its two ingredients—tin and copper—does not stop at the edge of this continent. Across North America are remnants of a lost civilization, which American archaeologists have been slow to appreciate—so slow that the real truth of who built some of these structures might forever have become lost.

Archaeologists have somewhat reluctantly accepted that much more copper was used than what they have been able to attribute to European mines. So where did an extremely large part of the copper come from? The answer, as bizarre as it may sound, could be America. It is known that, during the European Bronze Age, large quantities of copper were mined in North America. However, no one is able to answer where the copper that was mined there was used on the American Continent. It simply has not been found there.

If we were to add the two problems together, do we have the solution? Of course, the answer for the reigning scientific dogma is no, as it argues that there were no transoceanic contacts in the Bronze Age, and hence copper could not have been traded from the New to the Old World. But perhaps there is sufficient scientific evidence available that will challenge these assumptions of the scientists.

The chief ingredient for bronze is copper. The era around 3000 BC saw more than 500,000 tons of copper being mined in the so-called Upper Peninsula, in the American state of Michigan. The largest mine was on Isle Royale, an island in Lake Superior, near the Canadian border. Here, there are thousands of prehistoric copper pits, dug thousands of years ago by ancient peoples unknown. The Minong Belt on Isle Royale has a distance of 1.75 miles in length and is nearly 400 feet wide. The copper pits range from 10 to 30 feet deep with connecting tunnels; one archaeologist estimated that their digging would take the equivalent of 10,000 men working for 1,000 years.

After two centuries of speculation, no one has ever satisfactorily explained where the world's purist copper might have gone. Extraction from Isle Royal began in 5300 BC, with some even claiming that it began as early as 6000 BC. Evidence for smelting is known to exist from "only" 4000 BC onward.

The exact size of how ore was mined here is perhaps never going to be exactly determined, but what is known, is that c. 1200 BC, all mining activity was halted. Is it a coincidence that in 1200 BC Europe was plunged into a continent-wide recession that would last several centuries? It would take until c. AD 1000 before mining was restarted; it lasted until AD 1320. During this period, a moderate 2,000 tons were removed.

In North America, not even 1 percent of the mined ore has been recovered. Some individual pieces of ore that were removed weigh 34,000 pounds, which equals the combined weight of all bronze or copper artifacts found in the United States. Other stones, such as the Ontonagon Boulder, weigh 3,700 pounds. One 5,720-pound mass found near McCargo's Cove was raised partway to the surface on cribbing in the same way others were found in other mines. The ancient workers were raising these stones, but the archaeological evidence reveals that some were left abandoned mid-task, showing that the mining efforts were suddenly and unexpectedly called off.

Octave DuTemple, one of the first archaeologists to investigate the site, stated that the miners left their tools behind, as if they had thought that the following morning, they would return to their quarry and continue their work.

These miners were experienced laborers. The mines were efficiently run, producing large quantities of ore that could be quickly transported to the surface. Between 1,000 and 12,000 tons of material were removed from one mine, resulting in approximately 50 tons of copper. Their technique was basic, but efficient: They created large fires on the veins of the copper ore, heating the stone, then pouring water on top of it. This cracked the rock and with the aide of stone tools, the copper was removed from the rock.

About 5,000 mines have been discovered, in an area that is c. 140 miles long and 3 to 7 miles wide. The area mined on Isle Royale measures 5 to 40 miles. If all mines were placed in one consecutive row, it would measure five miles, and be 25 feet wide and 30 feet deep.

Every mine that was opened in the past 200 years showed some previous, prehistoric mining activity. This included mines where the copper ore did not protrude to the surface—showing evidence of the advanced knowledge tht allowed the prehistoric miners to identify subterranean ores. It also worked the other way around, for sites that showed evidence of ancient mining were in modern times considered to be good omens, as they were often the best sites to find copper—lots of copper.

How the miners knew which stones contained copper is a mystery. They obviously did, but where they learned this information is unknown, as it remains unknown who was responsible for the mining activity.

If there were no transoceanic contacts, is it not highly remarkable that both continents, completely independent from each other, at the same moment in time, began to mine and use copper and tin to create bronze, yet America did nothing sensible with it—apart from a few artifacts that have been recovered?

The Menomonie Indians of north Wisconsin possess a legend that speaks about the ancient mines. They described the mines as being worked by light-skinned men, who were able to identify the mines by throwing magical stones on the ground, which made the ores that contained copper ring like a bell. This practice closely resembles a similar practice that was used in Europe during the Bronze Age. Bronze with a high concentration of tin indeed resonates when a stone is thrown against it. The legend might have confused the start of the process with the result of the process. Even so, S.A. Barnett, the first archaeologist who studied Aztalan, a metropolitan site near the mines, believed that the miners originated from Europe. His conclusion was largely based on the type of tools that had been used—tools that were not used by the local people. Another piece of "hard" evidence so far uncovered is a statue discovered in c. 1660 by a missionary, Allouez, who traveled through the region and stumbled upon a 1-foot-tall copper statue, depicting a man with a beard. The native Indians do not have beards.

With a vast workforce—possibly as many as 10,000 people— some must have died. It is also likely that at least some laborers came with families to the area. In short, there must have been a number of dead people, but where are the burials? The answer, it seems, is nowhere. There is no evidence of cremation or burial near any of the sites or the Upper Peninsula; the only things that were left behind were their tools—millions of them.

In 1922, William A. Ferguson discovered a harbor on the north coast of Isle Royale. Ships could load and unload, aided by a pier that measured 1,500 feet in length. This suggests that the type of ships that anchored here were large ships—and that there were many. The most likely explanation as to the purpose of this harbor was that they formed the point where the copper was loaded to be transported to other regions. The presence of a harbor was further proof that the people working the mines were not local, as the local Indians only used small canoes.

It is likely that the mines were only worked during the summer, with the workforce moving further south during the winter months. This could explain the absence of buildings: People living here in the winter need buildings to survive, but that is not necessarily so during the summer months.

Equally interesting is the fact that there are no signs of copper smelting factories, required for its future use. This means that the copper was transformed elsewhere, as copper required further handling for it to be useful.

Could we find out where the miners went for the winter months? Though back to Europe is a possibility, it is also unlikely. Their most likely habitats were probably Aztalan and Rock Lake, where some years ago, buildings and a temple were discovered just below the water surface. These sites are a mere 30 miles south of the snowline, which makes them ideal places to settle for the winter. Furthermore, their winter residence and summer work site were connected via rivers, allowing for convenient transportation.

Most interestingly, it is around Rock Lake that many graves have been discovered. No less than 70 funerary hills containing the cremated remains of thousands of individuals have been discovered there. One of the better preserved graves contains the body of a man with a hammer; a similar hammer was discovered at Isle Royale.

So, is the problem of the copper trade fully answered with the discovery of their remains around Rock Lake? The problem is that though Rock Lake seemed to house the workforce, nowhere is there any evidence that they, or other people nearby, used the copper. So the problem of where the copper went remains. Furthermore, the copper was definitely worthy of a transoceanic voyage. The copper around Lake Superior was the best and most important copper found in the world. Between AD 1000 and AD 1400, the copper was exported to the Mexican Toltecs—and perhaps other civilizations further south. But who were the buyers several millennia before?

When we look to the problem on a global scale, there are only a handful of possible cultures that possessed the advanced knowledge to mine copper ore. The most likely candidate, however, remains Bronze Age Europe. The mining techniques in America are also identical to those used in the British Isles, from where the other component, tin, originated. Together with Spain, the British Isles were the main sources of tin, and the depletion of the Cornish tin mines in 1200 BC clearly meant that there was no further need for copper. Indeed, after the Bronze Age came the Iron Age, but this was a development that occurred out of necessity, not desire, because our ancestors somehow felt iron was superior to bronze.

Western Europe in the Bronze Age was largely driven by the sea. The areas that were most populated and the furthest developed were all coastal, with many, such as the Orkneys, strangely off the beaten track—yet the Orkneys are perfectly situated if there was trans-oceanic contact.

More and more scientists are agreeing that Bronze Age Europe was a maritime system. Is it that impossible to suggest that travelers who sailed from Spain to Scotland would not have been able to cross to America? Some might argue that the waters of the ocean were far rougher than those coastal waters, but anyone sailing around Land's End in Cornwall—where the ships had to pass to take tin—will know these seas there are extremely rough. Would it be impossible to assume that a world economy of copper and tin existed in 3000 BC? The archaeological record on two continents suggests this was indeed the case.

THE SMOKING GUN?

Finding evidence of prehistoric, transoceanic contact is very much like looking for the smoking gun. One man who may have come upon the best evidence for transoceanic contact is Russell Burrows. He accidentally discovered a cave along a branch of the Little Wabash River near his home town of Olney, Illinois, in 1982. Hunting for discarded archaeological relics, he found a shallow cave leading into a subterranean corridor, the likes of which you'd not expect to find in rural Illinois. The passageway was lined with oil lamps, the ceiling black from smoke. The 500-foot-long tunnel had several chambers along it.

The Burrows Cave, as it is now known, is famous for its large numbers of inscribed stones, often containing profiles of people who look African, Egyptian, and European as well as Native American. On first sight they look crude: the work of an amateur or someone meeting an imminent deadline. Furthermore, preliminary analyses of the writing on the stones revealed a mix, if not a mismatch, of various styles, words, and languages that archaeologists and linguists quickly labeled as obviously fake ("obvious" being a preferred word that scientists use to underline what they can easily, obviously, see is fake, though amateurs are fooled by it, obviously). As early as 1983, Burrows placed a very small collection of the artifacts on sale in a local antique shop—but if he created the entire collection, he created so many that he could never have gotten rid of them all. Moreover, it was not until 1997 that he or anyone else would cash in on the stones themselves. If Burrows wanted to get rich from creating fake artifacts, his hoax was obviously ill executed.

A rare photograph, taken by Russell Burrows, from the inside of Burrows Cave, of an area that is labeled as crypt 4. Burrows found this enigmatic cave complex in Illinois. The cave was a tomb complex, occupied by what appears to be European nobility that fled Europe long before Columbus ever discovered America.

But the cave is more than just a collection of inscribed stones. Burrows allegedly found and removed many gold artifacts. These look genuine and contain the same mismatch of writing. You can only wonder why a fraud, if Burrows were indeed one, would use gold—which, to begin with, is costly to obtain. It is true that there are conflicting stories about this gold. Burrows at one point stated that some of the gold had been melted down and then sold. Swiss author Luc Bürgin claimed that Burrows removed huge quantities of gold, had it melted down, and then sold it, depositing a grand total of $15 million (U.S. dollars) into

Swiss bank accounts. If true, this indicates that Burrows did indeed get his hands on tremendous amounts of gold and decided to sell for the gold's monetary value—not the archaeological value. Others have stated that Bürgin was merely told this information by a fellow researcher and possesses no evidence for his assertion.

Some skeptics claim that the gold never existed—that it has never been seen. That's not true, because early researchers did see it. I have been shown color photographs of apparently gold artifacts by Burrows himself. Other critics argue that the "gold" was just metal, finished off with gold paint to make it look real. If they are correct, then Burrows merely created these artifacts to fool archaeologists, amateur scientists, and the media, and he could never allow any direct contact with or testing of the artifacts. It would also mean that he could never have regarded the gold artifacts as part of a quick money-making scheme. In short, this conclusion is incompatible with the other skeptics' argument, which is that Burrows tried to make money from a hoax.

Burrows claimed that inside the complex, he discovered a male human skeleton in the first crypt. The second chamber had a funeral bier with the remains of a woman and two children. A golden spearhead lay in the woman's ribs, where the heart would have been. The skulls of the children showed signs of perforation. The scene suggested that the woman and children had been murdered at the time when the male, her husband, died. In total, there were 12 crypts. The central chamber, containing the golden sarcophagus, was closed by a stone that had to be rolled away. The room, including the ceiling, was decorated and white marble was seen throughout. The golden sarcophagus inside the stone tomb resembled the ancient Egyptian form of burial. It displayed the same style of wearing the hair as well as the crossed arms on the body, and the hands were holding the ankh symbol. It is said that Burrows was able to open the sarcophagus and saw that it contained human remains as well as a death mask, also thought to be of Egyptian origin. Although the sarcophagus was of tremendous value—to be compared with the golden sarcophagus of Tutankhamun—it could not be removed from the cave by just Burrows with the help of his brother-in-law. Furthermore, Burrows was unsure as to whether he might face prosecution if he disturbed the human remains he'd found in the cave or if he tried to sell any of its contents.

Burrows was obviously totally unprepared for such a find (who wouldn't be?), and his volatile character did not help in a situation where patience is a virtue. On July 27, 1984, the local *Olney Daily Mail* ran a small article identifying Burrows as the discoverer of a local cave, but provided little more except for this hope: "[T]he university [with which he was in contact] will probably begin the dig next year. At that time, more information can be given."[1] Though Burrows sought help from the scientific world, he received mixed reactions from it. Soon afterward, one amateur archaeologist after another pressed his doorbell. Each one almost immediately asked to see the cave. It's like a person in a plaster cast getting constantly asked whether someone can see or sign his/her plaster; at some point the answer will be no, because it feels as if no one is interested in you but only in your plaster. For Burrows, it felt like all they wanted was to see the cave; they had no basic respect or regard for his own wishes, often not even bothering to ask about them. People such as these came away disappointed, hurt because Burrows did not want to play their game, and they often voiced scathing opinions. In this regard, amateur archaeologists suffer from the same human frailties as professional archaeologists.

Others wanted to use the Burrows Cave to substantiate their own pet theories. One of these was Joseph P. Mahan, author of the 1983 book *The Secret,* who suggested in a 1991 lecture that the cave was connected with "sun-related semi-divine mortals [who] were the descendants of extraterrestrial immortal progenitors who had come to Earth in fire ships, had resided for a while [and] had upgraded the humanoids they found here by modifying the genes of these children of Earth, thus producing a hybrid progeny."[2] Such a nonsensical conclusion is not based on anything at all that Burrows ever said about the case, but it rubbed off badly on Burrows's image and the cave.

Another example of how the cave became a hostage in other people's battles is the story of Richard Flavin, who used the cave to persecute Frank Joseph. For more than 15 years, Joseph had nothing to do with the story until, in his position as a writer for *The Ancient American* magazine, he became interested and eventually wrote a book about it (*The Lost Treasure of King Juba*). But Flavin instead focused on Joseph's past as a neo-Nazi (dating back to the early 1970s) and uses this as ammunition to "prove" that anyone suggesting the cave could be real is hence a neo-Nazi. Flavin met Burrows on a few occasions, but his interpretation of events is spurious at best and his account reads more like that of a Christian missionary in the lands of the "primitives" or a communist witch-hunter of the 1950s than a scientific approach to the subject.[3]

In the final analysis, the story of the Burrows Cave is typical for a finding of this nature. Just look at other similar discoveries and replace the names; the general storyline would hardly alter. The same basic stand-off is here, with the scientific experts quick to condemn the artifacts they were shown as obvious forgeries. By default, the artifacts could not be genuine, for we all "know" that Columbus was the first to reach America. When it came to the amateurs, Burrows was unprepared for and unaware of the amount of in-fighting and controversy that exist in most amateur organizations. In the process, he was eaten alive—and so was his story.

Unfortunately, Russell Burrows's personal disillusionment apparently led him to dynamite the entrance to the cave. He reportedly did this in 1989, three years before his cowritten book, *The Mystery*

Cave of Many Faces, was published. It's an extremely level-headed account of his discovery of the cave and the artifacts inside—and something that he considered to be his final word on the topic. But though Burrows often claimed to have lost interest in his discovery (largely because of the difficult people he had to deal with), he still returned to it. The fact that he could not let go, even though there was nothing in it for him anymore, should perhaps be seen as the best evidence that Burrows had indeed made a legitimate discovery. For if this discovery had started as a money-making scheme in 1982, by 1992 he had long abandoned such hope.

In 1993, diffusionist thinkers now had a new magazine to turn to, *The Ancient American,* which during the course of the subsequent decade continued to follow the story of the cave. In 1999, the magazine's founder/publisher, Wayne May, decided that if no one else could bring about a change in the situation, he would do so himself. Having reported on the subject for the previous six years, spoken to the man, and heard him out, May got Burrows to sign a contract and to disclose and show him the location of the cave—despite his initial belief that Burrows had lied about the location and had actually laid a false trail. From my personal dealings with Burrows in 1992 and 1993, I found him to be a man of honor. If he promised something, he would do it (cue for the critics to laugh at what they will see is my "obvious" gullibility). That, it seems, is what May felt as well. So, despite his initial reluctance to believe, May finally knew the location and persevered with his investigations. His ground-penetrating radar indicated that a cave was indeed there. The problem was how to get in, considering that Burrows's explosion a decade earlier had destroyed the entrance. Unfortunately, it soon became evident that the explosion had not only blocked the entrance but had also damaged the interior of the tunnel. During May's various attempts to gain access, each time he stumbled upon huge quantities of water. This seemed to indicate that the explosion had diverted the flow of an underground river and as a result had caused water to gush into the underground complex. It therefore looked like salvaging anything from the underground complex would be terribly complex—and largely outside May's capabilities.

In a nutshell, this is a nearly 30-year-long story that has left hardly anyone who has looked into it untouched or without an opinion. It is all too easy to label Burrows a hoaxer. People who have known and worked with him have called him many things, but not a fabricator of evidence or a liar. He has an explosive nature on occasion and has sometimes not been the best judge of character. No one is perfect, and we've observed the same human touches in Emile Fradin or Sam Osmanagic. But theirs and Burrows's character flaws are largely incidental in this narrative. Only his skeptics focus too heavily on them, whereas they should be focusing instead on whether or not he could actually have fabricated any, let alone such huge numbers of, inscribed stones. If we were placed in the same situation, the end result would be the same, for it is in the nature of such discoveries and how we react to them that they tend to produce the same kind of outcomes.

So, the fate of the cave was sealed, doomed from the moment that Burrows slid down into it. Where does this leave us? For skeptics to cry foul, they need to come up with better than "obvious" statements. There is no evidence that Burrows faked the stones. Skeptics argue that Burrows was known to work with wood and create wooden artifacts in his spare time. Indeed. This they see as evidence that he faked the stones. More importantly, there is evidence that a cave system exists where Burrows claims it exists. If it is all a hoax, the skeptics will need to provide evidence instead of repeatedly using the word "obvious." Still, even if the cave system is there, it may perhaps be lost to us forever. Any operation that could be mounted to provide a conclusive answer would cost an extraordinary amount of money—and such resources are "obviously" not in the hands of the diffusionists. So it seems that, once again, the establishment has won the fight and the status quo of how we look at our history remains standing—and that may be the only obvious thing about this entire story.

What sense can we make of all this? Could a golden sarcophagus, allegedly found in an Illinois cave, be evidence of pre-Columbian transoceanic travel between the Old World and the Americas, as so many people have claimed? While Burrows described what the cave looked like and what it contained, fortunately most of the artifacts removed from the cave were photographed early on, in part due to the efforts of James Schertz and Fred Rydholm. Various researchers have looked at this collection, and archaeologists have been quick to point out the mismatches. But most cultures are a mismatch of cultures! London and New York are prime examples of how various cultures create a new one. Both cities clearly exist! Things were no different in ancient times, the Egyptian city of Alexandria probably being the best example. Furthermore, this is all about the approach: Professional archaeologists will argue that all cultures developed in isolation, which would allow for easy identification of artifacts, whereas it is becoming evident that cultures exchanged goods and materials frequently, revealing what archaeologists call mismatches—artifacts that have signs of various cultures.

The Burrows Cave was a burial cave, but who was buried here? An important clue is that some of the stone slabs displayed a signature that was known in the Old World. It belonged to one Alexander Helios, son of Cleopatra and Marc Antony, and twin brother of Cleopatra Selene, the future co-ruler of Mauritania (in Africa's western Sahara). Among Burrows's earliest team of amateur researchers were Jack Ward and Warren Cook, the latter of whom died in 1989. Cook's analysis of the artifacts made him conclude that creating them would have taken thousands of hours. But more importantly, Cook continued Ward's analysis of their possible origin and argued that they were most likely the remains of a Libyan-Iberian expedition. He identified Mauritania's King Ptolemaeus I (1 BC–AD 40), son of Cleopatra Selene and King Juba II (52–50 BC–AD 23), as the man responsible for this transoceanic voyage. Could this have been possible?

The rulers of Mauritania had fallen foul of the Roman emperors, if only because of the economic power that Mauritania had become, turning the scales on who was in control of whom. When the Roman Empire decided to redress that balance, the Mauritanian king Juba II and his family had to flee. It's possible that he used the knowledge of the seas that his ancestors, the Phoenicians, had gathered. He knew the location of the Azores, whose goods he was able to sell at the highest prices in Rome and elsewhere. So, if the Burrows Cave artifacts are genuine and the interpretation correct, it's possible that the Phoenician-informed Mauritanian royal family sailed further west, beyond the Azores, to the Americas.

If they ended up in Central America, perhaps they entered the Mississippi River and traveled north until reaching Illinois—where they settled, far removed from the squabbles of the Old World. The cave artifacts are not the only evidence of the presence of an enigmatic people in the first century AD. According to one Native American legend, the region contains the tomb of a king who was not native to America. The tribe once knew the location, but this information is now lost. Could this location be the same as the Burrows Cave? Furthermore, it is known that Juba II ordered a golden sarcophagus to be prepared for the mausoleum that had been built for him in Tipaza (modern-day Algeria). This was one of the prized possessions that the Romans had tried to get their hands on, but they never did find the sarcophagus or the Mauritanian king. Official history is silent on the fate of both. King Juba II must have died, and he and his sarcophagus must have ended up somewhere, and maybe that was somewhere in Illinois.

THE LEGEND OF AKAKOR

On March 3, 1972, German journalist Karl Brugger met a local Amazonian Indian, Tatunca Nara, in the backstreet tavern Gracas a Deus. The meeting would result in Brugger's book *The Chronicle of Akakor,* published in 1976, which saw a number of foreign editions and created the legend of Akakor, a mythical town somewhere deep within the Amazonian jungle, still left to be discovered. In 2008, the story was incorporated in *Indiana Jones and the Kingdom of the Crystal Skull.*

The title of Brugger's book was supposedly the same title as the chronicle that the Amazonian Ugha Mogulala tribe (which also makes an appearance in the Indiana Jones movie) held sacred—or at least central—to their mythology and philosophy. Indeed, Tatunca Nara claimed to be a member of this unknown Amazonian tribe, the son of a native and the daughter of a German missionary—which was supposed to account for his impeccable German.

The mere notion that an Amazonian tribe had a written chronicle was remarkable, as the Amazon population is largely believed not to have a written language. A second bombshell was that Tatunca claimed that the Year Zero of the Chronicle was 10,481 BC—very much outside accepted archaeological dates for human occupation of the Amazon, but perfectly fitting in the Atlantis and Deluge theory that many alternative researchers favored as the anti-thesis to the Science-wrought framework and that was, at the time, already made popular due to the American "prophet" Edgar Cayce. The third bombshell was that the Gods came from a solar system known as Schwerta, and built an underground tunnel system in South America. Each element on its own and all together even more so made for a stunning revelation—or lie.

Tatunca Nara had made a series of tall claims, and they definitely required the caliber of an Indiana Jones to test them to reality. The best evidence in favor of them would be to discover any of the several cities in the Amazon jungle, including any of the 13 underground cities, which this civilization had allegedly left behind. Their most important ancient towns were said to be known as Akakor, Akanis, and Akahim, as well as Cuczo and Machu Picchu, the latter two known sites part of the Incan Empire. The first, Akanis, was built "on a narrow isthmus in the country that is called Mexico,"[4] at a place where the two oceans meet (Panama?). The second was Akakor (apparently derived from *Aka*, "fort," and *kor*, "two"—Fort Two) and lay far up the Purus River, in a high valley in the mountains of the border between Brazil and Peru: "The whole city is surrounded by a high stone wall with thirteen gates. They are so narrow that they give access only to one person a time."[5] Tatunca added that the city had a Great Temple of the Sun, that it contained documents, such as maps and drawings telling the history of the Earth. "One of the maps shows that our moon is not the first and not the only one in the history of the earth. The moon that we know began to approach the earth and to circle around it thousands of years ago."[6]

The third fortress was Akahim, which was apparently not mentioned in the chronicle before the year 7315 BC, was linked with Akakor, and was situated on the borders of Brazil and Venezuela. Tatunca Nara concluded that 26 stone cities were built around Akakor, including Humbaya and Paititi in Bolivia, Emin, Cadira in Venezuela, and so on. As stone is rare in these locations, it merely underlined that, if genuine, these were indeed extraordinary finds. Alas, Tatunca added, "[A]ll these were completely destroyed in the first Great Catastrophe thirteen years after the departure of the Gods."[7] It meant that there was very little left to check on the ground. It also meant that Tatunca's claims seemed to be unverifiable.

Was Tatunca telling the truth or was he a con artist? It was a very tall tale he told, and with the stakes being very high, Brugger decided to investigate and see where the rabbit—or Tatunca—would take him. The two decided to go on an expedition in search of Akahim, setting off on September 25, 1972, on a trip that would last six weeks. Akahim, however, was not discovered.

That was Act One. In 1976, *The Chronicle of Akakor* was published and the controversy was reignited. Part of the core message of the chronicle was the statement that there was a network of tunnels, some still in existence today and used by the Native Americans. On his part, during the summer of 1977, Swiss ancient astronaut author Erich von Däniken traveled for a third time to Manaus to meet with Tatunca Nara, in the hope that via Tatunca, he could produce evidence and vindicate himself. Apart from von Däniken and Brugger, a third European entered the scene: a former Swissair pilot Ferdinand Schmid, who was living in Brazil, and who contacted Tatunca Nara in 1975. In 1977 and 1978, the pair made several attempts to penetrate into the jungle, in search of Akahim. The 1978 expedition was joined by an archaeologist, Roldao Pires Brandao, added to the team by the Brazilian government. He was also the reason why the mission had to be abandoned: Brandao apparently shot himself in the arm, for unknown reasons. Once recovered, he got the Brazilian authorities sufficiently interested to set up an expedition of their own, and he eventually set off with six men.

In its August 1, 1979 edition, *Veja,* a Brazilian magazine, reported the discovery of Akahim, including a number of photographs. That same year, Tatunca and Schmid claimed to have found Akahim, too— sort of. Early on, Tatunca had stated that Akahim had three large pyramids and they claimed to have found these. Still, though seen, they had not visited the site itself and Schmid lost—or claimed to have lost—his camera and film.

Then began Act Two for real. It was the time frame when two legends merged: Tatunca stated that he knew Juan Moricz, a Hungarian-born Ecuadorian who had allegedly shown Erich von Däniken underground tunnels in Ecuador. So two separate stories of underground tunnels were now possibly linked. Tatunca stated he had met Moricz when he was staying in Venezuela in 1967. Moricz did spend time in Venezuela, a fact that is not often reported or known. As Moricz was also quite a high-profile visitor to the country (he befriended the president), that Tatunca met Moricz is therefore not an impossibility. But whether it is significant is an entirely different matter.

The legend of Akakor unexpectedly received an entirely new dimension when Karl Brugger was murdered leaving a restaurant in Rio de Janeiro on January 1, 1984. Though a life does not cost much in Brazil and armed robbery is even more violent there than in the rest of Southern America, some have queried whether his murder had anything to do with his book and/or knowledge of Akakor. So far, no one has been able to show a link. At the time, Tatunca Nara was apparently questioned, but was able to provide an alibi for his whereabouts.

Then came Act Three—an act that few people have seen or known about. Since the 1970s, the Amazon has become much more open to the world, and parts where Brugger had great difficulty in getting to are now less so. Akakor, however, remains undiscovered. At the same time, the question needs to be posed whether Tatunca merely drove with Brugger into the jungle, knowing that even though everything was an invention, they would at some point hit an obstacle, which would necessitate their return home—and would make his lie live to see another day.

After Brugger, Tatunca Nara took several others into the jungle, apparently all enthralled by the legend of Akakor, and trying to be the discoverer—or at least co-discoverer—of this mythical city. In 1980, Tatunca left with American John Reed on such an expedition, but only Tatunca Nara returned; what happened to John Reed is unknown, but it is assumed he died in the rainforest. In 1983, Tatunca left with Swiss explorer Herbert Wanner, and he didn't return, either. A few years later, a group of tourists came across a human skull, which was later identified as Wanner's. In 1987, Swede Christine Heuser also left with Tatunca on an expedition, and disappeared as well. Tatunca Nara later denied he traveled with any of these men into the jungle, but the site where Wanner's skull was found left no doubt whatsoever that he had left on an expedition, Tatunca Nara being the only logical guide that accompanied him.

Rumors of Tatunca's own death circulated on a number of occasions. In 2003, he had himself declared as mentally instable, but he nevertheless continued to offer his services as a tour guide for any willing parties.

What is less known—the Final Act—is that the story of Akakor turned out to be a fraud. The story was unraveled when Tatunca Nara was exposed as being one Günther Hauck, a German ex-pat. The discovery was made by the German adventurer Rüdiger Nehberg and film director Wolfgang Brög. Brög tricked Tatunca to take him onto an expedition, during which his story began to unravel. It was discovered that Tatunca had left Germany in 1967, which explained why he spoke perfect German, yet broken Portuguese. Apparently, he left Germany as he was trying to escape imprisonment due to unpaid alimony after a divorce in 1966. Since, his ex-wife has confirmed that Hauck is indeed the "Tatunca Nara" in Brugger's photos, and there are also pre-1968 German court proceedings that mention Hauck preferred to go by a nickname Tatunge Nare.

That, alas, is the unfortunate story of the legend of Akakor, which killed at least three people and which was, in origin, the story of a man who was able to con the world. However, no one doubts that there are still undiscovered settlements and tribes in the Amazon, and since the 1970s, when this story started, several have been discovered. But tunnels or stone cities in the heartland of the Amazon are unlikely for anyone who has been in the rainforest. To find a written chronicle here is unlikely, but not impossible. The appeal of his story was such that it sent men on a quest for Akakor, which very much became to them their private Grail Quest. Alas, for some, the fact that they did not ask the proper question about Tatunca before setting off, didn't result in them waking up in an empty castle in the morning, but that they never woke up ever again.

Lost Cities

The Amazon and South America as a whole continue to reveal its history to us. If we ever assume that Southern American history is known, that is simply not the case. It was as recent as 1911 that Machu Picchu was discovered. The "Lost City of the Incas" is only 50 miles from the ancient capital Cusco, but apparently no one ever found it—though new theories are emerging that suggest that, for several decades before 1911, the site was known but was kept secret, as gold and other treasures were secretly removed from it, to be sold. The traditional account has it that throughout the centuries, the surrounding jungle grew over the site, leaving no clear visible indication that a true lost city was located there.

On July 24, 1911, American historian Hiram Bingham announced the discovery of Machu Picchu to scholars. Bingham had actually been searching for another lost city, Vilcabamba, the last Inca refuge as the Spanish Conquistadors invaded Peru. It was an 11-year-old local boy, Pablito Alvarez, who took Bingham up to Machu Picchu. Today, Machu Picchu is one of the most desired travel destinations in the world and a truly wonderful experience to have.

In 2001, Hugh Thomson wrote *The White Rock,* his travel journal of how he heard of an Inca ruin that had been discovered, but whose location had subsequently been lost. Thomson made it his mission to rediscover the site, which he did. The White Rock, or Chuquipalta, is about 20 miles west of Machu Picchu, but what is obvious to anyone who has been to Peru's Sacred Valley, and maybe not so to someone who hasn't, is that distance in the Andes or Amazon is of no importance. The jungle rules and can hide anything, even if one were to stand 3 yards in front of it. Thomson's account reveals that even in the 21st century, discovering lost cities in the Andes is not yet an exhausted endeavor.

In 1952, Victor von Hagen set off to explore the old Inca road from Lake Titicaca to Quito in Ecuador, a formidable distance. Afterward, he wrote that he realized that the Inca had a road system that was a true master plan: a system that had a combined distance of 10,000 miles of all-weather roads, many of which were marvels of engineering. Many of the roads edged a territory, delineating an internal border. Rather than zigzag up a hill, they used steep stairways, for the animal used to carry weight on this system was the llama, which, unlike horses, had no problems with stairs.

Von Hagen's discovery fits in a larger framework that American author Charles C. Mann has brilliantly brought into perspective in *1491*: "Contrary to what so Americans learn in school, the pre-Columbian Indians were not sparsely settled in a pristine wilderness; rather, there were huge numbers of Indians who actively molded and influenced the land around them."[8] Mann shows that South America's history is up for reinterpretation with every new discovery. For example, early reports from explorers in the Amazon spoke of cities, some of them populated by tens of thousands of people. But a few decades later, subsequent explorers could not find a single trace of these cities, and therefore the consensus grew that the early explorers had merely told tall tales. Satellite imagery has now confirmed that there are indeed lost cities deep within the Amazon. What happened was that these tribes were also exposed to the Spanish viruses, to which they had no immunity.

Hundreds of thousands of people died in South America—which is why the big cities that the early explorers had found had been completely wiped off the face of the Earth.

In his book, Mann underlines the now-usual skepticism of professional archaeologists to truly appreciate the reality of the situation. Betty J. Meggers, of the Smithsonian Institute, wrote to him saying, "I have seen no evidence that large numbers of people ever lived in the Beni"—one of the areas that caught Mann's initial interest. "Claiming otherwise is just wishful thinking."[9] Mann highlights that there is a big difference between "not seeing evidence" and "reality" and that there is no wishful thinking at all involved in what is now being uncovered across South America.

The leading lights of Science are caught in what Mann has labeled "Holmberg's Mistake":

> The Siriono are the best known of a number of Native American groups in the Beni today. Between 1940 and 1942 a young doctoral student in anthropology named Allan R. Holmberg lived among them, and published an account in 1950 of his experience in *Nomads of the Longbow*. [...] He saw them as primitive humankind living in a raw state of nature that for millennia had existed almost without change. Quickly recognized as a classic, the book provided an enduring image of South American Indians to the outside world.[10]

Holmberg was wrong. What follows is a detailed account that reveals that—like Europe—the people of America were far less primitive than reported, and had extraordinary means of communication and transportation. This not only applies to the best known civilizations like the Maya and the Inca, but across the continent, from the deepest jungles of the Amazon, to the coast of Peru, where as recently as the 1990s, a few hills were misidentified as natural formations. Now, they are considered to be the oldest pyramids in the world!

131

THE OLDEST TOWN IN THE NEW WORLD

We call it the New World, because we believe it was discovered as recently as 1492 and because the civilizations that lived there appear to be far more recent that those of the Old World. But what if this were yet another illusion, projected by historians?

Sometime before 3200 BC, if not 3500 BC, something happened in the Norte Chico in Peru, an agronomical "no go" area, where hardly anything grows. This, however, is the site where the oldest traces of a genuine civilization—pyramids included—were found in America. And at 3500 BC, it is on par with the likes of Sumer and Ancient Egypt.

At least 25 large ceremonial/residential sites have so far been found, of which Caral has become the most famous. The North Chico, roughly 100 kilometers north of the Peruvian capital, Lima, consists of four narrow river valleys, from south to north, the Huaura, Supe, Pativilca, and Fortaleza. The ancient pyramids of Caral predate the Inca civilization by 4,000 years, but were flourishing a century before the pyramids of Giza were built. No surprise therefore that they have been identified as the most important archaeological discovery since the discovery of Machu Picchu in 1911.

The first full-scale archaeological investigation of the region took place in 1941 in Aspero, when Gordon R. Willey and John M. Corbert of Harvard investigated a salt marsh at the mouth of the Supe. They found a big trash heap and a multi-roomed building with no pottery and a few maize cobs under the pounded clay floor. They wondered how maize could have been cultivated in a salt marsh and why these people could have practiced agriculture, yet apparently had no pottery. Willey and Corbett also found six mounds, some of them nearly 5 meters tall. They were catalogued as natural eminences of sand.

Thirty years later, Willey, in the company of Michael E. Moseley, revisited the site and realized that these natural eminences were, in fact, temple-type platform mounds. He also realized there might have been as many as 17 such mounds, all of which Willey had missed on his first exploration of the site. "It is an excellent, if embarrassing, example of not being able to find what you are not looking for," he commented later.[11] As to its age: Carbon dating revealed that Aspero could go back to 3000 BC, whereby samples from a nearby site even revealed a date of 4900 BC. Those objective findings were nevertheless seen as impossible—far too old with "what was known" and hence not accepted, and no doubt waiting for another, future discovery that will show that maybe the impossible is true after all.

Caral is located 14 miles inland from Aspero. Even though Caral was discovered in 1905, it was quickly forgotten as the site rendered no gold or even ceramics. It required the arrival of Ruth Shady Solis in 1994 before a genuine paradigm shift would occur. She is a member of the Archaeological Museum of the National University of San Marcos in Lima. Since 1996, she has cooperated with Jonathan Haas, of the American Field Museum. Together, they have found a 150-acre array of earthworks, which includes six large platform mounds, one 20 meters high and more than 100 on a side. But Shady Solis did not make the same mistake Willey had made: She felt that the "pyramids" were just that; they were not natural hills, as some of her predecessor had catalogued the structures of Caral. Her subsequent research led to the announcement, in the April 27, 2001 issue of *Science,* of the carbon dating of the site, which revealed that Caral had been founded before 2600 BC. The "impossible" carbon-dating results of Aspero now seemed more likely—and Caral had become the oldest city in the "New" World, older than the Giza pyramids.

What is Caral like? The site is in fact so old that it pre-dates the ceramic period, the reason why no pottery was found. Its importance resides in its domestication of plants, especially cotton, but also beans, squashes, and guava. As mentioned, the heart of the site covers 150 acres and contains six stone platform mounds—pyramids. The largest mound measures 154 by 138 meters, though it rises only to a height of 20 meters; two sunken plazas are at the base of the mound and a large plaza connects all the mounds. The largest pyramid of Peru was terraced with a staircase leading up to an atrium-like platform, culminating in a flattened top housing enclosed rooms and a ceremonial fire pit. All pyramids were built in one or two phases, which means that there was a definitive plan in erecting these monuments. The design of the central plaza would also later be incorporated in all similar structures across the Andes in the millennia to come—thus showing that Caral was a true cradle of civilization. Around the pyramids were many residential structures. One house revealed the remains of a body that was buried in the wall and that appears to have been a natural death, rather than evidence of human sacrifice. Among the artifacts discovered are 32 flutes made from pelican and animal bones, engraved with the figures of birds and monkeys. It shows that though situated along the Pacific coast, its inhabitants were aware of the animals of the Amazon, showing once again that our South American ancestors traveled across vast distances much earlier and far more prominently than largely assumed.

How did Caral begin? It is suggested that several small villages merged in 2700 BC, quite possibly based on the success of early agricultural cultivation and fishing techniques. The invention of cotton fishing nets—the cotton grown in the Supe valley—must have greatly facilitated the fishing industry. It is believed that this excess of food might have resulted in trade with the religious centers. But apart from an economic model of exchange, the new social model also meant that a labor force existed that had in essence little to do. This labor force could thus be used for religious purposes. Caral might have been the natural result of this process—just like pyramids elsewhere in the world, whether Bosnia or Egypt, seem to have been the result of an available workforce.

The discovery of Caral has therefore reintroduced a powerful enigma: At the same time, on two different continents, agricultural advancements created a new style of life. The available workforce that agriculture had created was reemployed in the construction of pyramids. This "template" is visible in Peru, Sumer, and Egypt, all in the 3rd millennium BC. Coincidence, or evidence of design? Alternative researchers will certainly soon reopen this debate, but archaeologists steer well clear of it for the moment, even though the third millennium BC is precisely the period that in North America, people were engaged in the transoceanic copper trade.

Even without a European connection, Caral is hard to accept. It is very old. Still, its dating of 2627 BC is beyond dispute, based as it is on carbon dating reed and woven carrying bags that were found in situ. These bags were used to carry the stones that were used for the construction of the pyramids. The material is an excellent candidate for dating, thus allowing for a high precision.

The town itself had a population of approximately 3,000 people. There are 17 other sites in the area, allowing for a possible total population of 20,000 people for the Supe valley. Indeed, the Caral archaeological team broke up to investigate some of the other sites, such as along the Pativilca River, the next river to the north, and the Fortaleza, just north of the Pativilca. All of these sites share similarities with Caral. They have small platforms or stone circles, and all were major urban centers on par with Caral—though some of them were even older than Caral. Haas believes that Caral was nevertheless the focus of this civilization, itself part of an even vaster complex, trading with the coastal communities and the regions further inland—as far as the Amazon, if the depiction of monkeys is any indication.

But Norte Chico may have far more discovery in store for us. One site, Huaricanga, saw a first paper published in December 2004.

The team of Haas, Winnifred Creamer, and Alvaro Ruiz found evidence of people living inland from the coast as early as 9210 BC, with the oldest date associated with a city being 3500 BC. Other urban sites in the region are now dated as being older than Caral: Caballete at 3100 BC, and Porvenir and Upaca at 2700 BC. Charles Mann writes how "individually, none of the twenty-five Norte Chico cities rivaled Sumer's cities in size, but the totality was bigger than Sumer."[12]

Haas describes the civilization of Norte Chico as the second experiment humanity did with government: surrendering personal freedom and liberty to a centralized authority, which then apparently decided to create a ritual center—a city, asking those who had surrendered their freedom to work hard—if not very hard—for this common or greater good. The cities were not sited strategically, nor did they have defensive walls; no evidence of warfare has been found. It seems that cooperation existed, because the population realized that cooperation would benefit the individual and the community as a whole. Though Haas and his colleagues put forward several logical reasons, Caral is primarily a religious cult center. And no one seems to dare to suggest the perhaps obvious reason: that these people built Caral because of their belief and adoration of one or more deities they held in common worship.

That the workforce involved was not slaves or oppressed is supported by the archaeological evidence. Haas and Creamer believe that the city rulers encouraged the workforce during construction by staging celebratory roasts of fish and achira root. Afterward, the remains of these feasts were worked into the fabric of the mound. Alcohol is suspected of having been consumed, and music seems to have been played: At Caral, Shady Solis's discovery of 32 flutes made of pelican wing bones tucked into a recess in the main temple provides the evidence for that conclusion.

The creation of a religious complex implies the existence of a pantheon. Little evidence has been uncovered of what these gods may have been, other than a drawing etched into the face of a gourd, dated to 2280–2180 BC. It depicts a sharp-toothed, hat-wearing figure who holds a long stick or rod in each hand. The image looks like an early version of the Staff God, a fanged, staff-wielding deity who is one of the main characters in the Andean pantheon, the deity that is figured prominently on the Gateway of the Sun in Tiahuanaco, on the shores of Lake Titicaca, hundreds of miles away.

For an unknown reason, Caral was abandoned rapidly after a period of 500 years (c. 2100 BC). The preferred theory as to why the people migrated is that the region was hit by a drought, forcing the inhabitants to go elsewhere in search of fertile plains. But the fact that the Staff God is found two millennia later elsewhere in Southern America shows that these people did not disappear; they merely moved elsewhere, and seem to have built other religious centers on their travels.

The harsh living conditions have not disappeared, however. According to the World Monuments Fund (WMF), Caral is one of the 100 important sites under extreme danger. Shady Solis argues that if the existing pyramids are not reinforced, they will disintegrate further and money from tourism, as well as private donations, will help preserve the site. Conservation will go hand in hand with exploration. And though Caral continues to steal the limelight, other nearby sites, such as Aspero, are older. Indeed, Aspero might one day lay claim to the title of the world's oldest city.

Shady Solis came to Caral looking for the fabled missing link of archaeology: a "mother city." Today, she is still trying to convince people that Caral was indeed the oldest urban civilization in the world: "The discovery of Caral challenged the accepted beliefs. Some historians were not ready to believe that an urban civilization existed in Peru even before the pyramids were built in Egypt," she says. "This place is somewhere between the seat of the gods and the home of man."[13]

Still, the fame of Caral as the oldest pyramid complex might be short-lived. Archaeologists have found a 5,500-year-old ceremonial plaza at Sechin Bajo, in Casma, 229 miles north of Lima, the capital. The discovery occurred by a team of the Latin American Institute at the Freie University in Berlin, under the auspices of Professor Dr. Peter Fuchs. It contained a platform pyramid that was originally possibly up to 100 meters tall. Carbon dating shows it is one of the oldest structures ever found in the Americas. Nearly 2,000 years later, another structure measuring 180 by 120 meters was added onto it. The discovery at Sechin Bajo means this pyramid complex is now even older than Caral, and it means that the dawn of civilization in the New World is continuously pushed back, revealing that the New World is just as old as the Old World. Maybe older?

Jurassic Library

May 13, 1966 was the 42nd birthday of a local physician, Dr. Javier Cabrera Darquea, and his old friend, photographer Felix Llosa Romero, had presented him with a seemingly innocent gift: a curiously marked stone. Cabrera lived in Ica, the capital town of a small Peruvian coastal province, some 185 miles south of the capital Lima.

Dr. Cabrera, who had a long-standing interest in the prehistory of the region, examined the design on the stone and identified it as a species of fish that had become extinct millions of years ago. News of his excitement reached the ears of Carlos and Pablo Soldi, brothers and well-known collectors of pre-Inca artifacts. They showed Cabrera thousands of similarly marked stones found in the nearby Ocucaje region and told him that they had repeatedly failed to interest archaeologists in investigating the area. Cabrera bought 341 stones from them for the equivalent of $50.

Cabrera's private museum included a collection of stones belonging to his father, Bolivia Cabrera (a Spanish aristocrat), gathered from the fields of the family plantation in the late 1930s. They resembled his new acquisitions, and soon he found another supplier—a farmer named Basilo Uschuya—and bought many thousands more from him. By the late 1970s, Cabrera estimated, he had more than 11,000 of these anomalous engraved stones.

Among the Ica stones are depictions of humans apparently fighting dinosaurs. Quickly considered to be fake by many, for others the question is why impossible encounters such as this were created by someone to try to pass off a collection of stones as genuine. It is a question that has made the Ica stones extremely controversial for a number of years.

Image copyright Brattarb. Made available as part of the Creative Commons License on Wikimedia.

The stones vary in size from pebbles to hefty boulders and have a dark patina into which the designs are incised. They bear an astonishing variety of images (including some showing bestiality, which have been described as pornographic) and Cabrera arranged his collection into groups, including star maps, maps of unidentified lands, scenes of complex surgery, men using telescopes to observe stars and comets, and what seem to be humans in flying machines. Here, too, are depictions that challenge the accepted view of the history of life on Earth. They show people interacting with extinct animals; hunting and domesticating a variety of dinosaurs, in particular the brontosaurs, Tyrannosaurus Rex, stegosaurs, and flying pterodactyls. According to connoisseurs, the real gem of the dinosaur series is a scene in which men use hand-axes to kill a dinosaur. What impresses, they say, is that the hunters seem to display a knowledge of the animal's anatomy in chopping at a critical nerve center in the dinosaur's spine that would inflict a quick and sudden death. In short, it seemed that the stones were testimony that Jurassic Park had been real: that humanity had somehow lived at the time of the dinosaurs—or vice versa.

Cabrera's medical career was distinguished—he'd retired as professor and head of the department of medicine at the University of Lima—so it is natural that, at first, he kept quiet about his so-called dinosaur stones, preferring to draw attention to those that displayed advanced scientific knowledge, such as the astronomical and medical images. The surgery-themed stones imply that the makers possessed an advanced knowledge of medicine millions of years before the earliest modern civilization, for here, in gory detail, are scenes of heart, liver, and kidney transplants, a cesarean section, a brain operation, sophisticated equipment, acupuncture, and genetic engineering. In short, this highly controversial "library in stone" is an archaeological anomaly—a prime example of what the Fortean pioneer Ivan Sanderson called oops-art, or out-of-place artifacts.

In the late 1960s, after he had bought thousands of the engraved stones from farmer Basilo Uschuya, Cabrera tirelessly promoted his discovery, telling anyone who would listen about his speculations, and it soon came to the attention of revisionists such as Erich von Däniken and Robert Charroux. Riding in the slipstream of von Däniken's *Chariots of the Gods?*—a worldwide best-seller in 1969—a spate of similar books emerged in the early 1970s, almost all of them including the Ica enigma. Most claimed it was straightforward, if puzzling, evidence of an advanced civilization from a time before the dinosaurs perished 65 million years ago. More recently, Creationists—who place the Bible above Darwinian theory—have used the Ica stones to substantiate their beliefs that the behemoth of the Book of Job is, in fact, a dinosaur. Rejecting the mooted antiquity of the stones, they believe the stones show, instead, that dinosaurs survived into relatively modern times, co-existing with early man, and offer proof of the Genesis account of the Creation some six millennia ago.

According to the reigning scientific opinion, a span of some 60 million years separates the living dinosaurs from our earliest human ancestors. This huge gap in time, supported by geological evidence and modern dating methods, makes the idea of the co-existence of dinosaurs and man hard to entertain scientifically. But we know from history that historians love isolationism, whereas the true imagery of our past is that there were no such clear distinctions. Cremo's research has furthermore shown that humans have been around much longer than we think and, whereas it might appear that pushing our presence back from 100,000 years to one million years still falls far short of 65 million years, at least, there is an ever-increasing possibility that Jurassic Park might have been real.

Then, it seems, the bubble burst. A BBC TV documentary was severely critical of the Ica stones, drawing the attention of the Peruvian press and resulting in the arrest of Uschuya by the local authorities.

Interrogated, he admitted he had carved the stones himself; he wanted to bilk the tourists and claimed he never thought it would get out of hand on such a large scale. Remarkably, after his release, Uschuya continued to make and sell stones, presumably with official knowledge.

The Ica stones were now considered to be a hoax and officially a branch of the tourist industry. It was over—or was it? When dealing with controversies of this sort, nothing is ever simple. Believers in the antiquity of the stones claimed that the farmer admitted to the hoax for a very simple reason: If the stones were genuine, he had been selling government possessions. Peruvian law dictates that archaeological discoveries should be turned over to the government and he faced prison if found guilty. By admitting it was a simple hoax, the farmer was let off the hook—and was able to provide his family with an income. When von Däniken visited the farmer in 1973, Uschuya confirmed to him that he had faked the stones, but later, in an interview with the German journalist Andreas Fischer, Uschuya claimed the opposite. They were genuine, he insisted, and he admitted to a hoax to avoid imprisonment.

It is sometimes alleged against Cabrera that he colluded in the making of fakes and must have profited from them, but there is no evidence of that. In any case, Cabrera's original motive—to preserve the stones—is clear from the record. Along with the Soldi brothers, he tried to attract the attention of a top-level archaeological investigation into what he believed was a genuine pre-Incan mystery. Indeed, though Cabrera is often singled out, he was not the only one interested in these stones, or convinced that they were genuine. The Soldis's interest began in 1961 when, according to Herman Buse, the Ica River flooded and "uncovered in the Ocucaje region a large number of engraved stones which ever since have been an object of commerce for the huaqueros who found them."[14] Also interested in the objects was an architect, Santiago Agurto Calvo, then rector of the Universidad Nacional de

Ingenieria, who bought many and, in 1966, began excavating pre-Inca tombs around Ocucaje. In an article that year, he described the designs as "[u]nidentifiable things, insects, fish, birds, cats, fabulous creatures and human beings [...] in elaborate and fantastic compositions."[15] In 1968, Calvo donated a great number of engraved stones to the Ica museum but failed to have the province's cultural department declare the Ocucaje region a special preserve to prevent the illegal removal of ancient objects.

The earliest Peruvian artifacts seem to date back to around 20,000 years ago, and discoveries of engraved stones in the Ica region go back to Spanish records of the mid-15th century. The curator of the Ica museum accepted Calvo's collection at first as examples of pre-Inca burial art, but they were withdrawn from open display in 1970, when Cabrera's ideas gained international notoriety. As a general rule, museums hate controversy. When Cabrera visited the museum to compare his artifacts with Calvo's, the curator said he withdrew them because he now believed the huaqueros (grave-robbers) had made them, which is remarkable, for grave-robbers normally get their material from the graves they rob, which would make the material genuine.

Despite Uschuya's damning admission, Cabrera continued to feed the cult of the dinosaur stones—he called them gliptoliths—and became their biggest promoter. He put his collection on display in his house. Shelves lined every wall, organized by subject: the races of the planet, ancient animals, lost continents, and so forth. Cabrera considered that his hypothetical ancient people—Gliptolithic Man—had larger brains than ours (even though no skeletal remains exist) and were therefore more intelligent than us. These humans supposedly used a form of concentrated psychic energy with which they were able to influence celestial events and record on their stones the approach of a great comet. Further, he believed that some of the "machines" depicted look like spacecraft and probably traveled through space without consuming fuel. Now, Cabrera ascends into a realm all his own, leaving behind his puzzled and more conventional colleagues for the increasing isolation of his contemplation among the strange stones. He believes he has come to know what they are saying. "I can only deduce," he wrote, "that the men who carved these stones co-existed with these animals. This means, of course, that man is at least 405 million years old."[16]

Cabrera's reading of the stones has little support; especially as the engraved images lend themselves to other, less dramatic interpretations and there is not enough corroborating detail to substantiate any of them. For example, even if we assume they are genuine and millions of years old, they do not necessarily contain the type of information Cabrera maintains; the heart and brain transplants could just as well be mutilations or acts of cannibalism, and the flying machines resemble birds more than high-tech craft. American archaeologist-publisher David Hatcher Childress said, half in jest, that the scene showing ancients using telescopes could equally show them playing a game of prehistoric tennis.

On February 25, 1996, NBC TV showed a documentary titled *The Mysterious Origins of Man*, which included the work of Michael Cremo. Neil Steede, an independent archaeologist and director of the Early Sites Research Society, was one of its researchers who, in 1995, traveled throughout Southern America, gathering material for the program. He investigated the Ica stones firsthand, but thought they should not be included in the original documentary because they did not add any scientific weight to the debate.

In 1997, the documentary's producer, Bill Cote, decided to repackage two controversial items dropped from the original broadcast. The segment concerning the Ica stones was called "Jurassic Art" and was marketed for cable television and the video sales market. The production focused on Steede's research, as he was the latest archaeologist to investigate the collection. When Steede met Basilo Uschuya, the farmer confirmed that he had engraved the stones from drawings that Cabrera had brought to him. Why? "Making these stones is easier than farming the land."[17] Uschuya stated that Cabrera had about 5,000 genuine stones—in other words, stones that Uschuya himself had not made—and that he had not fabricated all of the others, contrary to what he had previously stated.

Cabrera explained Uschuya's implication by admitting that a large number of stones had indeed been copied, but they were only for sale to tourists. There is of course little harm in creating replicas, a position most museums will be happy to agree with. Indeed, there is no hard evidence that Cabrera ever said he was selling genuine artifacts, suggesting what was occurring was not faking stones, but creating replicas for sale. As Uschuya stated: Cabrera had 5,000 genuine artifacts. Cabrera also claims he was shown a cave in which the cache of stones had remained hidden for millions of years. This cave was revealed, he says, after a severe rainstorm washed open a new area near the Ica river. (This may or may not be the event referred to by Herman Buse in 1965.) Cabrera remains tight-lipped on who took him to the cave and, as no maps or pictures of it exist, we have only Cabrera's word for it. Interestingly, Cabrera has stated that he hopes it will not be found. Even Erich von Däniken, who describes Cabrera as a warm friend, was denied the privilege. Steede, who offered to be blindfolded throughout the journey to the cave, was also rebuffed and now believes the cave never existed.

Surely, you ask, couldn't the matter be settled once and for all by dating the stones? Unfortunately, though some testing was done, the results remain inconclusive. Cabrera himself sent stones to the universities of Lima (Peru) and Bonn (Germany) and to NASA scientist Joseph Blum. At Bonn, a Professor Frenchen apparently confirmed that the stones were andesite (an extremely hard volcanic rock composed mostly of silica) and that the oxidized patina on their surface indicated significant age.

In 1967, Cabrera asked friend Eric Wolf, a mining engineer, to arrange an analysis and published the results in his book. The stones were indeed andesite, worn smooth in ancient rivers. "I have not found any notable or irregular wear on the edges of the incisions,"[18] Wolf notes, concluding: "These etchings were executed not long before they were deposited in graves or other places where they were discovered."[19] Cabrera adds, specifically, that "the coating of natural oxidation covers the incisions as well."[20] This would suggest the stones were indeed ancient. However, this has to be balanced by the firsthand observation by Neil Steede that, even though the stones he examined did have this patina, there was no patina in the grooves. This suggests that, although the stones were certainly very old, the carvings were of far more recent origin.

Though some investigators claim that they were refused permission to see the Calco collection in the Museum of Ica stash, Neil Steede was granted access. He concluded that these definitely genuine stones show a finer workmanship and have less deep cuts than Cabrera's stones. This is an indication of a more highly skilled manufacturer than Cabrera's artisan. Furthermore, they are restricted to depicting conventional humans and existing animals, not extinct animals; nor do they include any examples of the more exotic motifs of the Cabrera stones. It suggests that a cache of inscribed stones was found, but that more imaginative scenes were later added to the collection, no doubt in efforts to gain a larger audience for these artifacts.

In the same year that *The Mysterious Origins of Man* documentary aired, the German cable channel Kabel 1 broadcast its own investigation. The team had filmed secretly as Cabrera took them into one of his "secret" rooms. Here, instead of incised stones, were astonishing clay sculptures: small dinosaurs crawling out of an egg, kangaroos, people with odd-shaped heads, and other similar themes. The team decided to confront Basilo Uschuya with this new footage. He claimed to have made these sculptures as well, for what in his opinion was a minimum salary, and showed the team such a sculpture, which seemed indistinguishable from those in Cabrera's secret room.

The story became stranger when, that same year, Erich von Däniken launched the German version of his book *Arrival of the Gods,* in which he reported on his 1996 trip to Peru—and said that Cabrera had allowed him to visit and photograph the figurines! Von Däniken stated that he was first shown these clay figures during his visit in 1983. The point is that, unlike the stones, these clay figurines can be tested. Von Däniken sent one to the University of Zurich for carbon dating and they reported that the figurine was modern. His fellow researcher, Johannes Fiebag, sent two other samples to the University of Weimar, which likewise concluded that the samples were relatively young and still contained water. Conclusion: These figurines were not a hundred thousand years old, as Cabrera claimed; they could have been made 20 years ago.

It seems increasingly likely that the Ica stones have been fabricated, but it is difficult to believe that they are all—estimates run to 50,000 pieces—made by one poor, uneducated farmer. No independent study has been made, if only to separate any possibly authentic artifacts from the fakes. Nor do we know to what extent Cabrera's interpretations have been based on any of the fakes. The one researcher who has known Cabrera the longest, Erich von Däniken, has repeatedly stated that some stones are definitely fakes. He has also cast doubt on the origins of the entire collection. In the end, perhaps von Däniken understands Cabrera's motive best. He is convinced Cabrera tells stories: "And stories is the right word, for they do not fit in with any scientific scheme of things. The old man uses engravings which he must know are fake to substantiate his beliefs. Why? Has he become so enamored of his own theories that he thinks imitations will back them up?"[21]

Cabrera's interest in medicine and archaeology might have made him susceptible to an ingenious fraud, but if so he is not the one who has profited from it. Or perhaps he has fooled himself, seeing evidence of his wishful thinking everywhere. In 1966, the media were rife with the theme of men and dinosaurs interacting, especially in the movie *One Million Year BC* (1966). Was Cabrera inspired by this? Or was he inspired by the so-called Acambaro figurines, named after their place of origin in Mexico where, in 1925, Waldemar Julsrud, a Danish storekeeper, found hundreds of clay figurines of dinosaurs that—as their Ica counterparts were some 40 years later—are cavorting with men? More research must be done to settle the doubts about the Ica stones, but the forecast is not looking promising, all the more so as no research has occurred on them since Cabrera's death in 2001.

GOLD RUSH

From the time of the Spanish Conquistadors to the present, there have been persistent accounts of lost cities. Often, these were linked with fabled treasure, especially large golden deposits waiting for the man who would stumble upon them. The most famous of all legends, no doubt, is that of El Dorado, which in origin was not so much a city, but a man.

El Dorado, "the golden one," was the name given to a Colombian Muisca tribal chief who covered himself with gold dust at the time of his coronation and dove into the highland lake of Lake Guatavita, near present-day Bogotá. Soon, the man became a city, then a kingdom, if not an empire. In 1541, Francisco Orellana and Gonzalo Pizarro departed from Quito toward the Amazon Basin, in search of it. Though El Dorado remained elusive—ever since, to everyone—Orellana did become the first person known to navigate the Amazon River all the way to its mouth.

As El Dorado never was a city, the City of Gold was of course never found. The story is nevertheless absolutely true; few if any doubt that this tribal leader covered himself in gold dust and performed this ceremony. But El Dorado was never the only City of Gold. In the 16th century, rumors traveled around Mexico about the "Seven Cities of Gold," called Cíbola, which was located across the desert, hundreds of miles north. The story is thought to have come about as a combination of two myths, one of them a Portuguese legend of seven cities on the island of Antillia, the other the factual discovery of pueblo sites in what are now Arizona and New Mexico.

The rumors have been traced back to four shipwrecked survivors who, upon their return to Mexico, spoke of having heard stories from Natives about cities with great and limitless riches. When he heard this news, Viceroy Antonio de Mendoza organized an expedition headed by Franciscan friar Marcos de Niza, who took one of the four survivors, one Estevanico, as his guide. When Estevanico apparently heard that Cíbola was nearby, he did not wait for de Niza and reached Cíbola (what is now identified as Háwikuh, New Mexico), where, at the hands of the Zuni tribe, he met his death, while his companions were forced to flee.

Marcos de Niza returned to Mexico City and claimed that he had seen Cíbola from a great distance, and that it was larger than the Aztec capital of Tenochtitlan. He said that the people used dishes of gold and silver, decorated their houses with turquoise, and possessed gigantic pearls, emeralds, and other gems.

The Viceroy wasted no time and mounted a military expedition, led by Francisco Vázquez de Coronado, taking de Niza as his guide. Coronado left with a small group of explorers from Culiacán on April 22, 1540. When they arrived at the New Mexican pueblo, he soon realized that the friar's stories were lies. Still, even though Cíbola was not a city of gold, it was clearly a civilization. The friar may have realized that the Viceroy would only ever be interested in sending troops if there were stories of gold, although the friar's ambitions may have been purely to convert the locals to the Christian faith. The Zuni Native Americans would have remained outside the reach of the Spanish Conquistadors for much longer if there had not been rumors of gold. The Zuni soon realized how to play the game. While among the Zuni, Coronado heard another rumor from a native that there was a city with plenty of gold, known as Quivira, located on the other side of the great plains. Now believed to be modern Kansas, Nebraska, or Missouri, he of course found no such golden city, but did find more Native American cultures. Though they were not El Dorado, they were indeed a lost civilization, until discovered.

Both Inca and Pueblo people were masters at sending the Spanish Conquistadors on wild goose chases, as they knew they would give their right arm for gold. But you cannot blame the Spanish Conquistadors too much, for when they entered the Inca capital of Cusco in 1533, and especially the Coricancha, the central religious temple, there was gold everywhere. Literally.

The Coricancha, meaning "the corral of gold," was dedicated primarily to Viracocha, the Inca creator god, and Inti, the Sun god. The south-facing walls of the temple were covered with gold, in order to reflect the light of the sun and illuminate the temple. It is said that there were more than 700 sheets of pure gold, weighing about 4 pounds each. Inside the temple was the Punchaco, a solid-gold disk inlaid with precious stones, which represented the sun and which was probably the most sacred object in the Inca Empire.

Pizarro's men stripped the 1.5 tons of gold from the walls. They gathered hundreds of gold sculptures and objects from the temple, including an altar big enough to hold two men and an extraordinary artificial garden made of gold, including cornstalks with silver stems and ears of gold. At the center of the Coricancha, marking a place known as Cusco Cara Urumi (the "Uncovered Navel Stone"), was an octagonal stone coffer, which at one time was covered with 55 kilograms of pure gold. That, too, was removed.

Tragically, everything was melted down within a month and put on boats that sailed for Spain. The fleet became embroiled in a naval battle, all the gold sinking to the bottom of the seas. Everything was lost, except the Punchaco, even though its whereabouts remain unknown to this day. As to the Coricancha itself: That was converted into the monastery of Santo Domingo, where once 4,000 Inca priests had officiated masses for Viracocha and Inti, now the Dominicans worshipped Jesus Christ.

At the time of the Spanish Conquest, several items of tremendous importance were nevertheless hidden by the Inca themselves, including the Punchaco. The collective of this lost treasure is often labeled the "treasure of Inca King Atahualpa" and rumors had it that it was taken out of Cusco into the Amazonian jungle; other stories argue it was secreted away in tunnels below Cusco itself. This rumor has been linked with stories about a tunnel leading from the Coricancha and exiting near Sacsayhuaman, the fortress that towers above the city. This exit was known as Chinkana Grande ("Big Cave," though it is also the Quechuan word for "labyrinth"), which upon closer inspection seems to be nothing more than a big hole a few meters deep. In 1989, archaeologist Fernando Jimenez del Oso tried to film the entrance of the cave, but failed in his efforts due to the narrowness of the opening and the rubble inside. But...

In 1600, Jesuit Friar José de Acosta said:

The celebrated cave of Cusco, called Chinkana by the Indians, was made by the Inca kings. It is very deep and runs through the center of the city, its mouth or entrance being in the fortress of Sacsayhuaman. It comes down on the side of the mountain where the parish of San Cristobal is situated and, with varying degrees of depth, ends at the Coricancha. All the Indians to whom I have spoken have told me that the Incas made this costly and laborious cave to enable their kings and armies to go in times of war from the fortress of Sacsayhuaman to the Temple of the Sun to worship their idol Punchau without being detected.[22]

In the 17th century, an effort was made to find the treasure supposedly secreted away under the Inca capital. After a team spent several days underground, only one person came out alive. Interestingly, he emerged from an opening under the main altar of the church of Santo Domingo, the former site of the Coricancha. Most importantly, the survivor brought with him an ear of corn made of solid gold, definitive proof that the legends were at least partially true.

A century later, in 1814, Brigadier Mateo Garcia Pumakahua showed his superiors part of the treasure. He took an officer blindfolded through the main square of Cusco to a stream and then, after removing some stones, proceeded down a stone stairway into Cusco's underworld. Once the blindfold was removed, the officer saw large silver pumas with emeralds, "bricks" made of gold and silver, and much more. As incredible as it may seem, it is indeed likely that some of the treasure of the Coricancha was secreted away—though some was left behind, leaving the Spanish with the impression that they had captured everything.

Interestingly, Pumakahua stated that, when witnessing these treasures, he could hear the clock of the Cathedral of Cusco ringing above. It seems everyone in Cusco was walking on gold, without knowing it.

Spanish journalist and novelist Javier Sierra cooperated with Vicente Paris in his efforts to retrieve the treasure. Paris noted that the Coricancha, the convent of Santa Catalina, San Cristobal church, and Sacsayhuaman were aligned; if there was a tunnel, it would run perfectly straight. In 1993, they decided to test the ancient accounts and their new hypothesis. They chose the main altar of Santo Domingo to check whether an opening was indeed present there. Father Benigno Gamarra, abbot of the Convent of Santo Domingo, confirmed: "Your information is correct, but the tunnel in question extends much beyond Sacsayhuaman, since it ends in some place underneath Quito, in Ecuador."[23] The abbot was thus claiming that the underground network extended for hundreds of miles, which might seem difficult to believe, but is therefore not untrue.

Still, there was—no doubt not unexpectedly—a problem: The main altar entrance to the underground system was partially closed after the earthquakes that hit the city in 1950. When work had been carried out to strengthen the foundation of the church, though, a UNESCO report had cataloged four crypts in the monastery. Furthermore, one Spanish explorer, Anselm Pi Rambla, claimed that he had entered the structure as recent as 1982.

So far, everything looked positive. To quote Sierra:

The priest met me in his study a little before daybreak on March 21, in order to resolve the mystery of the golden corn. "'I'm only going to tell this to you, I will let you take photographs and ask questions on one condition," he warned, "That you do not reveal what I'm about to tell you until I am no longer here." I accepted. Gamarra then unwrapped a small bundle on the table of his study in which two elaborately encrusted gold crowns had been protected.[24]

153

Sierra also became convinced that the tunnel had a special function: "Every 24th of June the interior of the tunnel was totally illuminated by the rays of the sun being reflected on the surface of the famous solar disc and were in time deflected towards the interior of the Chinkana. There, a series of mirrors of highly polished metal sheets conducted the light to Sacsayhuaman."[25] Gamarra added that the original walls of the Coricancha had been excavated. He found out that there was a stream originating in the main square, running to the old walls of the Coricancha, under the church. To him, it showed that a natural passage connected the various structures.

In 1999, Anselm Pi Rambla negotiated with the National Institute of Culture, the palace of Government and Father Gamarra to arrange the conditions for the exploration beneath the Monastery of Santo Domingo in search of the Inca tunnel. Sponsored by Texan financier Michael Galvis (at a cost of $760,000), the project got underway in August 2000, using ground-penetrating radar to map the underground tunnel. The project revealed that "beneath the altar of Santa Rosa, about four or five meters down, we located a cavity two meters wide that we believe can be the entrance to a great tunnel."[26] The fourth crypt that had been identified by UNESCO, had since disappeared.

Though part of the Inca treasure was therefore apparently hidden underneath Cusco, another part of the treasure (including 14 gold-clad mummies of the former Inca emperors removed from the Coricancha) was said to have been sent by llama caravan into the Antisuyo, the mountain jungle area east of Cusco. The caravan's destination was a mountain-jungle city called "Paikikin"; the Spanish called this city El Gran Paititi—and hence a name was born that would soon become one of the most enduring legends. The mention of gold and/ or the drive to be remembered as the man who revealed the pride of the Inca empire—on par with Carter's discovery of the Tomb of Tutankhamun—has had a lasting appeal on many Lara Crofts.

Though there is little doubt that Paititi did exist, where it was, is unknown. Former Peruvian journalist Nicholas Asheshov argues that Peru is so littered with ruins that there's something seriously wrong if an area doesn't have any; either no one's looked hard enough or they're just incompetent. Furthermore, whether Paititi was just the city to which part of the treasure was transported, or whether there was something special about the city, is another big question mark. If the former, any old ruin of a small town or settlement might in theory be Paititi, yet unless there is somewhere a name or further reference, an actual discovery of a ruin might bring no hard confirmation.

In 2001, Italian archaeologist Mario Polia came across a Jesuit document in Rome, written in 1600 by missionary Andrea Lopez, who vividly describes a large city, rich in gold, silver and gemstones, located in a rainforest and called by its inhabitants Paititi. Andrea Lopez described waterfalls and deep forests around the mysterious city, and the information was presented to Pope Clement VIII.

In 1681, a Jesuit missionary named Fray Lucero spoke to the Indians in the Rio Huallagu area of northeastern Peru, who told him that the lost city of Gran Paititi lay behind the forests and mountains east of Cusco. He wrote:

> This empire of Gran Paytite has bearded, white Indians. The nation called Curveros, these Indians told me, dwell in a place called Yurachuasi or the 'white house'. For king, they have a descendant of the Inca Tupac Amaru, who with 40,000 Peruvians, fled far away into the forests, before the face of the conquistadors of Francisco Pizarro's day in AD 1533. He took with him a rich treasure, and the Castilians who pursued him fought each other in the forests, leaving the savage Chuncho Indios, who watched their internecine struggles, to kill off the wounded and shoot the survivors with arrows.

I myself have been shown plates of gold and half-moons and ear-rings of gold that have come from this mysterious nation.[27]

The testimony suggested that a century and a half after the Spanish Conquest, Gran Paititi was still an operational Inca city, beyond the reach of all.

Another treasure hunter was Pedro Bohorques, a penniless soldier who pretended to be a nobleman. In 1659, after serving in Chile, Bohorques re-baptized himself as Don Pedro el Inca, swearing that royal Inca blood flowed through his veins. Bohorques set himself up as emperor of a Native American kingdom at the headwaters of the Huallaga River south of Cusco. He converted almost 10,000 Pelados Indians into his service, and declared all Spaniards fair game. All of this was no doubt merely a prequel to his real intentions: to send some of his followers on a search for Paititi. Alas, his team did not return with gold, whereupon Bohorques left his empire behind and went to Lima. There, the Spaniards threw him in prison and sentenced him to death. Knowing the Spaniards were even more interested in gold than he, he promised to reveal the location of Gran Paititi if he was released. The judges refused, but many treasure hunters visited him in prison, begging him to share his secret with them. He refused, and went to the gallows in 1667.

So where is Gran Paititi, generally speaking? Gran Paititi is believed to be in the Paucartambo area of Peru, east of Cusco, toward the Madre de Dios River. Indeed, on first impression, the area where to look seems well-defined, yet that has not made the search easier—enabling some to suggest Gran Paititi simply does not exist.

One of the more recent expeditions was organized by Boston anthropologist Gregory Deyermenjian and British photographer Michael Mirecki, who mounted their first expedition in 1984. Their specific goal was a jungle mountain in eastern Peru called Apucatinti, as various accounts stated that the mountain on which Paititi is located was called Apucatinti. Alas, which mountain is the real Apucatinti is open for debate, as there are several carrying that name.

However, historically, Gran Paititi was not reported as being located on top of a mountain, but by a lake—and of course there is more than one lake, too. Still, in August 1986, Deyermenjian made it to the summit of Apucatinti with his Indian guides. To their disappointment, neither Paititi nor any other structures were at the summit of the mountain. Since, Deyermenjian has continued to explore the jungles, and beginning in 1994, allied himself with Peru's foremost living explorer, Dr. Carlos Neuenschwander, who had been conducting his own investigation into Paititi and the significance of the Pantiacolla plateau since the 1950s. None of his expeditions have been successful either.

French explorer Thierry Jamin, too, has organized almost yearly expeditions in search of the city. Jamin's interest began with the search for pyramids that satellite imagery had revealed in December 1975. Situated at the foot of the Sierra Baja du Pantiacolla, the pyramid field was apparently 4 kilometers long, orientated north-south, with apparently two lines of pyramids (20 in total), and some 150 to 200 meters in length.

In 2001, with a team of 22, including the Franco-Peruvian explorer Herbert Cartagena (who had discovered the lost city of Mameria in 1979), he set out for the pyramids. When he arrived on the site, the first impression was that the structures were natural, and were an anomalous geological formation. Still, the structures suggested to have known some human intervention, if only because various Inca tools were located in the area. Furthermore, the locals, the Machiguengas, considered these pyramids to be a sanctuary of the ancients, known locally as the Paratoari. They used certain valuables as everyday instruments, leaving Jamin to speculate that a treasure was nearby: Gran

Paititi. Since, Jamin has made a number of repeat voyages, but despite some interesting, though rather mundane petroglyphs, he has not discovered the golden Paititi.

Jamin walks in dangerous footsteps. In 1970, journalist Robert Nichols went on his search for Paititi. Nichols had traveled to some of the toughest places in the Peruvian jungle, so he seemed well equipped to have a go at locating Paititi.

Nichols wanted to explore the area around La Convención, but no news of him was heard for several months, before Nicholas Asheshov decided to search for his colleague. It was learned that Nichols had entered the jungle with two young French travelers and a dozen Mashco Indians as guides. These guides had returned shortly afterward, refusing to go on past the Shinkikibeni petroglyphs. Throughout the next six months, Asheshov searched both for Nichols and Paititi, finding neither.

Two years later, Yoshiharu Sekino, a Japanese law student, went into the jungle alone and learned that Nichols and the Frenchmen had been murdered; apparently, the Frenchmen had made advances to local Machiguenga women, resulting in the murder of all three. Sekino had even made a photograph of the killers with Nichols's machete and some of his surviving possessions. Sekino tried more than once to follow up on Nichols's leads, setting off into the jungle armed with satellite photographs that showed the same curious series of dots that had inspired so many others.

Paititi is not just an obsession for foreigners. In Peru, Juan Carlos Polentini Wester has left a powerful legacy, including one organization known as Paititi Peru, which organizes adventure holidays, but which also firmly believes in the reality of Paititi. Maria del Carmen, the company manager, has organized a number of expeditions based on information provided by Polentini, whom she has been a disciple of, as well as accompanying him on his own treks. Polentini, an Argentine priest, trekked the jungles for more than 25 years in search of the city. For del Carmen, "Proving the existence of Paititi in Peru is only a matter of time. If this is real, our Peru would become the most visited country in the world. Our Manu National Park and the Kcosñipata-Pilcopata area would become the launching point for all the expeditions and tourists."[28]

Some might call her deluded, or overly optimistic, but it is a matter of fact that the jungles of Southern America are still giving up their secrets. Each year, new sites are being discovered. On January 16, 2008, *National Geographic News* even reported that Paititi might have been discovered. On January 10, 2008, Peru's state news agency reported that an archaeological fortress had been discovered in the district of Kimbiri and that the district's mayor suggested it was the lost city. Mayor Guillermo Torres described the ruins as a 40,000-square-meter fortification near an area known as Lobo Tahuantinsuyo. Few other details about the site were offered, but initial reports described elaborately carved stone structures forming the base of a set of walls.

Francisco Solís from the Peruvian government's Cusco-based National Institute of Culture nevertheless stated that "it is far too early to make any definitive judgments."[29]

If ever Paititi is discovered, it will outshine most other archaeological discoveries, including Machu Picchu, if only because of all the gold that is supposedly part of this treasure. And thus, the gold mummy of Tutankhamun would be rivaled by another gold mummy from an Inca king.

This form of archaeology is of course more the bailiwick of treasure hunting a la Indiana Jones and Lara Croft. What is a matter of fact is that almost five centuries after the Conquest, large sections of South America refuses to surrender their secrets and stories of lost cities and entire lost civilizations continue to make the rounds, and be discovered. As a whole, the only conclusion we can draw now is that, as is the Old World, the New World is far older and far more homogenous than standard history is wont to tell us. There is solid archaeological evidence that the New World is just as old as the Old World, and the pyramid complex at Caral is probably the best evidence for that. Caral was explored less than two decades ago, and even that story is not yet fully uncovered from the dust of time.

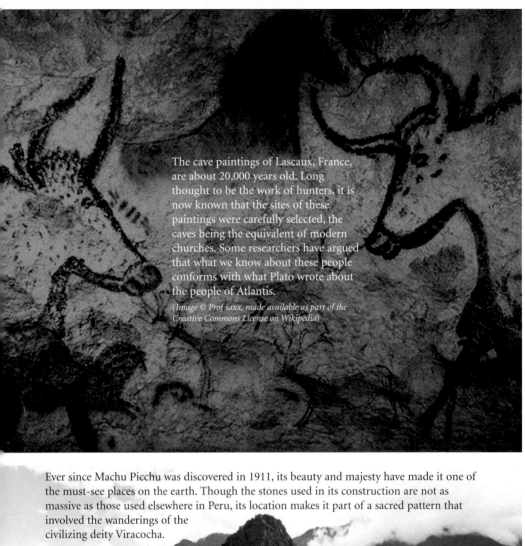

The cave paintings of Lascaux, France, are about 20,000 years old. Long thought to be the work of hunters, it is now known that the sites of these paintings were carefully selected, the caves being the equivalent of modern churches. Some researchers have argued that what we know about these people conforms with what Plato wrote about the people of Atlantis.

(Image © Prof saxx, made available as part of the Creative Commons License on Wikipedia)

Ever since Machu Picchu was discovered in 1911, its beauty and majesty have made it one of the must-see places on the earth. Though the stones used in its construction are not as massive as those used elsewhere in Peru, its location makes it part of a sacred pattern that involved the wanderings of the civilizing deity Viracocha.

(Image courtesy of Philip Coppens)

The Nebra sky disk, dated to 1600 BC, shows stars and phases of the moon. It was found in Germany in 1999. (*Image © Dbachmann, made available as part of the Creative Commons License on Wikipedia*)

The Layard Lens in the British Museum was used by our ancestors for stargazing. (*Image © geni, made available as part of the Creative Commons License on Wikipedia*)

Göbekli Tepe is one of the oldest archaeological sites ever uncovered. This temple complex in Turkey dates back to 10,000 BC, and reveals that our ancestors were quite capable of working with carefully hewn stone thousands of years before is commonly accepted. Each of the stones (*below*) of Göbekli Tepe is expertly crafted, revealing animals and other images. The artwork is so delicately crafted that it is sometimes difficult to believe that the carvings were done more than 7,000 years prior to the dawn of Ancient Egypt. (*Image © Teomancimit, made available as part of the Creative Commons License on Wikipedia*)

This tranquil courtyard in the center of Cusco is all that remains of the Coricancha, the golden temple that was once the very heart of the Inca Civilization. All its gold was removed by the Spanish Conquistadors, though various reports claim that some of the treasure was secured. (*Image © Philip Coppens*)

The rock paintings of the Tassili are thousands of years old, dating back to a time when the Sahara was fertile and populated. Some researchers now argue that it was these peoples who moved to Egypt when the Sahara became desert, and who were instrumental in sparking the Egyptian civilization. (*Image © Philip Coppens*)

The Oracle of Delphi was one of the greatest oracular sites of the ancient world. The Pythia brought visitors into contact with other-worldly realities. It was part of a series of initiation centers that were designed to teach humanity that there was much more to reality than what could be seen with the naked eye. (*Image © Philip Coppens*)

The Bosnian Pyramid of the Sun (*right*) dominates the skyline of the town of Visoko, just outside of Sarajevo. Aligned with the cardinal points, the structure was only identified as a pyramid as recently as 2006, making it the tallest and oldest pyramid ever discovered. The Pyramid of the Moon (*below*) is the second largest pyramid of the Visoko complex—and in the world. Excavations on its top have revealed a "floor" of perfectly shaped stones. There are a number of interesting geometrical and solar alignments between the various pyramids of the complex. (*Images © Philip Coppens*)

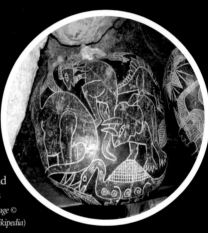

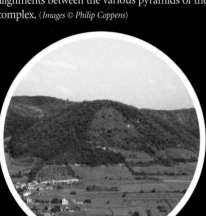

The Ica Stones (*right*) comprise a remarkable collection of about 50,000 stones. Some show dinosaurs fighting with men, forcing the question of whether our ancestors coexisted with the dinosaurs, and whether the currently accepted dating, which separates these two species by millions of years, is erroneous. (*Image © Brattarb, made available as part of the Creative Commons License on Wikipedia*)

The island of Santorini (Thera) is put forward by many as the actual site of Atlantis. However, neither its size nor its location match Plato's description of the sunken civilization, even though the ancient towns of Thera were destroyed when the volcano erupted in the middle of the 15th century BC.
(*Image courtesy of Philip Coppens*)

Chapter 4

THE BIG A: ATLANTIS

Atlantis. The world's most famous lost civilization. In the fourth century BC, the Greek philosopher and historian Plato wrote about this lost civilization, and ever since, it has more than intrigued humanity.

The "Island of Atlas" was first mentioned in Plato's dialogues *Timaeus* and *Critias,* written about 360 BC. He wrote that Atlantis was a naval power that had conquered many parts of Western Europe and Africa. After it failed to attack Athens, it sank, "in a single day and night of misfortune."[1]

Plato gave specific information about its time frame—9,000 years before the time of Solon, which would make it c. 9600 BC—and location, in front of the Pillars of Hercules, today's Strait of Gibraltar, at the southernmost tip of Spain.

In *Critias,* Plato identified Greek statesman Solon as the original source for the story of Atlantis. He had learned about this lost civilization during a visit to Egypt. Solon had met a priest of Sais, who translated the history of ancient Athens and Atlantis, recorded on papyri in Egyptian hieroglyphs, into Greek.

Ever since Plato wrote about the story of Atlantis, the world has been divided into believers and skeptics. The skeptics have no uniform approach other than to say it is impossible that Atlantis could have been real. They "know." Hence, Atlantis is explained away. Many underline Plato the philosopher, rather than listing him as a historian (such distinctions didn't exist in Ancient Greece), and argue that he invented Atlantis, as some type of ideal society, to offset it with Ancient Greece. What they fail to address is the issue that Plato wrote about the lost civilization in a book that is all about history, not philosophy.

Others argue Plato or Solon were mistaken, and that Atlantis was actually a memory of a more recent event, such as the Thera eruption that signaled the end for the Minoan civilization on nearby Crete in c. 1450 BC, or the Trojan War.

The truth of the matter is that Atlantis was definitely a possibility. We know that in 9600 BC the sea levels were lower, as the world was coming out of the last Ice Age. For several thousand years, the sea levels rose, so for a civilization to be swallowed up by the ocean in 9600 BC is not only possible, but we ourselves have seen this occurred to a number of places, such as Doggerland.

Furthermore, it is little known that in his own time, Plato had supporters who reported on the validity of Plato's account. Crantor, a student of Plato's student Xenocrates, came out in his defense. Crantor's work, a commentary on the *Timaeus,* is now lost, but fifth-century AD Neoplatonist Proclus reported on it. He wrote:

> As for the whole of this account of the Atlanteans, some say that it is unadorned history, such as Crantor, the first commentator on Plato. Crantor also says that Plato's contemporaries used to criticize him jokingly for not being the inventor of his Republic but copying the institutions of the Egyptians. Plato took these critics

seriously enough to assign to the Egyptians this story about the Athenians and Atlanteans, so as to make them say that the Athenians really once lived according to that system. Crantor adds, that this is testified by the prophets of the Egyptians, who assert that these particulars are written on pillars which are still preserved."[2]

The final sentence, however, is debated by the skeptics, for it is of course hard evidence that Plato's account was historical, not imaginary, as they argue. The skeptics argue—correctly—that in the original, the sentence does not start with Crantor, but with "he." Obviously, most translators have identified this as Crantor, but the skeptics argue it should be Plato—thus offering them an escape from an otherwise-harsh reality.

Indeed, throughout ancient times, many were convinced of Atlantis's existence and Plato's truthfulness. These included Strabo and Posidonius, both expert geographers. This is in sharp contrast with the claims made by Plato scholar Dr. Julia Annas, Regents Professor of philosophy at the University of Arizona, who argues:

> The continuing industry of discovering Atlantis illustrates the dangers of reading Plato. For he is using what has become a standard device of fiction—stressing the historicity of an event (and the discovery of hitherto unknown authorities) as an indication that what follows is fiction. The idea is that we should use the story to examine our ideas of government and power. We have missed the point if instead of thinking about these issues we go off exploring the sea bed.[3]

Clearly? The only clear thing here is that Annas clearly prefers to reach conclusions that are not supported by the historical evidence. In *Timaeus,* Plato has the speaker Critias twice emphasize that his story is about something that actually happened!

THE HALL OF RECORDS

Though Plato never mentioned it, today it is widespread belief that survivors of Atlantis settled in Egypt and were responsible for the dawn of the Egyptian civilization. Though I personally do not adhere to this point of view as it is expressed in many popular theories and books, in general, of course, it is possible. We know that Ancient Egypt had connections with the lost civilizations of the Sahara before it became a desert, and it is entirely possible that these people fled from a lost civilization that had been destroyed a few thousands of years before a bit further to the west.

According to Edgar Cayce, there is a hidden Hall of Records located near the Sphinx on the Giza Plateau. Though there is no archaeological evidence of its existence, for many years, explorations of the subterranean aspects of this pyramid complex have occurred in great secrecy, and it is equally clear discoveries have been made that have not been shared with the general public.

Image copyright the author.

164

The popular theories, however, argue that at Giza, at the foot of the pyramid plateau, the Sphinx is said to guard over a Hall of Records, which is said to contain information about this lost civilization. The phrase *Hall of Records* originated with the early-20th-century American psychic Edgar Cayce, who stated that five human races (white, black, red, brown, and yellow) had been created separately but simultaneously on different parts of the Earth. The red race had developed in Atlantis.

In 1933, Cayce made a series of predictions about the discovery of this Hall of Records, stating that we would come to a momentous moment in human history, which he identified as the year 1998, during which an ancient time vault in Egypt would be opened. He argued the time vault—the Hall of Records—had been installed in 10,500 BC and claimed that the materials inside would prove that the legend of Atlantis was true and that human civilization was tens of thousands of years older than believed. We now know that in recent years, even without the discovery of such a Hall of Records, the latter statement is definitely true.

Cayce's claim about Atlantis is well-known, but what is little-known is that most of his predictions never came true. Together with Lynn Picknett and Clive Prince, I investigated Cayce for their 1999 book, *The Stargate Conspiracy,* in which they showed that most of Cayce's predictions never materialized. He argued that China would invade the United States in the 1920s, an apparently outrageous claim—but not when we realized that Cayce was close friends with the head of the American Secret Service, which just happened to fear such an attack. After our exploration into the life and times of Cayce, we came away with the knowledge that Cayce's prediction could be safely disregarded, and the fact of the matter is that the existence of a Hall of Records was never announced before 1998.

In the 1990s, Hugh Lynn Cayce reportedly said, according to Edgar Cayce biographer A. Robert Smith: "I got him [Zahi Hawass] a scholarship at the University of Pennsylvania in Egyptology, to get his PhD. I got the scholarship through an ARE person who happened to be on the Fulbright scholarship board."[4] Dr. Hawass, then head of the Supreme Council of Antiquities of Egypt, strongly denied this, though it is a fact that he was admitted to the University of Pennsylvania through this scholarship. (Note: ARE is the Association for Research and Enlightenment, an organization set up to promote the work of Edgar Cayce.)

For many years, Hawass was both in Egypt and abroad identified as a man who suppressed new findings. Some even wondered whether he or his fellow Egyptologists had indeed found the Hall of Records, but had refused to release this information to the general public.

The Stargate Conspiracy was one of three books (*Giza: The Truth* by Chris Ogilvie-Herald and Ian Lawton and *Secret Chamber* by Robert Bauval being the other two), which in 1999 provided an overview of the controversy that was believed to surround the Giza Plateau and the pyramids, and whether there were any undiscovered, or purposefully kept hidden by the Egyptian authorities, chambers, whether inside the pyramids or under or near the Sphinx.

The previous decade had seen a renewed interest in the plateau, partly because of the theories of Robert Bauval and Graham Hancock and the discovery of a door in an inaccessible part of the Great Pyramid. It was found on March 22, 1993, by German robotics engineer Rudolf Gantenbrink during the installation of an air conditioning system. Anyone would think that Egyptologists would jump upon this discovery and quickly investigate what lay behind. Instead, it was an extremely slow development that took years and that made it appear that Egyptologists were truly not at all interested in this new discovery or what was behind the door. Were these impressions correct, or was it part of a larger framework—if not cover-up?

One source I contacted when Hawass was still in power—he resigned as Minister of Antiquities in 2011, in the aftermath of the Egyptian Revolution—said:

> I am a frequent visitor to Egypt and when I speak to government officials, most don't like Hawass. There are many archaeologists in Egypt that do excellent work. Anyone who visits Egypt and follows Egyptology sees this first-hand. The only problem is Hawass and the SCA. Why? Because Hawass has been imposed upon Egypt by certain foreigners, and this for a very long time. They have chosen an ignoramus, have flattered him, given him a PhD through the ARCE [American Research Center in Egypt]. He's a puppet.[5]

Pressed as to why that is, the source added:

> So that the secrets will not get out and that they have the best archaeological concessions. If Hawass is still there, it's only because he knows how to play with nationalism. I hear him say every day how foreigners want to steal from the Egyptians and that the antiquities are Egyptian. It's clever, because it makes it appear as if he is fighting the Egyptian cause and he won't be pushed aside.[6]

The source also noted: "The SCA follows the orders of foreigners from whom it has received help in guarding their interests."[7] Indeed, though one might think that the Egyptians are in control of their own country, archaeologically speaking, that appearance can be deceptive.

The puppet master organization that was identified was the American Research Center in Egypt. The ARCE's Website states: "Among ARCE's many great achievements is our relationship with the Supreme Council of Antiquities (SCA) within the Egyptian Ministry of Culture, without whom our work would not be possible. ARCE is viewed as making important contributions that serve to help Egypt directly in its pursuit of cultural heritage preservation."[8]

ARCE was founded in 1948 by "a consortium of educational and cultural institutions," and the organization underlines that it is also there to "strengthen American-Egyptian cultural ties" and especially to "establish an official 'presence' for North American scholars in Egypt."[9]

Interestingly, ARCE's Website adds: "Encouraged and aided by the US Department of State, in 1962 ARCE entered into an expanded and more structured consortium, and was charged with managing and distributing over $500,000 yearly in Public Law 480 (Food for Peace) funds."[10] This means that ARCE fulfills both scientific and social functions. However, seeing that it works with the U.S. Department of State, one could ask whether at one point ARCE was used or abused for other political purposes, seeing as Egypt has had an intriguing political past in the battle between East and West. Interestingly, one source contacted me, claiming that frequently the SCA (Supreme Council of Antiquities) receives from the U.S. National Security Agency (NSA) satellite imagery containing information as to whether or not there may be subterranean structures at certain sites.

But back to Hawass and the Sphinx. The previously noted operational framework was in evidence in April 2009, when Hawass reported: "Under my direction, the Supreme Council of Antiquities is working to reduce the groundwater level around antiquities sites throughout Egypt. We have completed a USAID-funded effort to de-water Karnak and Luxor temples, and work is underway in many other places. One of our greatest recent successes has been the development of a system to prevent the Great Sphinx at Giza from getting its paws wet!"[11]

Rather intriguingly, he added in his report, titled "The Story of the Sphinx," a discussion about mysterious underground tunnels and chambers carved below the Sphinx by so-called ancient civilizations. Some, including John Anthony West, Robert Bauval, and Graham

Hancock, claim that secrets were buried beneath the Sphinx by survivors of a lost civilization 10,000 years ago. They also claim that water caused the erosion of the Sphinx, and that this means that it dates to "long before the Old Kingdom."[12] Supporters have suggested drilling holes to find such hidden chambers. Hawass noted: "I have always refused to permit such a project in the past, because there was no scientific basis for it. Because such drilling was a necessary part of our work to protect the Sphinx from groundwater, however, we did finally drill in the vicinity of the statue, and we found that there were no hidden passages or chambers there."[13]

Despite all the usual hype that Hawass uses to underline his most mundane accomplishments, this is an unfortunate—and totally unscientific—conclusion. There are several studies, such as seismic work from 1992 and the Schor radar survey from 1996, that show geological anomalies (read: cavities), most of which are natural, but that is somewhat beside the point.

In fact, one might argue—and some have—that Hawass specifically tested for groundwater in those particular locations where he was sure that no such cavities, natural or "hidden passages or chambers," would be found. It would make sense to test for groundwater, but Hawass's glib statement "that there were no hidden passages or chambers" cannot be reached from the limited research this test carried out. Without doubt, there are cavities. Full stop. In fact, Hawass himself announced to the Egyptian press on April 14, 1996, that there are secret tunnels under the Sphinx and around the pyramids. He stated his belief that these tunnels would prove to "carry many secrets of the building of the Pyramids."[14] Although people are allowed to change their minds, they should perhaps, 13 years to the month, highlight their new position. Not Dr. Hawass.

However, Hawass's "Story of the Sphinx" report is also contrary to findings from scans carried out by Dr. Abbas and team, published by

169

NRIAG (National Research Institute of Astronomy and Geophysics) in 2007. But rather than comment on a fellow academic who has had his results published in a scientific publication, Hawass—for reasons that have nothing to do with science, but are likely to do with grandstanding if not more sinister motives—has a go at the likes of West, Bauval, and Hancock. Why the age of the Sphinx determined through water erosion has anything to do with the presence of chambers beneath the monument it is not altogether clear, either. Considering the other unscientific jumps Hawass makes, though, nothing should come as a surprise.

When one looks at Hawass's reports rather than at his statements to the press, an even more interesting picture emerges. We learn that in early 2008, the Supreme Council of Antiquities cooperated with Cairo University's Engineering Center for Archaeology and Environment to drill four boreholes, each 4 inches in diameter and about 20 meters deep, into the bedrock at the base of the Sphinx. A camera was lowered into each borehole to allow examination of the plateau's geology.[15]

The "Story of the Sphinx" report contains several gems, some of which Hawass should address, but instead he creates a smoke-and-mirrors show. One might almost wonder whether he does not want this material to be noted; judging from what happened upon publication, the few who reported on the announcement indeed focused on the "West-Bauval-Hancock sidebar" and not on the main show.

A separate scientific update states that 260 cubic meters of water are being pumped out every hour through drainage tubes. That's 6,240 cubic meters, or 6,240,000 liters, of water per day. An Olympic swimming pool has 2,500,000 liters. In short, water of a quantity equal to almost three Olympic swimming pools is pumped away on a daily basis from underneath the Sphinx! Indeed, the Sphinx could roughly fit inside an Olympic swimming pool. The report continues that, as such, the water in front of the Sphinx has been reduced to 70 percent of its original volume. But wait: "No fewer than 33 monitoring points were established to inspect the movement of the body of the Sphinx and the surrounding bedrock, this over a period of a month, and this monitoring proved that they are steady."[16]

Unless I am seriously mistaken, for such serious amounts of water to be moved hourly, there would need to be at least one cavity, roughly the size of a small swimming pool, that could fill up continuously with water. In short, an underground lake. So the report strongly suggests the fallacy of Hawass's own conclusions!

This brings us to the next question: Why are the Egyptian archaeological authorities emptying an underground lake? For stability, or for something else? One might argue that removing the water will reduce the stability of the Sphinx, which was an obvious concern, as this is why the stability of the Sphinx area was being monitored. Apparently, though, based on a month-long observation, emptying this underground cavity does not endanger the stability of the surface structures. But why empty it in the first place? To keep the Sphinx's paws dry?

One source, when confronted with Hawass's reports and my observation, has gone so far as to argue that Hawass, accompanied by Egyptologist Mark Lehner, had actually found this lake several years ago. The lake is under the entire plateau, the area contained within the concrete wall (construction of which began in 2002). He added that, in his opinion, these projects were preparation for an exploration of the Giza underworld.

The Egyptian Revolution of January 2011 was largely the result of known and widespread corruption throughout the government, and Egyptology was not immune from this. On October 8, 2008, the former Head of Restoration in Islamic Cairo and two other Egyptian Culture Ministry officials were jailed for 10 years for receiving bribes from contractors. The Cairo court ordered Ayman Abdel Monem, Hussein Ahmed Hussein, and Abdel Hamid Qutb to pay fines of between LE 200,000 and LE 550,000 [U.S. $33,000–91,000].[17]

Abdel Hamid Qutb was actually the head of the technical department at the SCA and reported to Hawass. The contracts under suspicion were worth millions of dollars and involved the restoration of some of Egypt's most famous monuments. Hawass was quick to defend Qutb at the time of his arrest in September 2007, claiming that the accused was not in a position to give out contracts. Hawass told the BBC's Arabic Service that contracts are only handed out after a "rigorous procedure" and that Qutb had no decision-making power.[18] The court obviously ruled differently, and if Hawass made a comment at that point, I could not find a reference to it.

In the interview at the time of Qutb's arrest, Hawass also told the BBC that he takes "immediate action against any employee with the slightest shadow of suspicion hanging over them, even if the person turns out to be innocent."[19] Guilty until proven innocent, it seems, is the modus operandi within the SCA. No wonder there are reports that Hawass is unpopular within Egypt.

This was not the first time that Hawass found himself in murky waters. In fact, at the same time that Gantenbrink's robot uncovered the hidden door inside the Great Pyramid on March 22, 1993, Hawass was suspended from his then-position as chief inspector of the Giza Pyramid Plateau. Synchronicity, or did Gantenbrink make use of the power vacuum to announce his finding in April 1993, knowing that otherwise it might be suppressed?

What happened next is also interesting and revealing. Upon the announcement, Gantenbrink was banned from resuming his work. The Egyptian Antiquities Organization (EAO), the predecessor of the SCA, claimed that Gantenbrink had broken a rule of archaeology by speaking for himself rather than through the proper channels—which are obviously there, by its own admission, to control what gets out and what doesn't. What happened next is also interesting and revealing. Graham Hancock writes: "The [then] Director of the German Archaeological Institute in Cairo, Dr Rainer Stadelmann, sided with the Egyptians and condemned Gantenbrink for his press action. Dr Stadelmann was adamant about the nonimportance of the find. 'This is not a door; there is nothing behind it.'"[20] The president of the EAO, Dr Muhamad Bakr, went so far as to claim the announcement a hoax. He stated: "The orifice of the shaft is too small for the robot to go through."[21] History has shown Bakr to be wrong on both counts.

It was Bakr who removed Hawass from his position, claiming that a valuable ancient statue had been stolen from Giza under Hawass's watch.

To quote again from Hancock: "Three months later, in June 1993, Dr Bakr himself was fired and replaced by Dr Nur El Din. Amid accusations of malpractice and fraud, Dr Bakr spoke of a 'mafia' which had been involved with the Pyramids for 'the last twenty years'. Refusing to give names, Dr Bakr said, 'I wanted the whole matter investigated by the prosecution authorities, but my request was refused.'"[22]

In early 1994, Hawass was reinstated to his position. Though Bakr is not the most credible source, there are nevertheless clear echoes of the ARCE. Hawass's reinstatement was "said to have been brought about by American intervention," according to Chris Ogilvie-Herald, writing in the British magazine *Quest for Knowledge.*[23] At the very least, Hawass seems to be quite fortunate in that no matter what, whether it involve stolen statues or his technical department head being fined and imprisoned, he remains immune to it all.

Gantenbrink never returned to work inside the Great Pyramid. He even offered the Egyptian authorities the use of his robot—because only a robot can penetrate the air shaft—and volunteered to train an Egyptian technician to operate it, but his suggestions were not taken.

However, Hawass eventually argued that the discovery of the door was extremely interesting and would be further explored. In March 1996, he stated that the door would be opened in September of that year. The month was right, but it was on September 17, 2002, that the door was finally opened. The event was broadcast live on Fox TV in America and transmitted to 140 countries via the National Geographic Channel. The end result was the discovery of another door, which Hawass claimed would be opened soon. The world still waits.

During the 2002 live broadcast, Hawass made some intriguing throwaway remarks. For instance, he argued that "'it was not 'slaves' who built the pyramids, but 'great Egyptians'."[24] Afterward, he told the Arabic newspaper *Al Gomhoreya* that "[t]he results of the robot's exploration refute the allegations reiterated by Jews and some western countries that the Jews built the pyramids."[25] Of course, the exploration of an air shaft does no such thing. But an equally serious scientific faux pas is that no one actually claims that the Jews, as slaves, ever built the pyramids. Roughly speaking, if this were a historical event, it would have occurred c. 1,000 years after the building of the pyramids. Practically anyone of some education in the Western world is aware of this. Yet one of the leading archaeologists and the protector of Egypt's heritage is not, it seems.

Hawass frequently abuses nationalism, but some journalists and observers have gone further, positing that in their opinion Hawass is anti-Semitic. In my opinion, Hawass suffers from a severe case of verbal diarrhea whenever a camera or a microphone is placed in front of him.

On a more serious note, the SCA (read: Hawass) for years had a stranglehold on most of the research occurring in Egypt, and whether and how it gets reported. This is in evidence in the case of Gantenbrink, who broke the rule, and also in the case of Dr. Abbas, whose official Giza report has been stopped from publication for a very long time.

Sources I contacted said that they, too, had several reports waiting to be published, but that there was always one delay or another. This kind of treatment, of course, is not science but control, if not a gag order. Some might argue that there is a serious backlog; others might shout "cover-up."

Indeed, why did the SCA place such stringent penalties on the publication of scientific reports without its consent—the penalty often being the denial of access to Egyptian archaeological sites? These are the measures of a dictatorship at best and are far removed from any scientific approach, but then the SCA operated within the framework of a dictatorship.

No one will argue that Egypt alone is in charge of deciding who digs when, where, and to what extent, even though it is obvious, in light of the SCA's connection with ARCE, that this is not truly the case. But once permission has been given, the participating scientists and organizers surely should have the power to decide when and where to publish the results, rather than being literally gagged by the SCA until it—if ever—deems it appropriate to release the results, and even then sometimes demanding editorial changes. All of this is occurring without any external overview.

One source went so far as to argue that Hawass's approach is one of disinformation: that Hawass carefully twists scientific results that do not conform to the standard history of ancient Egypt and that, as he exercises sole control and makes himself the medium, he can almost singlehandedly maintain the status quo of Egyptian history. This "Hawass touch" is also in evidence in the spin in his 2009 Sphinx groundwater report. But the important question is: Why?

The answer has already been given: Hawass tried to maintain the consensus view of ancient Egyptian history. This is why he often singled out Hancock, Bauval, and West. Hawass realized that these are the most vociferous and dangerous parties that can go against him, but they are not alone in feeling his wrath. Hawass denied findings when they didn't fit with his agenda, and defamed any individual for daring to have a different idea and not releasing it through his office.

In 2008, Professor Barry Kemp reported on his research at the city of Amarna, created by rebel Pharaoh Akhenaten. The Pharaoh was obviously despised and, in the decades following his death, the ancient Egyptians tried to remove any mention of his existence. It was reported that Kemp and his team found skeletal remains at Amarna that show "signs of malnutrition, extreme labour, and the lowest age of mortality witnessed at excavations of Pharaonic sites."[26] This evidence goes a long way to confirm that Akhenaten created a brutal regime, one of which few were proud.

However, the findings were immediately subjected to criticism from Hawass, who used the Egyptian state news service to accuse the excavators of distorting history. He claimed that their findings were "not based on any admissible scientific proofs" and added that "[b]uilding Akhenaten city was an obsession for ancient Egyptians like the Giza Pyramids and workers wanted to realise a national achievement to be proud of."[27] Hawass, by his comments, was later described as "indulging in empty chauvinism."[28]

Hawass is also proud that he "worked to strengthen Egypt's antiquities law" and that in 2002 he "worked to have a new law enacted forbidding excavation in Upper Egypt...to encourage documentation and preservation rather than excavation."[29] Indeed, Hawass is proud of the fact that he has stopped all excavations in Upper Egypt! One can only wonder why. No one will argue that documentation and preservation are important, but to the exclusion of everything else—and to make it a law, rather than just an internal guideline?

Finally, when interviewed about geologist Robert Schoch's theory that the Sphinx is much older than the pyramids, Hawass stated: "If geologists prove what Schoch is saying, still in my opinion, as an

Egyptologist, the date of the Sphinx is clear to us."[30] In short, no matter what the evidence, Hawass claims it is all clear to him. It is clear that for Hawass, Egyptology is a religion, not a science.

Though Hawass can and should be blamed for many things, it is equally a matter of record that Egyptology as a science is seriously in need of spring cleaning. It might perhaps come as a surprise to learn that since c. 1840 the paradigm of Egyptian history has remained firmly in place. Serious scientific evidence has often been put aside to maintain a dogma, and Hawass and many other "scientists" are religiously sticking to it.

In 1984, 85 samples were taken from the Giza Plateau, including five from the Sphinx, which were submitted for carbon dating. The results showed dates from 3809 to 2869 BC. This meant that the accepted Egyptian chronology for the building of the Giza pyramids was off by 200 to 1,200 years. Bauval quotes Mark Lehner: "The Giza pyramid is 400 years earlier than Egyptologists believe."[31]

Equally, in the 1950s, Zakaria Goneim, then chief inspector of Egyptian Antiquities, found the inviolate sarcophagus of Third Dynasty Pharaoh Sekhemkhet inside his pyramid. When the sarcophagus was opened, there was no mummy inside. It was an empty sarcophagus. In this case, grave robbers could definitely not be blamed. In fact, in many instances, including with the Great Pyramid, Egyptologists have identified grave robbery as the reason for an empty sarcophagus. If it were a crime scene investigation, few detectives would reach a similar conclusion based upon the available evidence.

Egyptology, in fact, looks with disdain upon ancient records such as those of first-century BC historian Diodorus Siculus, who wrote that not a single pharaoh was buried in a pyramid that he had constructed for himself, but that the pharaohs were buried instead in a secret place. Egyptologists prefer to argue—despite evidence that proves otherwise—that the pyramids are but tombs.

Dutch author Willem Zitman ponders why today's scientists do not want to admit that the Ancient Greeks were all schooled in Ancient Egypt, as they themselves claimed. Instead, he says, they prefer to pretend as if the Greeks discovered everything by themselves, and thus they can make claims that the Egyptians did nothing whatsoever to further science or knew nothing of astronomy. Zitman adds that, although archaeo-astronomy has been taught as a scientific discipline since 1983, Egypt has hardly been discussed—a notable exception. It is precisely when such a vacuum is created that it will be filled by theories of the likes of Robert Bauval. If Egyptologists do not like that fact, they should not blame Bauval.

In the end, Hawass does stand for, and sums up, the current state of Egyptology. He blames the likes of West, Bauval, and Hancock for making ridiculous statements, but in August 1996—unsurprisingly, while in front of a camera—Hawass was scrambling through a tunnel leading under the Sphinx, stating: "No one really knows what's inside this tunnel. But we are going to open it for the first time."[32] This is further evidence that his 2009 statement is a complete and utter distortion—if not of the truth, then at least of what he said before.

So, in 1996, there were tunnels. But in April 1999, Hawass appeared on Fox TV and denied the existence of tunnels going out from the Tomb of Osiris, an underground structure near the Sphinx. In April 2009, he repeated this story, as if he needed to do so once per decade. Yet, as mentioned, in August 1996 he was actually filmed walking inside a tunnel under the Sphinx!

As Bauval points out in *Secret Chamber,* the controversy involving Hawass and the Giza Plateau dates back many decades: "Meanwhile something unusual happened involving Zahi Hawass. For reasons that are not clear he started a dig in front of the Sphinx temple, apparently in connection with the Institute of Underground Water of the

Egyptian Ministry of Irrigation. A drilling through some fifty feet [15 meters] of debris struck red granite instead of the natural limestone of the area."[33])

Red granite is not native to the Giza Plateau; the only source is Aswan, hundreds of miles to the south. The very presence of red granite, discovered in 1980 in the vicinity of the Sphinx, proves that there is something underneath the Giza Plateau. If Hawass says anything different, it should first be seen as a case of "methinketh he protesteth too much." Whether whatever is hidden underneath the Giza Plateau has anything to do with Atlantis, or—more likely—with a forgotten dimension of the history of Ancient Egypt, is a question that only time will be able to answer.

THE QUEST FOR ATLANTIS

Atlantis is a unique word, a translation from the Egyptian word *Keftiu* into Greek. Keftiu was a translation of an original Atlantean word—thus said Plato. As it is a unique name, and a unique account, the story of identifying Atlantis is difficult; had it been easy, the mystery would have been solved long ago.

When Plato wrote *Timaeus* and *Critias,* he would probably never have imagined that Atlantis would create a controversy in the following millennia. Though the civilization is often believed to be located in the Atlantic Ocean, numerous locations have been proposed, from America to the Middle East. One of the many researchers who claim to have located Atlantis is American researcher Robert Sarmast. Though his story may not be as spectacular as some of the other theories, it does have the advantage that his possibility is likely—and thus might be the key that unlocks the problem.

One of the most remarkable facts about the disappearance of Atlantis is that the "continent" slowly sank. It was the end result of a series of disasters, which include earthquakes. According to Sarmast, this is a clue in determining the location. Briefly, Sarmast has identified the Mediterranean Sea as the location for Atlantis, specifically the area immediately to the southeast of Cyprus, currently buried underneath 1,500 meters—about a mile—of water. It is known that the Mediterranean has not always been a sea, at least not as large as its current size. At least three times, earthquakes and the continental drift have closed the Strait of Gibraltar—the Pillars of Hercules. As a consequence, water began to evaporate, turning the sea into land. This is now an accepted scientific fact, testified by various geological remains, including the visible routes of the Nile, continuing its course much further.

Graham Hancock is one of the authors who has gone in search of evidence that buildings and cart ruts around the island of Malta are now buried underneath the water's surface, evidence that even relatively recently (5,000 years ago) the water level seems to have been lower than today.

Sarmast argues that approximately 10,000 years ago, the Strait was closed off, which resulted in one of the biggest waterfalls the world has ever seen—a hundred times bigger than Victoria Falls. But when earthquakes reopened the corridor, millions of tons of water slowly entered the Mediterranean, whereby land began to sink underneath the water. Sarmast believes that Atlantis was lost in this catastrophe.

Atlantis has a number of characteristics that Sarmast feels he has been able to confirm apply to Cyprus. The presence of elephants and copper are two important characteristics that fit within his hypothesis. Copper was so abundant in Cyprus that the island was actually named after the metal.

But what about the so-called Pillars of Hercules, where Atlantis was said to be located beyond? Criticism against the identification of the Pillars as Gibraltar predates Sarmast; Eberhard Zangger was one of those who argued that various locations around the Mediterranean Sea carried that description. Gibraltar should not be considered the sole candidate for that title, some argue.

But could Atlantis be an island, if the Mediterranean Sea was not a sea? Even though most of the sea was turned into land, the rivers still emptied inside the area—and some ocean must always have remained at the bottom, unless the period in which the Mediterranean was cut off from the Atlantic Ocean was extremely long.

It is a fact that the shores of the Mediterranean Sea show signs of the origins of civilization, whereby the eastern shores have many remains that are dated to 8000 BC—relatively shortly after the sinking of Atlantis, which the Ancient Egyptians had dated to approximately 9500 BC. It thus seems likely that that region indeed had an unknown civilization. If Atlantis was located in the Atlantic Ocean, would we not have seen those signs in the western Mediterranean, or even on the western shores of the Atlantic Ocean, along Spain and Morocco?

Sarmast adds that Cyprus still has a yearly Festival of the Flood, whose origin has been lost in the mists of time. Is it a remembrance of the catastrophe? The festival is even named Kataklysmos, and even though it is now celebrated at Pentecost, this was an old festival that the Church Christianized.

It is not the only potential link with Atlantis. The highest mountain on the island is now almost 2 kilometers above sea level and is named Olympos. Is this the original Olympos, the sacred mountain of the Greek gods?

Sarmast touches upon, but does not extensively discuss, the possibility that the demise of Atlantis may be connected with the story of Noah and the Flood. A catastrophe of this sort—the filling of the Mediterranean basin—and the Ark of Noah beginning to float on water, until it finally reaches land, are very similar. Indeed, once the waters had risen to a new level, the world had been transformed and the evils of the old world had been washed away. The evil was also in Atlantis, as the disaster that befell it has been identified as God washing the slate clean of the evil that the civilization had begun to wreak upon its neighbors.

Whether it was God or a natural disaster, the refilling of the basin must have created a massive reaction—panic—with the people that lived inside it. Some must have been confronted with a rising sea level, and some may even have experienced a tsunami. Many must have died. Atlantis had a further problem, in the sense that it was a plain, located next to the sea. If it had been a mountain civilization, they may have survived, or had more time. Among all the victims that the disaster must have made, a civilization along the shores must have been its major victim. And the Egyptians remembered them.

However, Sarmast's hypothesis remains, for the moment, just that. At best, it highlights that there is likely a lost civilization waiting to be discovered below the waters of the Mediterranean Sea. It will be another lost episode, and might provide interesting insights as to how Jericho, Malta, and maybe even Old Europe were all once related and part of a larger whole. But the fact of the matter is that Cyprus is likely not Atlantis. Though there were several Pillars of Hercules, and the one Plato would have referred to was Gibraltar. Equally, Plato listed the dimensions of Atlantis, and these measured almost 1,000 miles in width—a civilization that one cannot place everywhere, and especially not on the tiny Mediterranean volcanic island of Thera as some have tried to make do. It therefore seems that the quest for Atlantis is not over.

ATLANTIS: THE LOST WALHALLA

In the eighth century, Viking ships left their Scandinavian homeland and set sail for distant shores. By the end of the 11th century, the end of the Viking Age, their longships had reach as far west as

Iceland and Greenland, as far south as Northern Africa, and as far east as Constantinople and the Volga River. Throughout the ninth century, the Vikings would attack and slowly take control of the British Isles, as well as many other countries in Europe, including France, reaching Paris in AD 845. By 900, major towns and abbeys across the continent had been sacked; the vanquished countries would never be the same again, and distant memories of the Viking raids continue to live on in popular legends to this day.

What caused the Vikings to invade so many European countries remains an unanswered question, though historians have speculated wildly on the subject. Early theories focused on overpopulation and the need to expand the Viking territory. This proposal has now been abandoned, though there is currently no new theory held as the consensus view as to why the Vikings invaded Europe. Missing from the gamma of possibilities is that they might have gone in search of their mythical homeland, Walhalla, which, according to their legends, was somewhere to the southwest. Walhalla is often called the Hall of the Gods, but in myth it was inextricably linked with an island where the gods had supposedly granted its inhabitants the gift of immortality. That the Vikings had indeed left their homeland in search of Walhalla was the conclusion reached by Belgian historian Marcel Mestdagh. After years of retelling the same traditional story of the Viking conquest of Europe to his students, he realized that there was logic to the Viking methodology, in which they invaded first England and then France. Mestdagh had noticed something that no one had seen before.

After their initial conquests, mostly of islands and coastal regions, the Vikings gathered their so-called Great Army. In England, the Great Army was formed in 866, the core of it created by soldiers brought by boats from Denmark. Their mission was to conquer the major towns and cities, a task that was accomplished in 879 when the army crossed the Channel to continue their campaign in France.

Mestdagh realized that the way in which the Great Army moved about through England was not haphazard, but rather involved a type of pattern. It was almost as though something in the landscape—something in the topography, perhaps—was leading them from place to place. Whatever it was, it was something that was still present or visible at that time but has long since been lost to us.

Many years and a great deal of research later, Mestdagh realized that this missing clue was still present in the landscape, though we no longer recognized it as such: It was an ancient road network that fanned out from two towns, one in England (Nottingham) and one in France (Sens). Mestdagh was able to show that the network of roads in England centered on Nottingham, but that the Vikings hadn't been able to find there what they were looking for. After the conquest of Nottingham, new recruits came from Denmark, and the Viking Army crossed the Channel into France. There they made use of the same system of roads, whereby all roads led to the French city of Sens, which the Viking Great Army reached in late 886.

Interestingly, Sens was the only city that the Vikings did not sack. Instead, it was taken after a peaceful siege, which lasted only about six months. The history books make special note of the fact that no one was injured or killed during the siege of Sens. When the Great Army arrived, the people of the town had settled on the islands in the river Yonne, fully expecting that they would be brutally invaded like any other town. Some historians have argued that the archbishop of Sens had bought peace with the Vikings, but there is no evidence to support this. In short, there is no known reason why the Vikings would have been so respectful. Mestdagh wondered: Was Sens, the former stronghold of the Celtic tribe known as the Senones ("the Elders") somehow sacred to the Vikings? Was Sens what the Vikings had been looking for and had now found? Could it be that Sens was their mythical Walhalla? And was this the reason why they did not sack the town?

The French City of Sens, southeast of Paris, has been identified as the center of an enormous megalithic civilization, which Belgian historian Marcel Mestdagh identified as Atlantis. The local Celtic tribe was later known as the Senones ("the Elders") and the region, despite being hundreds of miles from the sea, is known as the Ile-de-France ("the Island of France").

Image copyright the author.

What the Vikings encountered in northern France was an old and long-forgotten system of roads. Mestdagh believed the road network had originally been the work of the Romans, who were known to have been road builders par excellence. The notorious Roman conqueror Julius Caesar had chosen Agedincum—Sens—as the town where he stationed his armies, though it became only an administrative center in the late fourth century AD.

It soon became clear, however, that the Romans had not constructed this network of roads, as it was interlaced with a network of megalithic stones and therefore dated back thousands of years earlier, long before the Romans ever invaded Gaul. Standing stones and other megalithic constructions are known to have been used as boundary markers by the Celts, a people that came from the Eastern parts of Europe in the first millennium BC. It is well known that the Celts made active use of these megalithic sites, and when places such as Stonehenge were analyzed in the 18th century by the likes of William Stukeley, it was thought that the priestly class known as the druids performed elaborate ceremonies inside and among these monuments. Caesar in his conquest of Gaul specifically targeted and hunted down the druids, thus ensuring that nothing of their knowledge survived.

No such extermination had occurred in the Scandinavian countries, which were equally rich in megalithic sites. In fact, northern Europe had a relatively peaceful transition from megalithic times all the way to the Vikings. This meant that the knowledge associated with these megaliths survived well into the era of the Vikings, which meant that when they landed in Europe they knew far more about these ancient markers than the local people did. The Vikings had effectively maintained an active link to a former world, and by AD 800, when they set out to find their Walhalla, they managed to do so largely on the basis of this link, which, sadly, had been severed, first by the Romans and later by Christianity in England and France. As a consequence, very little of the Viking knowledge was passed down to us, so Mestdagh had to spend years driving through the countryside of northern France, mapping megaliths, road networks, and ancient monuments, as well as cataloging ancient legends—all of this at a time (the 1970s and 1980s) when there was no GPS nor the modern miracle that is Google Earth. It was a monumental task that would be a contributing factor to his early death, though not before he could publish the astonishing conclusions his research had revealed to him.

When he looked at the results of his painstaking research, he realized that this network of roads and megaliths was only part of the story. He also discovered a series of tremendously long ditches, which had at one time formed a series of vast, concentric ovals with Sens at its center. No one had ever figured out what these ovals signified. In fact, the raised sides of the ditches had once been used to construct roads, many of which survived and are still in use to this day. But Mestdagh's on-site investigations showed that enormous ditches had once been located there, and that oftentimes, they could still be described in the landscape. Because the ditches were made of sand, their integrity had slowly degenerated during the more than 3,000 years that they had not been in use. Detailed analysis revealed that they were actually ditches with raised borders. In the center of each was a depression or trough that had probably contained water at one time. These inner ditches probably functioned as canals and were often connected to rivers; indeed, portions of the concentric ovals that surrounded Sens were comprised of actual rivers—the portion of the river Marne between Meaux and Châlons-sur-Marne, for example.

The true extent of knowledge that Megalithic peoples—the ones responsible for the thousands of megaliths in western Europe—possessed has not yet been discerned either by archaeology or history. But in the 1970s, archaeologist Alexander Thom made an amazing discovery. After performing detailed studies of more than 600 megaliths in Britain, Ireland, and Brittany, he realized all of them had been built with a standard unit of measurement, which he called the Megalithic yard. He also concluded that there was a central form of government, "because there must have been a headquarters from which standard rods were sent out but whether this was in these islands or on the Continent the present investigation cannot determine."[34] That headquarters might be Sens. Mestdagh had realized that the creation of the sacred center at Sens had been done in accordance with the cardinal points, by someone with a detailed understanding of geography. The main axis of this geometrical pattern ran east-west and went through the center of the city of Sens, extending to the east, with the center of the road system located about 1.5 miles east of the city.

The end result of Mestdagh's investigation was multifold, many of them outside the scope of this book. First, there were a total of 64 roads, extending as far as 200 miles in either direction. He had found hundreds of miles of this road network still in use in the 1980s, with numerous megaliths and sacred sites along the way. Second, Mestdagh also realized that many of the names of the towns and villages situated along these roads contained the Marc- or Merc- prefix—literally, "marker." One of the better-known sites is located on the southern road, which skirted the Puy-de-Dôme, a famous extinct volcano, which was commonly regarded as sacred since Celtic times, if not earlier. Its summit holds a temple dedicated to the Roman god Mercury, a further reference to the merc- prefix. Is it a coincidence that Mercurius was thought to be the protector of travelers on the road?

This system of four concentric ditches would have required an extraordinary amount of work to construct, for the circumference of Oval I, the first and smallest oval, is already an incredible 400 miles. Oval IV has axes of 297 and 370 miles, and a circumference of 1,106 miles—staggering dimensions, but definitely still within human capabilities, particularly when we remember that the Great Wall of China stretches for more than 5,500 miles.

On a map of France, Oval III is almost visible to the naked, untrained eye: Take any map from France and find the town of Rouen; follow it down to Le Mans, Tours, and Châteauroux. Further north is a small section between Amiens and Poix; between Poix and Rouen there is a section missing on modern maps, but it is known that there was once a Roman road here. Far from being mere figments of the imagination, these ovals are very real.

When you map the old Celtic tribal boundaries, they coincide with the ovals and the fanlike road network centered on Sens. When we know that this Megalithic system incorporated standing stones and that the Celts used these stones as boundary markers, the enigma of why certain standing stones were built in certain places is explained. Mestdagh had essentially discovered a Megalithic civilization, a civilization that had once been lost to the sands of time. But had it? There were the easily identifiable references to an island, remembered in the name Ile-de-France, but could this place really have been the mythical lost island of Atlantis?

Fortunately for the trained historian, Mestdagh did not have to take this on faith. We now know that the story of Atlantis was told to Plato by Solon, who had visited Egypt and heard about the lost city from some temple priests there. They had provided Solon with precise dimensions—3,000 stadia (333 miles)—of this island, which Plato then incorporated in his account, part of an unfinished work known to us as *Timaeus*. And here is where it gets interesting: Oval IV can be inscribed inside a diamond (as any oval can) comprised of equal sides that are 333 miles long. This distance corresponds perfectly with the 3,000 stadia that Plato mentioned as the dimensions of Atlantis! There is more. Plato locates Atlantis on relatively flat land, and situates it between the mountains and the sea. Oval IV is indeed located on relatively flat land, and sits between mountains (the Alps) and the sea (the Mediterranean). Plato adds that the distance from Atlantis to the sea is 2,000 stadia, or 222 miles—precisely the distance from the southernmost point of the diamond to the Mediterranean coastline. Finally, using the system of roads, Mestdagh was able to retrace the 10 kingdoms of Atlantis mentioned by Plato, concluding that the area within Oval I was the "middle kingdom" and that the area between Oval I and Oval IV contained the nine other kingdoms. Another Greek philosopher, Proclus, referred to a text of Marcellus, which stated that the width of the middle kingdom of Atlantis was 1,000 stadia, which is actually precisely the width of Oval I! And can it be just a coincidence that there is a town named Avalon, the name of a lost mythical land in Celtic tradition, located on this very oval?

Mestdagh also found supporting evidence that the Megalithic civilization was Atlantis from the Megalithic Era itself. Petit-Mont is a famous tumulus (a mound of earth and/or stones over a grave or graves) around the Gulf of Morbihan, a region that is known today mainly for its more than 4,000 standing stones, most of them aligned into rows in and around the town of Carnac. The tumulus dates back to 4600 BC and is one of the most significant, but also most brutally damaged, cairns in Brittany. Z. Le Rouzic was one of the first French archaeologists who actively investigated and restored the Megalithic monuments of Brittany in the first half of the 20th century. Inside the tumulus, Le Rouzic identified a series of stones that carried inscriptions along the interior walls. Stone M is an ellipse with 18 spokes and is traditionally interpreted as a solar wheel. Mestdagh contended that this was actually a map of Atlantis, which showed the nine-plus-one kingdoms of the lost civilization. An analysis of the carvings around the solar wheel added weight to this interpretation, as it showed mountains to the south, as well as the shores of East Anglia and Kent, and the Rhine and Main river system, thus revealing the "solar wheel"—Atlantis—was rendered in a location that makes it geographically fit with Mestdagh's Megalithic civilization.

For Mestdagh there was no doubt that the lost civilization of Atlantis had been found. It would have taken our ancestors centuries to build this truly gigantic and sophisticated civilization. The Megalithic city had also been an island surrounded by an astonishing system of canals. But the etymology of the word *island* provides us with perhaps the best clue as to its shape. For example, the word *island* in Dutch is eiland, which means "egg land" or "the land in the shape of an egg"—an oval. The English word *island* comes from is-land, or ys-land, and it is in Brittany that the story of the drowned land of Ys is recorded. In the story, dikes are used to protect the island from the sea, and, incredibly, dikes are precisely what Mestdagh found.

It is my belief that Sens was the capital, the sacred spiritual center of Atlantis. No doubt this is why its inhabitants were known as the Senones, "the Elders," in Celtic times. Its sacred nature was also apparent during medieval times, when its archbishops held the prestigious title of Primate of Gaul and Germany, an extraordinary honor that the history books have had great difficulty explaining. The fact that Caesar himself stationed his army in Sens gives further support to the idea that Sens was of great historical importance. Caesar knew that the druids were his most dangerous opponents. He made it his mission to silence and exterminate them, famously giving chase and then cornering them in England on the island of Anglesey. Did Caesar station his army in Sens because that was their French headquarters?

Sens as the center of the Megalithic world might seem odd, given our modern perspective on the history of that area. Today the megaliths in Carnac are far better known. This is something for which the tourism industry is partly to blame. An inventory of all extant French megaliths was established in 1880 and printed in the *Bulletin de la Société d'Anthropologie de Paris*. The report shows that by far the largest concentration of megaliths—261 out of 509 pockets—can be found in and around Sens. Though most of these disappeared by the turn of the last century, due to the encroachment of civilization and the contingencies of our modern age, the area around Sens was once literally littered with megaliths. It was the center of a lost world—Walhalla.

Archaeologists tend to see megalithic monuments in total isolation. For example, the gigantic stone circles of Avebury are located a mere 12 miles to the north of Stonehenge, which is probably the best-known megalithic monument in the world. Hardly any research has been undertaken by professional archaeologists to find what common ground, if any, exists between the two structures, even though it's very straightforward that the people of Stonehenge knew of Avebury, and vice versa. Mestdagh's research methodology showed that we should not look at megalithic complexes in isolation—as archaeology tends to do—but as a coherent whole. This idea is also in line with the conclusions drawn by Alexander Thom that the megalithic civilization had headquarters—a capital—somewhere. That capital has now been identified as Sens. What this means is that from c. 4500 to 1200 BC, a major civilization existed in Europe about which we know very little.

What we now call the inhabitants (the Megalithic people) shows that we have given primacy to this aspect of their culture—the stone cutting and technology behind it. But Mestdagh's discovery unveiled several more facets of this civilization that were on par with, if not superior to, Ancient Egypt. In fact, this is precisely why Solon was told of this city when he visited Egypt. Whereas there are thousands of books about ancient Egypt, though, there is hardly any knowledge about the Megalithic civilization of northern Europe. It is missing from the pages of history altogether, and if it had not been for a few Egyptian priests, Solon, and Plato, it might have been lost forever.

When Mestdagh focused his research on Stonehenge and Avebury, he found remnants of a road that connected the two sites, which was equally of oval design. The road actually extends beyond the two sites. When traced on a map, he found that two-thirds of this oval still existed and that its dimensions were precisely one-tenth of the dimensions of Oval II in France. With this mathematical information, he had undeniable proof that the megalith builders of France knew the megalith builders of England. Everything that happened for more than three millennia in northern Europe was executed according to a plan so great in design that it defies belief. That is precisely what the lost civilization of Atlantis was.

The ancient Egyptians knew about the lost civilization of Atlantis. In Egyptian mythology, the Afterlife was identified as an island in the west, intersected by canals, and was represented as an enclosed oval formed by the body of Nut, surmounted by Osiris holding aloft the Solar Disk. This Egyptian equivalent of Walhalla was known as the Sekhet-hetep, the Field of Offerings. Egyptologists have interpreted these "myths" as the products of the imaginations of the ancient Egyptians. An alternative interpretation is available—one that shows that Sekhet-hetep was once real and existed in France.

That there was some kind of communication between the Megalithic civilization and Egypt was once accepted in archaeological circles. Italian anthropologist Guiseppe Sergi recorded finding the sign of the ankh and other hieroglyphic signs on several French dolmens. Professor J. Morris Jones confirmed the suggestion of Sir John Rhys that Celtic languages preserved an Egyptian Hamitic syntax: "The pre-Aryan idioms which still live in Welsh and Irish were derived from a language allied to Egyptian and the Berber tongues."[35] French archaeologist Letorneau noted in 1893 in the *Bulletin de la Société d'Anthropologie* that "the builders of our megalithic monuments came from the South, and were related to the races of North Africa."[36] In modern archaeological circles, however, this is a most unpopular opinion, as its political correctness suggests that all cultures developed totally independent of each other, simply because it is now seen as an outdated colonial perspective that some cultures were incapable of accomplishing extraordinary feats such as building the Great Pyramid on their own. When it comes to the Megalithic civilization of Atlantis, this stance is turned on its head, and archaeologists argue that there was no such thing as one monolithic civilization at all!

Mestdagh's material was only ever made available to a Dutch audience; therefore follow-up research after his death in 1990 has been limited. Dutch researcher Wim Zitman has studied Mestdagh's conclusions and has noted that the dimensions of the Atlantean civilization contained a series of numbers that are mathematically related to the star Sirius. Sirius is the brightest star in the sky and is sacred in many cultures, but in none more so than in Ancient Egypt. Zitman argues that the ancients worked with the notion that time was equal to distance—a concept that is essentially correct, as we now know that time and space are identical—and that when one measures the distances between ancient monuments, one often finds numbers that correspond to certain astronomical measurements. The ancients, he argues, observed the sky and astronomical events, and incorporated them in their earthly constructions, to reflect one aspect of the famous maxim: "as above, so below." In this case, what was seen in the skies was also depicted on the ground in the sacred layout of these structures. Zitman, in his book *Egypt: Image of Heaven,* has demonstrated how this occurred in Ancient Egypt. For certain astronomical bodies and constellations to be mapped, not everything could be done from Egypt, and Callanish may be the best example of this.

Of course, it was 12,000 years ago that Atlantis sank, at least according to Plato. Yet all the information we've gleaned so far suggests that it ended sometime around 1200 BC. So although it is an undeniable fact that the Megalithic civilization of Sens bore the same dimensions and was situated in the same location as Plato's Atlantis, the timing doesn't add up. What are we to make of this?

For Mestdagh the answer is in the possibility that the number of years that was quoted to Solon did not refer to solar years, but lunar years. If this is true, that would yield an end date of c. 1200 BC, which would conform with the information provided to Solon by the Egyptian temple priests. We cannot be sure that this is the correct approach. If we take Plato's information as gospel, there are several possibilities: Someone was confused and in error about the dates of the Atlantean civilization; two separate legends were somehow made one, with another lost civilization somewhere to be found that is 12,000 years old; or the Megalithic civilization of Sens was not, in fact, the real Atlantis. The dimensions of Atlantis are identical to those of this Megalithic civilization at Sens. Unless the various analyses of the Megalithic civilizations are wrong, the megaliths of northwestern Europe do not date back to 12,000 years ago. This leaves one option, which for the moment needs to be the working hypothesis: that the Megalithic civilization, itself a truly lost civilization, was constructed as a copy—a perfect replica—of another civilization that was once lost itself and that was indeed far older—in other words, the original Atlantis.

Apart from the time frame, everything about the Megalithic civilization fits Atlantis. The dating of the Megalithic civilization itself is by proxy (that is, by the material found around the various standing stones). Could it be that there were two phases—one extremely old (12,000 years old), and that from c. 4000 BC onward, people came and repaired the structures, re-creating Atlantis? It is a hypothesis that is currently impossible to validate, but that quite often means that it is the truth, waiting to be proclaimed.

The Arms of Orion

The Great Pyramid. Stonehenge. Teotihuacan. Tiahuanaco. Four of the most important and best known ancient monuments on the surface of the Earth. What if those four monuments were able to locate the lost civilization of Atlantis?

That is the conclusion that Willem Zitman has reached, following years of research. Zitman knows that uttering the name Atlantis in connection with Ancient Egypt—or anything else—will not enchant him with Egyptologists, but wherever he has turned in his studies, the distant shadow of Atlantis has always loomed on the horizon—or has been the only logical conclusion to draw.

Each of these sites is the center of its own civilization: Teotihuacan was the site where the gods were said to convene in 3114 BC, the mythical creation date of the Maya. Tiahuanaco was the place of emergence of the Inca creator deity Viracocha. The Great Pyramid hardly needs an introduction, and Stonehenge is one of the most famous mega-lithic monuments, featuring prominently in the work done by Marcel Mestdagh.

Zitman believes that the four sites need to be connected by a series of lines, though one central feature needs to be added: a center point—the location of Atlantis. When this is drawn in the middle of the Atlantic Ocean, the resulting image is the constellation Orion.

To attain this center point, one needs to work with Stonehenge and Giza: On a Mercator Projection of the world, draw a longitudi-nal line through Stonehenge, and on the latitude of Giza, measure the distance from where both lines cross. Mark the same distance to Giza on the other side of the longitudinal axis. You end up in the Atlantic Ocean, at 30.30 North—the latitude of Giza—and 35.07.30 West. Interestingly, the resulting image is—of course—a triangle, but one that looks identical to a cross-section of the Great Pyramid, featuring the same internal angles. Coincidence? Most likely, design.

To this point in the Atlantic Ocean you need to connect two lines, one from Teotihuacan and one from Tiahuanaco, and the end re-sult is indeed the constellation of Orion. Is it a coincidence that Orion's Belt was incorporated in the layout of the Pyramid complex of both Teotihuacan and Giza? Both sites are often linked with somehow con-taining knowledge of a lost civilization; the Maya legends speak of an island in the East and how survivors reached the New World. Though it is clear that it is not a coincidence that two pyramid complexes both were designed in the image of Orion's Belt, that both sites—and three others—were carefully mapped so as to make the outline of the constel-lation of Orion and that this was likely linked with the lost civilization of Atlantis, suddenly has added far more weight to this speculation.

Zitman measured the design and noted that the distances con-necting the various sites, when added up, also revealed information about diameter of the Earth—which shouldn't come as a surprise. For anyone to have created this almost-worldwide design, that someone must have mapped the Earth and must have been aware of the dimensions of the Earth. That mapping must have occurred at least in c. 3000 BC—and more than likely thousands of years before, at the time of Atlantis.

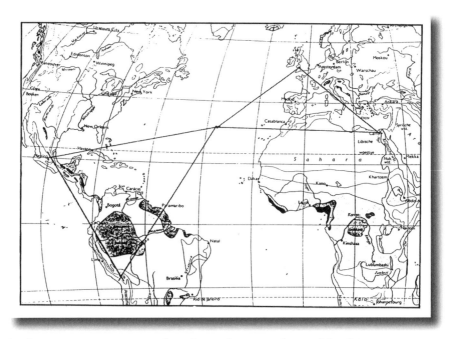

The four most important archaeological sites in the world—Giza, Stonehenge, Teotihuacan, and Tiahuanaco—when mapped on the world, reveal that they are laid out in the formation of the constellation of Orion. The position of Orion's Belt is in the Atlantic Ocean, making one wonder whether this is the site of Atlantis.

Image copyright Willem Zitman. Used with permission.

The Giza–Atlantis–Teotihuacan distance measures 12,748 kilometers, which is only 8 kilometers difference from the currently accepted diameter of the Earth on the equator. The total length of this design is 31,316 kilometers, or 10,000 Pi, or 60,000,000 royal els (the Egyptian royal el is 52.36 cm), or 12,000 Phi x Phi. Coincidence, or evidence of advanced mathematics—and hence an advanced, lost civilization?

Plato: Prehistorian

In the book *Plato, Prehistorian,* archaeologist Mary Settegast argues that Plato's Atlantis provides accurate insights into what archaeology is uncovering. First, she argues that the existing model of prehistory is in desperate need of change, but that few archaeologists are willing to let go of the unilinear approach. She points to the caves of Lascaux, dated to c. 20,000 BC, a culture that had harnessed the horse by 12,000 BC, while Barbary sheep were managed in North Africa as early as 18,000 BC. Several grains recovered at the Palestinian site of Nahal Oren suggest that grain was under cultivation as early as 14,000 BC. These discoveries show that settlements such as Göbekli Tepe and Jericho are actually quite recent, compared with these findings, and that the path of human civilization is far older than commonly accepted—the mythical date of 4000 BC.

Settegast argues that all the available archaeological evidence suggests that there was "civilization" pre-10,000 BC (thus conforming with Plato's Atlantis), that these people lived in areas of the world that are currently under sea level, and that they were furthermore competent seafarers. She argues that "catastrophic floods would not be inconsistent with the archaeology of Greece and Anatolia midway in the eighth millennium B.C.,"[37] to which she adds "the wave of inexplicably sophisticated settlers that appeared in the Near East in the last half of the eight millennium B.C. [e.g. Jericho] may actually have been refugees from Plato's ruined cultures in the west."[38]

She argues that what has done the Atlantis hypothesis a disservice is the endless speculation about where Atlantis would be. Instead, she feels, everyone should have focused on land that was still above sea level, for Plato argued that southwestern Europe, including Italy and Greece, was under the control of the Atlantean kings. Is there any evidence, she wondered, that in c. 9000 BC, this territory and its land were as Plato described them?

198

The short answer reached by Settegast is yes. She refers to the Magdalenian Culture—best known for its cave art—"which for several thousand years had graced Europe as far as Italy with an artistic tradition of uncommon excellence and unity, a devotion to the horse [...] and possibly a system of written communication."[39] Archaeologists have mapped this culture but have failed, Settegast argues, to see that it perfectly corresponds with the Atlantean Empire as described by Plato. Furthermore, Plato noted the Atlanteans' reliance on the horse, equally apparent in the Magdalenian Culture. Settegast adds that the archaeology has shown that in c. 9600 BC, the Magdalenian civilization indeed was showing signs of decay.

Archaeology is never going to be able to answer all questions. But Settegast suggests that if we put archaeology and the legend of Atlantis together, a homogenous picture emerges that makes sense of European history in c. 10,000 BC. This is a picture in which there was indeed a large civilization, somewhere in the west and likely somewhere in the Atlantic Ocean, which had parts of western Europe under its command. The cave paintings of Lascaux and several others are evidence of this advanced civilization. When it tried to stretch ever further east, probably for climatological reasons, the very heart of its civilization collapsed—swallowed by the rising sea levels that were the consequence of the end of the last Ice Age. This left Atlantean inhabitants homeless in western Europe, and it is my contention that these survivors were instrumental in creating the Megalithic civilization, re-creating Atlantis in France.

The rising sea level that destroyed Atlantis also influenced the Mediterranean civilizations. Rather than assume civilization began here in c. 4000 BC, it is now abundantly obvious that there were highly civilized centers in Turkey and what is now the Mediterranean coastline of the Middle East. Equally, in the Sahara, climatological conditions were far better for human settlements, as evidenced in the Tassili.

In short, within this new framework, civilization is at least twice, and potentially four times, as old as the standard history textbooks are telling us. Clearly, they are in need of an urgent rewrite.

Chapter 5

Prehistoric Genius

The World's First Computer

In 1900, a Greek sponge diver named Elias Stadiatos, working off the small Greek island of Antikythera, found the remains of a Greek ship at the bottom of the sea. The wreck was 50 meters long and was located 15–25 meters off Point Glyphadia, lying in 43 meters of water. At the time, diving had to be done without the aid of any modern technology currently available to the diving community. It meant the work was highly dangerous. In fact, when the authorities began to remove objects from the wreck, out of the 10 divers, one was accidentally killed and two other divers became permanently disabled. Conditions had vastly improved when Cousteau visited the wreck in 1953, but by that time, the Greek government had long removed everything from the sunken boat.

The rewards of the initial team's work were marble and bronze statues, gold jewelry, amphorae, and other artifacts, all dating from the first century BC, when the ship was believed to have sunk, on what is believed to have been a delivery from Rhodes to Rome.

In early 1902, Valerio Stais began sorting through the recovered material, all donated to the Museum of Athens. On May 17, 1902, Stais noticed a calcified lump of bronze that did not fit anywhere and that looked like a big watch. He guessed it was an astronomical clock and wrote a paper on the artifact. When it was published, he was ridiculed for even daring to suggest such a thing. His critics argued that sundials were used to tell the time. A dial mechanism was unknown at the time, even though it was described on what Science considered to be a purely theoretical basis. The status quo was that "many of the Greek scientific devices known to us from written descriptions show much mathematical ingenuity, but in all cases the purely mechanical part of the design seems relatively crude. Gearing was known to the Greeks, but it was used only in relatively simple applications."[1]

So they could do it, but they did not do it. So, had Stais rightfully identified what some called the "most complicated piece of scientific machinery known from antiquity,"[2] or was it too good to be true? The future would tell, but it was for the moment definitely too good to be believed.

In 1958, Yale science historian Derek J. de Solla Price stumbled upon the object and decided to make it the subject of a scientific study, which was published the following year in *Scientific American.* Part of the problem, he felt, was its uniqueness. De Solla stated: "Nothing like this instrument is preserved elsewhere. Nothing comparable to it is known from any ancient scientific text or literary allusion. On the contrary, from all that we know of science and technology in the Hellenistic Age we should have felt that such a device could not exist."[3] He likened the discovery to finding a jet plan in Tutankhamen's tomb and at first believed the machine was made in 1575; a date of the first century BC remained hard to accept, let alone defend.

Still, Price must have realized that whereas its age was a dangerous subject to discuss, it was safe to explore the mechanism and function of the instrument. He thus concluded that the object was a box with dials on the outside and a series of gear wheels inside.

At least 20 gear wheels were preserved, including a sophisticated assembly of gears that were mounted eccentrically on a turntable. The device also contained a differential gear, permitting two shafts to rotate at different speeds. Doors were hinged to the box to protect the dials inside. As to its purpose, the mechanism appeared to have been a device for calculating the motions of stars and planets—a working model of the solar system.

This was not just speculation on his part. Price noted that the front dial was just clean enough to read its function:

> It has two scales, one of which is fixed and displays the names of the signs of the zodiac; the other is on a movable slip ring and shows the months of the year. Both scales are carefully marked off in degrees. [...] This dial showed the annual motion of the sun in the zodiac. By means of key letters inscribed on the zodiac scale, corresponding to other letters on the parapegma calendar plate, it also showed the main risings and settings of bright stars and constellations throughout the year.[4]

Price knew he had merely postponed the inevitable and would have to tackle its age. Evidence of its ancient origin could be found in the device itself: the Greek inscriptions. Price was helped in this work by George Stamires, a Greek epigrapher. To quote Price: "Some of the plates were marked with barely recognizable inscriptions, written in Greek characters of the first century BC, and just enough could be made of the sense to tell that the subject matter was undoubtedly astronomical."[5] There was no way back, and scientists could only pretend the device and Price's analysis did not exist—or accept the undeniable truth: It was ancient. It was Greek. Embedded belief systems of what the ancients were, could do, and did would have to be adjusted.

There was also circumstantial evidence, which created a historical framework into which the device fit nicely: Similar mechanisms were described by Cicero and Ovid. Cicero, writing in the first century BC—the right time frame—mentioned an instrument "recently constructed by our friend Poseidonius, which at each revolution reproduces the same motions of the sun, the moon and the five planets."[6] He also wrote of a similar mechanism that was said to have been built by Archimedes and that was purportedly stolen in 212 BC by the Roman general Marcellus when Archimedes was killed in the sacking of the Sicilian city of Syracuse. The device was kept as an heirloom in Marcellus's family.

Despite these literary references, scientists were doubtful, and Price summed up their thinking:

> Even the most complex mechanical devices described by the ancient writers Hero of Alexandria and Vitruvius contained only simple gearing. For example, the taximeter used by the Greeks to measure the distance travelled by the wheels of a carriage employed only pairs of gears (or gears and worms) to achieve the necessary ratio of movement. It could be argued that if the Greeks knew the principle of gearing, they should have had no difficulty in constructing mechanisms as complex as epicyclic gears.[7]

Still, someone had obviously applied the theory and had come up with a practical tool. But who had created the machine? The likely suspect may have been Greek astronomer, mathematician, and philosopher Geminus, a student or late follower of Poseidonius. The latter, of course, was the one whom Cicerco credited with inventing exactly what the device was.

Geminus was a Stoic, from a school founded by Zeno, and lived from 135 to 51 BC, teaching on Rhodes. Rhodes was the center of astronomical research. Geminus not only is known to have defended the Stoic view of the universe, but in particular to defend mathematics from attacks by Skeptic and Epicurean philosophers. The Antikythera device would have been right up his alley, as it combined astronomy and proved the powers and the excellence to which applied mathematics could excel: Science and mathematics could mimic the motions of the universe.

Most importantly, he lived in the right time frame. Furthermore, the date for which this calculator was set was the year 86 BC, which some researchers have argued can be seen by the positions of the dials and pointers. As five conjunctions of planets in four zodiacal signs occurred that year, an ideal time to set an astronomical calendar, 86 BC was an important astronomical year. This date has also influenced the dating of the ship wreck, as many believe it will not have been much later; otherwise the clock would have been reset to an astronomical event at a later date. Many thus argue for a date of 83–81 BC, though others posit dates such as 71 BC, adding that there is no guarantee the device was not idle for a number of years before being transported to Rome.

All of this understanding is intriguing, but for one researcher, Maurice Chatelain, one important ingredient was missing: logic. Chatelain argued that "if someone wants to construct an astronomical calculator by using intermeshing gears, the first condition is to find the number of cycles necessary to obtain an exact number of whole days. Some of these cycles are easily found but many are nearly impossible."[8]

Each gear is a cycle; this is how any mechanical clock works: Seconds turn to minutes, to hours, and in some clocks to days, if not larger cycles. To make such clocks work, not only do the cycles need to be known, but also the ratios between the cycles: how seconds relate to minutes (60:1), minutes to hours (60:1), hours to days (24:1), and so forth. It is difficult enough to construct such a device for the solar year, but the Antikythera device also incorporated the cycles of the moon and five of the nearest planets. No wonder scientists were skeptical that the device was…a device.

To make the system work, the system would have to be based on days, and thus the cycles would be expressed in full, whole days, with the ratios between the various cycles based upon the day counts of the cycles, too. The genius that created the artifact would thus have to be aware of the cycles of the heavenly bodies. This in itself was within the remit of the Greek scientific community—and many generations and civilizations older than that. A key question was what system was used, as each country had its own. The Greeks used the so-called Metonic cycle of 19 tropical years, but this, Chatelain felt, had no real value in creating a gear calculator.

According to Chatelain, only the Egyptian calendar system is suited for being used as a calculator—and he also found it was the one at the basis of the Antikythera machine:

> The seemingly complicated Egyptian calendar, based on Sirius, the Sun, and also the Moon, actually works like a charm. Every four years represents exactly 1,461 days which in turn represent 49.474 synodical moon months. This last number has to be multiplied only 19 times to give a number of whole days—27,759—equal to 940 months, or 76 Sothic years, which is the cycle of the Rhodes calculator!"[9]

Still, some do not share Chatelain's enthusiasm for an Egyptian origin. One inscription on the device itself significantly reads "76 years, 19 years." This refers to the Calippic cycle of 76 years, which is four times the Metonic cycle of 19 years, or 235 synodic (lunar) months. The next line includes the number "223," which refers to the eclipse cycle of 223 lunar months. Price reasoned that

> using the [Metonic] cycles, one could easily design gearing that would operate from one dial having a wheel that revolved annually, and turn by this gearing a series of other wheels which would move pointers indicating the sidereal, synodic and draconitic months. Similar

cycles were known for the planetary phenomena; in fact, this type of arithmetical theory is the central theme of Seleucid Babylonian astronomy, which was transmitted to the Hellenistic world in the last few centuries BC.[10]

Though all of this knowledge was not Greek in origin, the question remained whether it was Babylonian or Egyptian.

Price had injected a new life fluid into the device, and major breakthroughs occurred in the last decade of the 20th century. With the arrival of powerful computers, those machines were used to reminisce about what many considered to be the oldest computer—and the latest generation was used to shed light on what some considered to be the "Adam" of the line.

First, a partial reconstruction was built by Australian computer scientist Allan George Bromley (1947–2002) of the University of Sydney, working together with the Sydney clockmaker Frank Percival. This project led Bromley to review Price's X-ray analysis made in 1973 and to make new, more accurate X-ray images that were studied by Bromley's student, Bernard Gardner, in 1993.

Later, John Gleave constructed a working replica of the mechanism. According to his reconstruction, the front dial shows the annual progress of the Sun and Moon through the zodiac—against the Egyptian calendar. But, as if to remain neutral in the Egyptian or Greek debate, he stated that the upper rear dial displays a four-year period and has associated dials showing the Metonic cycle of 235 synodic months (19 solar years). The lower rear dial plots the cycle of a single synodic month, with a secondary dial showing the lunar year of 12 synodic months.

Another reconstruction was made in 2002 by Michael Wright, mechanical engineering curator for the Science Museum in London, working with the previously mentioned Allan Bromley. On November 30, 2006, the journal *Nature* published an article on Wright's and his team's analysis of the Antikythera device. It confirmed that the instrument had been used to predict solar and lunar eclipses. The article credited Derek de Solla Price, but equally stated that "although Solla Price's work did much to push forward the state of knowledge about the device's functions, his interpretation of the mechanics is now largely dismissed."[11]

The new analysis confirmed that the major structure had a single, centrally placed dial on the front plate that showed the Greek zodiac and an Egyptian calendar on concentric scales. On the back, two further dials displayed information about the timing of lunar cycles and eclipse patterns. Previously, the idea that the mechanism could predict eclipses had only been a hypothesis. The study also revealed some of the complexity of the engineering that had gone into this device. The Moon sometimes moves slightly faster in the sky than at others because of the satellite's elliptic orbit. To overcome this, the designer of the calculator used a "pin-and-slot" mechanism to connect two gear-wheels that introduced the necessary variations.

The team was also able to decipher more of the text on the mechanism, doubling the amount of text that can now be read. Some of the inscriptions mention the words *Venus* and *stationary,* suggesting that the tool could look at retrogressions of planets.

Wright also believes the device was not a one-off: "The designer and maker of the device knew what they wanted to achieve and they did it expertly; they made no mistakes. To do this, it can't have been very far from their every day stock work."[12] So it was probably mass produced at the time and must have been the product of previous, less fancy clocks. That those earlier models have been lost in the mists of time is understandable, but the big question by which everyone is baffled is why such clocks did not continue to be built in the centuries that followed—indeed, why it took more than a millennium before a clock of the same technological expertise appeared again.

Despite acceptance that this is a first-century BC planetarium, some questions remain. Price pointed out that he himself did not know whether it was operated manually, by turning, or automatically. He said:

> I feel it is more likely that it was permanently mounted, perhaps set in a statue, and displayed as an exhibition piece. In that case it might well have been turned by the power from a water clock or some other device. Perhaps it is just such a wondrous device that was mounted inside the famous Tower of Winds in Athens. It is certainly very similar to the great astronomical cathedral clocks that were built all over Europe during the Renaissance.[13]

—1,500 years later. Wright's team argues that it was manually operated, but this would somewhat work against a mass produced item, for it would require the most work from those people buying it; care for the device would be labor-intensive. So perhaps Price's hypothesis that it was to be used within a religious setting is more appealing—though every hypothesis is currently guesswork.

The discovery of the Antikythera device led to one gigantic realization: that our everyday clock started as an astronomical show-piece that happened also to indicate the time—and not vice versa, as most believed half a century ago. Gradually, the time-keeping functions of the clocks became more important, and the device that showed the cycles of heaven became subsidiary—only to be forgotten, and then reinvented all over again—all wheels inclusive.

Today, the device is worshipped by many as it is seen as the first calculator-computer. Price labeled the Antikythera device "in a way, the venerable progenitor of all our present plethora of scientific hardware."[14] It should not come as a surprise, then, that whereas the original mechanism is displayed in the Bronze collection of the National Archaeological Museum in Athens, accompanied by a replica, another replica is on display at the American Computer Museum in Bozeman, Montana. In substance, it is bronze; intellectually, it is a computer.

Of course, what the Antikythera device equally shows is that a highly technical device was accidentally found a century ago and that it took decades before the scientific community even deigned to consider it evidence of a scientific knowledge of our ancestors (in this case, the Greeks). Knowing that Science is actually quite quick and willing to grant such things to the Greeks, it becomes clear how reluctant Science is to bestow technological innovations on our ancestors. In fact, Robert Temple found an entire series of them completely lost within the walls of various museums.

CRYSTAL LENSES

Arthur C. Clarke provided the following endorsement for Robert Temple's *The Crystal Sun*: "should be read by all who have an interest in the history of science, and may well cause a revolution in this subject."[15] More than a decade since its publication in 2000, there are still no signs of a revolution (for all the reasons cited already), but the book is a remarkable collation of various artifacts—mostly lenses— that Temple identified in the museums of the world. His conclusion was that all of these museums had been sitting on artifacts that were evidence of a lost technology, dating back at least to the third millennium BC, involving making glass lenses that were often used for astronomical observations. Temple notes that, unknown to our modern archaeologists and historians, a science of optics and a sophisticated technology for the manufacture of lenses was widespread and fundamental in ancient times. Temple argues that it explains how the Egyptians surveyed their pyramids and hence were able to build them with such extraordinary precision; like modern surveyors, they used the equivalent of theodolites with lenses. But the use of lenses was not just in the building trade: Greek philosopher Democritus had a basic telescope through which he viewed the surface of the moon and described it having mountains.

Temple's interest began in 1967, when he met Derek de Solla Price, who told him about a crystal lens, of Babylonian or Assyrian origins, that was on display in the British Museum: the Layard Lens. The lens was excavated by Austen Henry Layard in 1849 in a chamber of the North-West Palace of the ancient Assyrian capital of Kalhu, in those days thought to be Nineveh (which is why another name for this lens is sometimes the Nineveh Lens). Layard straightforwardly identified it as a lens, adding: "it is, consequently, the most ancient known specimen of transparent glass."[16] Since its discovery, older lenses have been identified. The object was linked with Sargon II, King of Assyria, from 722 to 705 BC.

Once discovered and identified as a lens, criticism began to mount, including from classicist Thomas Henri Martin, who argued that "Sir David Brewster thinks that this little piece of quartz had been shaped to be a true optical lens, and not a simple ornament. This hypothesis of the English scholar seems to us improbable. The crystal was undoubtedly an ornament."[17] Martin, of course, used those fine scientific words of *improbable* and *undoubtedly* expertly. Fortunately, the likes of W.B. Barker, president of the College of Optometrists in London, came to the object's defense and argued for it being a lens, even outlining its potential usage in ancient astronomy.

Temple soon realized that various museums, as well as other sections of the British Museum itself, had dozens of lenses in their possession and even on display. They came from Ancient Greece and Babylonia, but also Egypt, where four such lenses were found at Karanis (currently on display in the Egyptian Museum in Cairo), though ascribed to Roman times.

Temple also found references to lenses in several ancient texts. The skeptics argue that Euclid did not mention lenses in his book *The Optics*. First, the work is incomplete, but what are we to make of this statement: "But things thought to be greater than themselves seem to be increased, and the things nearer the eye appear greater. So objects increased in size will seem to approach the eye."?[18] Is this not a reference to the magnifying effect of a lens? Quite straightforwardly, those cultures whose lenses are inside the museums had authors who spoke about lenses, as one would expect to find.

Greek geographer and historian Strabo wrote *The Geography,* in which he relates on his visit to the Spanish Cape St. Vincent, the most western point of Europe. He discusses optical effects of the setting and rising Sun (refraction), but notes that there are two methods used to study the Sun: one with the naked eye, the other observed through tubes. Temple uncovered that "tubes" was actually a substitution—the translators did not know or did not agree with the original text, or felt that the Greek writer had been mistaken in his word usage. Why? Because if a literal translation was made, the observation was not done through a tube, but through glass spheres! Why was the translated changed? Because the translator, G. Kramer, the German editor of the Strabo edition of 1844–52, had *pronounced* it to be corrupt. To repeat: A scientist singlehanded decided the original Greek text could not be true, as it showed the ancient Greeks possessed glass spheres to make astronomical observations, and hence pronounced it to be an error, and therefore substituted it with another word, which was in his opinion the right word! Evidence of lenses used for astronomical observations was written out of the source material by scientists! Why? Because "these spheres most assuredly could not have been employed as astronomical measuring instruments."[19] Why not? Because the scientists say so.

Thirteenth-century English philosopher Roger Bacon related that a lighthouse on the coast of Normandy had been used by Julius Caesar to study the English coastline prior to his invasion of the British

Isles. How was he able to do this? Through the use of a telescope or a large telescopic mirror. The telescope is truly only two lenses, held in a fixed position by a tube.

In short, Temple found numerous evidence, including archaeological evidence, such as Carthaginian towers, that showed that scientists both did not want to and often were incapable of recognizing ancient evidence that lenses were used far more frequently in ancient times, and that this went back thousands of years.

The use of lenses was not limited to the Mediterranean culture. Temple believes that the Megalithic culture made use of them and argues that Diodorus's description of Hyperborea implies the presence of a large telescope there, too. The account states that the mountains on the Moon could be seen and that "it appears to be but a little distance from the earth," which Temple notes "can only be satisfactorily explained on the basis of this being a description of a telescopic examination of the Moon"[20] and argues there was at least one telescope in Megalithic Britain. He also noted that Alexander Thom, in his survey of more than 500 megalithic sites, always underlined their accuracy, which Thom implied—and Temple extrapolates—could only have been achieved with the use of some technology—in other words, a telescope and similar devices.

Of course, the existence of ancient lenses also means that there was a capability of creating these lenses, and that largely remains a taboo subject within the scientific community. How were they made? Where? By whom? All of these questions are still waiting for someone to adopt them and nurture them toward an answer.

THE BIMINI CRYSTAL

Could there be a crystal pyramid in the waters off Bimini that is one of the sunken remnants of the lost civilization of Atlantis? The question could be purely theoretical, but the question is far more practical and pertinent: There is an eyewitness report from a source whose claim has never been disproven—and an artifact!

The story begins in 1970, when Dr. Ray Brown, a naturopathic practitioner from Mesa, Arizona, was scuba-diving near the Bahamas, 20 miles off a location that is known as the Tongue of the Ocean, according to an interview Charles Berlitz did with Brown for his 1984 book, *Atlantis: The Eighth Continent.* Brown and his group were looking for treasure, left on Spanish galleons sunken several centuries ago and known to be scattered on the ocean floor. A storm had hit just the area and had stirred up the ocean floor, which meant that new booty might be discovered, as sand had been moved about and might have exposed portions of these galleons. Apparently, the storm had also swept some of the team's equipment and possessions overboard—including, apparently, a camera—which is why we only have a story and no accompanying photographs.

Brown recounted that during the dive, he became separated from his fellow four divers. While trying to catch up with them, he noticed a pyramid shape appearing below him. In a televised interview in 1980, for the series *In Search Of,* Brown stated that "we found ruins and buildings everywhere," adding that "The buildings had an Egyptian or classic look to them."[21]

He calculated that the pyramid was 22 fathoms down (44 yards) and rose to 120 feet, while parts of it were obscured by the seafloor. He stated that the joints between the blocks of the buildings were almost indiscernible, thus attesting of the structure's good preservation and construction excellence. He described the capstone as resembling lapis lazuli, an intense and beautiful blue.

More importantly, Brown discovered an entrance into the pyramid, which he followed, to arrive in a small rectangular room with a pyramid-shaped ceiling. Though Brown was without a flashlight, there was somehow sufficient light inside for him to see. He described the room as having no algae or other material attached to the walls and bright. But it wasn't the walls that caught his attention. A metallic rod, 3 inches in diameter, hung down from the apex of the ceiling, the end of which held a multi-faceted gem. Below, on the floor of the room, stood a carved stone topped by a stone plate, which held two metal bronze hands. Inside the two hands was a crystal sphere, which Brown decided to take with him. Previously, he had tried to dislodge the metallic rod from the ceiling, but was unable to. Brown relates that as he left the structure, he heard a voice, warning him never to return.

A variation of the discovery emerges in *Prepare for the Landings,* in which authors Michaeel and Aurora Ellegion relate that they befriended Brown in the 1980s and that he disclosed that the discovery was made in 1968, not 1970; that he was on one of the boats with the famous French diver Jacques Cousteau; and that the site was not off the Bahamas, but 100 miles west, toward South Bimini. Despite different circumstances and location, all other details of the pyramid and what transpired inside are identical to accounts that Brown repeatedly told in public. When researcher Greg Little inquired with the Cousteau Society, he learned that Brown was definitely not part of any Cousteau expedition. As mentioned, though, in television and other interviews, Brown was consistent that he made the discovery in 1970, not 1968, and the fact that some retold his story differently, years after his death, is not Brown's fault.

Extraordinary treasures not only require extraordinary evidence, they also come with extraordinary emotions in the person who has discovered them. In the case of Brown, he said that there was fear—fear that the government, whether local or United States, would confiscate his crystal if he made it public. By 1975, it seems that the importance of the find and making it known to the world outweighed this fear. Still, in hindsight, he would only show the crystal sphere about a half dozen or so times, but each event was…eventful, with the visitors describing a series of strange activities associated with it. Then, less than a decade after going public, Brown disappeared off stage, taking his sphere with him. The story remained and became an often-repeated story of evidence of a lost civilization, but nothing more.

Part of the problem—and Brown's problem—was that even though there was an artifact, there was only Brown's word for it. There are no photographs of the pyramid, as Brown was diving without a camera. No one afterward was able to locate the site or find the structures Brown claimed he had discovered. The sphere is remarkable, but it is only a crystal sphere, with no irrefutable powers that would make everyone convinced we are in the presence of one of the most important ancient artifacts on the planet. In the interview with Berlitz, Brown related that "I'm not the only person who has seen the ruins—others have seen them from the air and say they are five miles wide and more than that in length."[22] But the problem was that if that were true, none of those witnesses were on record or had spoken out about it. Brown was one man with an artifact and a story telling a most interesting, but uncorroborated tale. It meant that in the final analysis, it all bore down to one question: Was he believable?

Then, Dr. Brown disappeared off the scene. He died in the early 1990s, and the story of the crystal was mentioned by some, but largely was just "one of those stories," with no proof, as the fate of the crystal sphere was unknown. Then, between 2005 and 2010, the crystal—today dubbed by some "The Atlantis Orb"—resurfaced, in the hands of Arthur Fanning, a resident of Sedona (Arizona), who refers to the object as the "Eye of God."

I met Arthur Fanning in Amsterdam, in early November 2009, when he was invited as a lecturer at the Frontier Symposium 2009.

I was able to meet the sphere in a private setting, as well as hang out with the new owner himself. Arthur was down to earth and relaxed, though did take the sphere with him everywhere, keeping it in a specially designed pouch on his belt. He lets people see and be around the sphere, even inviting members of an almost-500-big audience on to the stage to come and see the sphere for themselves.

When I contacted him to verify some details as to how he got the sphere in his possession, Fanning said that he had known Brown personally. After Fanning had held a channeling, "he invited me to a friend's house for a private showing of the sphere. Before Ray passed on, [D.J.] received the sphere. He had it for about a week but the energy was too intense and he gave it to me. He said he was guided to do so."[23] Fanning also inherited a picture that Ray had commissioned, which depicted how the sphere inside the pyramid was in the two hands that held it and the golden-colored rod that came down from the ceiling that had the red-faceted point hovering over the sphere.

There is no doubt that Fanning's sphere was Brown's, but it is also clear that it took Fanning some time after receiving the object before deciding he would show it. Like Brown, getting massive public attention to the object is not his desire, though once he has an audience, he allows everyone to see it—as per Brown's modus operandi. At each display, Fanning offers everyone the opportunity to verify the interesting characteristics associated with Brown's crystal: when turned into a specific position, in the center of the crystal, three pyramid-shaped objects become visible. From another vantage point, a single human eye was said to manifest itself.

During both Brown's and Fanning's exhibitions of the object, there were widespread interpretation and speculation of what all of this meant. An association with Atlantis was easily drawn, as it was, after all, discovered in a sunken pyramid. Experiments with compass needles also revealed that when the needle was placed next to the orb, it would spin counter-clockwise, but when moved as little as 2 inches away from the sphere, it would spin clockwise. On the *In Search Of* show, Brown showed how the sphere also magnetically repelled objects—showing that the sphere is definitely not an object he quickly bought in a shopping mall.

Could Brown's crystal be a remnant of Atlantis? Was the pyramid in which he discovered the object a remnant of Atlantis, too? The fact that Brown's story involved a sunken pyramid off the coast of Bimini obviously brings his story into the realm of American psychic Edgar Cayce, who proclaimed that, after 1968, evidence of Atlantis would be found off the coast of Bimini. Was Brown's story the fulfillment of this prophecy—however poor Cayce's track record for predicting the future was?

And what to think of Brown? He obviously did not do it for the money. Hoaxers often go for fame and if so, Brown definitely achieved his goal. There are no photographs. There are no corroborating witness reports. So the central question is always whether Brown can be believed.

Greg Little relates that after an appearance on the Coast-to-Coast radio show in which he tackled Brown's sphere, he received "an email from an elderly man who said he had been a friend of Brown since childhood. After exchanging a few emails he related that Brown confided to him that the entire affair was a hoax Brown concocted to take advantage of all of the media controversy that had been stirred up by the 1968 discovery of the Bimini Road."[24] Little adds that there is no evidence to support the claim that his contact knew Brown or speaks the truth. However, if Brown did want to be part of the Bimini Road as evidence for Atlantis controversy, he waited a long time—seven years—before he began to show the crystal. If he had immediately launched his story in 1970, it would seem logical. But with Brown's saga beginning in 1975, if it was a hoax, it was largely a stand-alone campaign.

Furthermore, Brown did not make many references to Cayce, the Bimini Road, or other buzz words that could make his story far more sensational and known than what he did.

Some of those who have looked into the story, such as Greg Little, have concluded it is a likely hoax and point out that the weakest element of the story is that none of the other four divers ever stepped forward. But there is a perfectly normal explanation for this, which Little seems not to have caught: When Brown told the basic story, of how he heard a voice say "You have got what you came for. Now leave and don't come back," he expanded that the other divers had heard the same voice and warning, even though they were not inside the pyramid. Apparently aware that Brown had found something, but they hadn't, they decided to return, but drowned during that dive. The possibility that the other divers died, of course, explains why no one of them ever stepped forward. It could also be the reason why Brown waited for five years before going public with the story and it could even be the reason why—if we are to accept the Ellegions' version as accurate on some counts—why on occasion Brown decided to change the location of where precisely it had happened. Indeed, one might argue that knowing that he was warned not to come back and that those who did, died, it would be prudent not to give an accurate location, knowing that future divers, even if only trying to verify Brown's account, could meet a similar fate. Of course—to ring the skeptical bell—the notion that four people had died and Brown remained the only eyewitness is also the perfect circumstance created if it were all a hoax. For a hoax, there needs to be motivation, and the one key denominator about the entire Brown and the Crystal Sphere saga is that no one has seen Brown as a trickster or a hoaxer, and that the entire methodology of how he went about it was that of a man who had a genuine artifact, and not someone who knew he had created a perfect hoax and was going to exploit it to the fullest.

With Brown, all we have today are a sphere and a mute object—except to those who can psychically connect to it—which has some anomalous capabilities, but which might need to be tested further in the near future. If so, then Brown's crystal sphere might finally make it into the ranks of truly amazing anomalous artifacts that challenge our current paradigm of what humanity's past looked like. Staring into it, when we see three pyramids, do we also see this future for this object?

TALKING TO GOD

The Ark of the Covenant. Indiana Jones went in search of it, and its fate and whereabouts continue to enthrall millions. It seems that its fame has overtaken some very basic observations about this... device.

In Exodus, God was said to have instructed Moses on Mount Sinai on how to construct the Ark. The account itself retained these detailed instructions, including its dimensions, material (gold-plated), and finishing. In fact, a great amount of specifics were retained in a book that is now largely seen as religious in nature, rather than engineering: Four rings of gold were to be attached (two on each side) to the central part of the Ark, and through these rings, staves of shittim-wood overlaid with gold were to be inserted, so that the Ark could be carried. It was stated these were not to be removed.

The Bible makes it clear that the Ark enables God to communicate with Moses, and so what we have is an account of divine technology: man building a device through which God can be contacted, the design apparently originating with God. The Bible itself contains evidence that this was indeed technology. For example, those carrying it had to wear specific clothing, and there are a number of incidents in which people were accidentally killed by the Ark. Equally, though the Ark was carried by the Israelites during their 40 years of wandering in the desert, when the Israelites camped, the Ark was placed in its own tent, outside of the main camp. This was not because God demanded privacy, but because the Ark was understood to be a dangerous device, to be kept away from people as much as possible.

The Ark also accomplished some miracles, which biblical scholars would ascribe to the Will of God, but which seem to have a more technological explanation. When Joshua crosses the River Jordan, the Ark was carried at the front of the community. During the crossing, the river dried up as soon as the feet of the priests carrying the Ark touched the water and remained so until the same priests left the river after all the people had passed. Some might argue this was clear evidence of God's direct intervention in this "miracle," but this was an effect of the Ark, not God, and the Israelites knew it. The Ark was carried into the River, the waters disappeared, and the priests, rather than advancing to the other shore, remained on the riverbed, as they knew that as soon as they would walk off, the waters would return. The effect was caused by the Ark, and its nature was technological.

Various designs as to how the Ark operated have of course been proposed, and it is unlikely we will ever know or be able to verify how the Ark truly functioned, but on a quite fundamental reading, it appears to be that the Ark was a device. Though many have written about the Ark being a type of "Manna Machine," in which it somehow dispensed food to the Israelites, my opinion is that this was a piece of technology that indeed allowed communication with the divine. We actually know that this is not the only device of this kind, though it is definitely the most famous one.

The Ancient Egyptians stated that they were able to "animate" statues of their gods, so that the gods could speak to them. Various ancient cultures did the same. In a number of instances, what has been discovered was that this were prehistoric special effects, in which the statue had a series of tubes installed, normally leading to a small room, where a priest was hidden who could then utter the divine words, as if they were emanating from the statue, the sound traveling from his hideout, via the tubes, to the statue.

Such examples do exist, but can they explain everything? For example, it was also said that this technology of animating a statue resulted in this statue being able to walk. Recently, in a Scandinavian museum, it was reported by the cleaning staff that they had observed some of the Egyptian statues moving in their display cases—all by themselves. One might think this is a tall tale, but it just happens to be precisely what the Ancient Egyptians said these statues could do.

The topic is also applicable to crystal skulls. Though many of these skulls are of modern origins, a handful, such as MAX and the Mitchell-Hedges Crystal Skull, are not.[25] "Psychics" who have worked with these skulls have come away with information that they claim these skulls have communicated to them.

My wife, Kathleen McGowan, communicated with MAX in March 2009, asking questions about a number of people she was about to meet, one of whom was me. At this meeting, we both fell in love and months later, Kathleen consulted her notes, in which MAX had told her "you will show Philip love," which at the time she thought meant me introducing to a friend of hers, which she fully expected to be the start of a relationship. MAX had a more direct relationship between Kathleen and me in mind, and he knew and told her, though she took no notice of it at the time.

In March 2011, we spent a weekend with MAX in Albuquerque, New Mexico. On Saturday of that weekend, several people came for 30-minute, private sessions with MAX, and many hung around after the sessions for a few minutes to speak with JoAnn Parks, the owner of MAX. None of these people knew each other, but those who said MAX had communicated with them on that day all came out of their private session with a highly consistent story, which was quite clear evidence that they were indeed picking up communications from this skull—MAX. This information was not generic (such as "respect your parents"), but very specific and also highly detailed about events that were happening, presenting them in a manner that these people could not have gleaned elsewhere. MAX's take on some current events was very unique.

Egyptian statues or crystal skulls are all made from materials that our modern society is using for information storage. We use quartz in our watches, and we use sand in our computers. Today's computer age is largely based on sand and rocks, and we know that these are capable of retaining information. That our ancestors figured out the same and that they may have used sand and rocks in similar fashion—though more artistically by making them physically attractive in the shape of a statue or a crystal skull—is a possibility that we should not all too easily disregard. Alas, no research at all has occurred or is occurring in this field, which means that answers as to how—and indeed whether or not—they did might still be a long time in the future.

Chapter 6

EARTH, SEVERAL TENS OF THOUSANDS
YEARS BC

THE LOST CONTINENT OF MU

James Churchward was a patented inventor, an engineer, and a man who claimed that he had found evidence of a lost civilization: Mu. Mu was said to have been the Pacific equivalent of Atlantis, though Churchward said Atlantis's origin was actually as a colony of Mu, a civilization that was much older than Atlantis.

The first man to write about Mu was Augustus LePlongeon, who in archaeological circles has the distinction of being the first to make a photographic record of the ruins of Chichen Itza. In his books *Sacred Mysteries Among the Mayans and Quiches* (1886) and *Queen Moo and the Egyptian Sphinx* (1896), LePlongeon related his decipherment of the so-called Troano Codex, which he claimed showed that the Maya were the ancestors of the Ancient Egyptians. He claimed that the document also revealed that the Mayans had originated from a lost civilization, Mu, which was on par with Atlantis, and which had been destroyed by a volcanic eruption. He added that Queen Moo—clearly linked with Mu—had traveled from this continent to Egypt, where she had gone down into the history books under her new name of Isis. Unfortunately, when the Mayan language was deciphered several decades later, it was learned that LePlongeon's interpretation of this document was completely erroneous, sometimes even using letters that were in fact no such thing. Jack Churchward, a descendent of James Churchward, states that LePlongeon relied on the translation of Brasseur de Bourbourg. Jack Churchward received an e-mail from one of de Bourbourg's descendants, who stated that the translation was done by channeling a spirit, which explains why LePlongeon erred so much when he interpreted the document based on this translation.

LePlongeon did put the lost civilization of Mu on the books, but left it to theosophist Helena Blavatsky to popularize the lost continent, claiming it was the mystical birthplace of occult traditions. But the man who brought Mu from theory and speculation to reality was James Churchward, who claimed to have found hard physical evidence for the continent's existence, when he was shown a secret library in India.

Born in Britain, Churchward eventually settled in the United States. It was years before, though, while living in Sri Lanka, where he owned a tea plantation with his wife, that he traveled to India. During this journey, he later claimed, he found a lost epoch of humanity's history. In India, he befriended a priest who taught Churchward to read an ancient dead language. Allegedly, the priest and two others were the only people in the world able to read it. The language was written down on numerous tablets, which the priest allowed Churchward to see and read. Churchward intimates in his books that he tricked the priest into showing him the tablets, as well as teaching him the meaning of the dead language. As he did so, Churchward claimed, he realized that the tablets he saw were not the complete library. Nevertheless, he was able to create a homogenous picture of the lost civilization of Mu by consulting other sources and people.

These events happened in the late 19th century, even though Churchward only went public with his Mu material in 1924—a very long time to remain silent about such a tremendous existence. Too good to be true? No, as it is known that Churchward had been interested in ancient civilizations long before the publication of his book. In the 1890s, he discussed the subject of Mu with LePlongeon and his wife, Alice. Jack Churchward states that an unseen publication from his ancestor is *Copies of Stone Tablets Found By William Niven at Santiago Ahuizoctla Near Mexico City.* It is known that in 1927, Churchward and LePlongeon exchanged letters.

Churchward's discovery became famous when a major article on it appeared on November 10, 1924, in the *New York American* newspaper. In it, the central framework of Churchward's claims about Mu was put forward. The civilization was labeled "Empire of the Sun." It was once a civilization that had 64 million inhabitants, known as the Naacals, the priestly brotherhood, keepers of the sacred wisdom, who lived 50,000 years ago. All known ancient civilizations—India, Egypt, and the Mayas—were decayed remnants of its many colonies.

In 1926, at the age of 75, Churchward published *The Lost Continent of Mu: Motherland of Man.* Where was Mu? It extended from north of Hawaii to the Fijis and Easter Island. Geologists find it hard to imagine dry land here, as the area is crossed by the so-called Andesite Line, making it geologically unlikely there was a landmass here.

As Churchward never produced any evidence for his visit to the Naacal Library, several people treat his claims with skepticism. So was Churchward a liar, or someone with genuine experiences? To understand the man better, it is noted that some aspects of the Mu legend are original to Churchward, and some aren't. It was LePlongeon who had first written about the Naacal, in 1896, where he identifies them as Maya adepts and missionaries, with the word *Naacal* meaning "the exalted." But LePlongeon identified their homeland as Central America, not Mu in the Pacific Ocean, which was specific to Churchward.

227

What about Churchward's relationship with Blavatsky? They both claimed that in India, they had been exposed to lost knowledge. In the case of Blavatsky, her source of lost knowledge was the Book of Dzyan, supposedly written in Atlantis and presented to her by the Indian Mahatmas.

Indeed, though it could be argued that Churchward merely copied from the likes of Blavatsky and LePlongeon in his exploit of Mu, at the same time, it could be said that his story is totally true, that it confirms Blavatsky's assertions, and that Churchward spent several decades cementing his case before he went public and wrote his series of books on the subject.

Churchward *was* living in India in the 1880s, before he moved to the United States in 1889. It is during his time in India when he allegedly made contact with these Indian adepts, allowing for a period of roughly a decade where he could befriend, learn, and study the language—more than sufficient time. Churchward said he studied the language that was said to be humanity's original language, which he had labeled Naga-Maya, for more than two years.

After having read the Naacal documents, he continued his searches for further information. In Burma, he visited an ancient Buddhist temple in search of the missing records, carrying letters of introduction from the Indian high priests with whom he studied.

What is lacking from Churchward's account is any verifiable information. His story truly hinges on whether or not he acquainted an Indian priest and saw numerous rare tablets. There is nothing to substantiate it, though, it has to be said, nothing to debunk it. It is simply a matter of belief: whether you believe it or not.

As a result, for years, the story of Churchward therefore remained a legend, while his books were reprinted as generation after generation was introduced to his writings. But never anything new was found that might change the status quo.

That changed when German independent researcher, author, and travel agency manager Thomas Ritter claimed he had entered a secret library underneath Sri Ekambaranatha temple in Kanchipuram, India, in which he has found evidence of the lost civilization of Mu. He claims that on July 23, 2010, he was contacted by one Pachayappa, who invited him to enter the underground complex—and even allowed him to photograph some of its contents! Ritter states that "at chamber no. 4 the priest only allowed me to take pictures from two tablets, not from all this books there. The two tablets he showed me, are a little bit damaged. But you can see clearly the inscriptions."[1]

The Temple Complex of Sri Ekambaranatha in India is where, according to Thomas Ritter, there is an underground complex that contains evidence of the mythical continent of Mu. Mu was allegedly a continent in the Indian or Pacific Ocean. Despite years of searching for evidence, there is no archaeological or historical evidence that Mu has ever existed.

Image copyright Ssiram mt. Made available as part of the Creative Commons License on Wikimedia.

These two tablets are the so-called Naacal tablets, which James Churchward claimed to have seen many decades before. When Ritter published the material, there was immediately a torrent of disbelief, not helped by the realization that what Ritter apparently showed was a tablet unearthed in Byblos (Lebanon), discovered by French archaeologist Maurice Dunand. Because of the small amount of writing on the tablets, they have so far not been deciphered, though the script is identified—Proto-Byblian—and therefore not related to India. Indeed, the tablet presented by Ritter is in the Beirut Museum (Cat. 16598) and not a secret library in India.

Ritter claims that on his trip in July 2010, he was not welcomed by the usual young priest Narjan, whom he knew well, but an elder man, Pachayappa, who, unlike Narjan, did not speak English. Pachayappa did immediately show him things Narjan never had. He took him down into the underground structures of the temple complex. Ritter states: "Before an iron-bound door he stopped and pointed with some gesture to the bottom: 'Rishi place!'"[2] Then he opened the door, behind which the Naacal library was located.

Whether Ritter is lying or not, he has at least specifically identified a temple as the location of the library: the Sri Ekambaranatha Temple in Kanchipuram, in the state of Tamil (India). The gate tower of the temple complex measures more than 60 meters tall, making it the largest temple tower in Southern India; is made from granite; and is decorated with the images of gods, goddesses, and heroes. The complex is a Hindu temple dedicated to Lord Shiva and is one of the five major Shiva temples, each of which represents a natural element. The Sri Ekambaranatha Temple represents the element earth. The temple's history dates back to at least AD 600, though it could be older and is notorious for its hallway with a thousand pillars, as the temple's inner walls are decorated with an array of 1,008 Shiva lingams, a symbol of the male energy.

Ritter has drawn attention to the subterranean system of this complex, where he claims there are 10 chambers. In nine of these chambers, they stored the tablets. Each room measured 25 meters long and 15 meters wide, with the ceiling quite low; he could touch it when he stretched his arm out. Pachayappa claimed that the inscriptions detailed the Rishi Puranas, the lives of the culture bringers of Ancient India. Inside were black granite tables, and there were tens of thousands of stone tablets. Ritter notes that "both sides of such postcard-sized stone tablets engraved with tiny lines were narrow characters covered in an unfamiliar script. Other plates showed fine geometric patterns on running, technical drawings, maps and astronomical images."[3] When he asked what they contained, he said it was the legacy of the Seven Sages.

In the first three chambers, the tablets are made from black granite; in the next three, from gold. Each golden tablet was 14 by 10 centimeters, and about 2 to 3 millimeters thick, and were bound together as in books.

In the final three rooms, he found silver and bronze tablets that were hard to read, so Ritter used a handkerchief to polish the tablet, restoring it to its original state.

Ritter claims he was only allowed to photograph two tablets. All of these chambers have inscriptions, describing the lives and deeds of the Rishis, and has produced photographs of these inscriptions.

The 10th room was located at the end of the corridor. In the middle of the room rose a column of about 1.5 meters high from a solid black material, and, according to Pachayappa, the material was not stone. Behind the lingam were statues of the Seven Rishis, placed in a semi-circle, and they were made from a shimmering metal, which Ritter thought could be gold or silver-plated. One of them he was able to identify as Aghasthiya, who is always depicted as a dwarf.

Throughout the rooms, Ritter also saw rolls of metal foils, one of which Pachayappa opened. He claimed they were easy to unroll and that the material was very thin, reminding him of titanium, as it did not tear or wrinkle. The characters inscribed on it were etched, rather than engraved, and Ritter realized that he had seen one of these rolls before: in Churchward's books.

At the back of this room was another door, but Pachayappa indicated that he would not open this for Ritter. He did learn that the door led to a large underground tunnel system, some of which are said to connect to towns several tens of miles away.

Ritter states that non-Hindus and foreigners normally find the library closed to them, and even access to the central part of the temple is forbidden. It is Ritter's conviction that it was here that Churchward was shown the Naacal tablets and that he, more than a century later, stepped into Churchward's footsteps.

Jack Churchward has studied the material of his ancestors in detail and remains skeptical of Ritter's material. Ritter claims that some of the scrolls he found were the same as Churchward found. Jack Churchward, however, adds: "If James was there, then the tablets would have been wrapped and put away in what James referred to as 'chatties,' and therefore not visible. James said as much in his books. Ritter does not say anything other than he saw a symbol, he doesn't know that the tablets James saw were unfired clay, or that the tablets would have been packed away. Just my two cents."[4]

Jack Churchward has been asking Ritter for more evidence, including photographs, to back up his extraordinary claims, but so far, Ritter has not been forthcoming, including missing a deadline upon which he promised he would deliver such material. My own two attempts to contact Ritter equally received no reply. German researchers whom I contacted argued that I should place no faith in Ritter's claims whatsoever and even suggested I should not speak of the man.

Even though there is no evidence for Ritter's or Churchward's claims, throughout the 20th century, these and other stories were able to inspire many people to leave the comfortable confines of the Western world behind and travel to Asia, in search of evidence of this lost civilization and its remnants, which were said to be found in secret parts. And the Indiana Jones stories were right to include the Nazis as part of those who were enamored by these legends.

The Quest for the Lost Civilizations

In 1938, a Nazi expedition set out to find the origins of the Aryan race, thought to be located somewhere in the sacred mountains of Tibet. Sponsored by SS chief Heinrich Himmler, the expedition was led by Ernest Schäfer, a naturalist, and Bruno Beger, an anthropologist. The expedition reached the Tibetan capital of Lhasa in the beginning of January 1939. From the middle of the 19th century, Tibet and its capital had been closed to foreigners. But the Nazi expedition made it, spending the next eight months in Tibet, before fleeing south to Calculatta, taking with them 120 volumes of the Tibetan bible, the *Kangyur*, hundreds of precious artifacts, and rare animals.

Many claims have been made, one of which is that the expedition was to discover a connection between Atlantis and the first civilization of Central Asia. Schäfer believed that Tibet was the cradle of humanity, where a caste of priests had created a mysterious empire known as Shambhala, adorned with the Buddhist wheel of life, the swastika, and that the men were magicians themselves, intent on forging an alliance with the Tibetan mystical cities of Agharti and Shambhala. In 1922, Polish explorer Ferdynand Ossendowski wrote *Beasts, Men and Gods,* in which he relates that on his travels through Asia, he was told of a subterranean kingdom that was known to the Buddhists as Agharti. There are definitely such traditions in Asia, as the Tibetan and Indian Buddhists speak of this subterranean kingdom, though they name it

Shambhala and locate it "somewhere" in Inner Asia. The place was originally seen as one of peace and happiness, though it would later transform into a place of purity. There were also various legends attached to it, especially prophecies about the fate of the world.

Shambhala was said to be ruled by a line of kings known as Kalki Kings, who were said to uphold the integrity of the Kalachakra tantra, deemed to be one of the most complex forms of tantric Buddhism. The Kalachakra prophecies state that when the world would be ruled by war and greed, the 25th Kalki king would emerge from the hidden kingdom with a huge army to vanquish the dark forces and usher in a worldwide Golden Age. Ever since the 17th century, people have been trying to locate it. Portuguese Catholic missionary Estêvão Cacella actually thought it was another name for Cathay or China. In 1627, he headed out on a mission to find it, but failed.

In Germany, Himmler was fascinated by lost civilizations, Indian wisdom, and alternative medicine. If he had lived in the 1960s, he would have been a leading man in the Flower Power movement, but as he was the head of the SS, he used his power to try and find answers in far more cruel ways, including experimenting on prisoners of war to test his theories on the ancient German super-race, which he thought somewhere lost. He founded the Ahnenerbe specifically to advance the study of the Aryan race and its origins. From 1935 onward, a series of expeditions was organized to find evidence in support of these and other theories that would uncover this lost Aryan race. In 1937, the Nazi government sent archaeologist Franz Altheim and his wife, photographer Erika Trautnann, to Val Camonica to study the famous prehistoric rock inscriptions that had been found there. Upon their return, Altheim claimed that they had found traces of Nordic runes on the rocks, arguing that Ancient Rome was originally Nordic, and hence Aryan. That same year, Himmler investigated the claims of Hans F.K. Günther—namely that early Aryans had conquered much of Asia, including attacks against China and Japan, in approximately 2000 BC. Günther went as far as to claim that Gautama Buddha was of Aryan offspring. But of all the expeditions Himmler sponsored or organized, the Tibetan expedition was the largest and most ambitious. He was likely inspired by the failed expedition of the great Russian mystic Nicholas Roerich, who in 1926 had tried to enter Tibet, but was instead detained and returned to the British.

In 1937, American Theosophist Gottfried de Purucker argued that the Gobi desert was once fertile and lush with cities, and where one would find the seat of the Fifth Root Race. Blavatsky described the Fifth Root Race with the following words:

> The Aryan races, for instance, now varying from dark brown, almost black, red-brown-yellow, down to the whitest creamy color, are yet all of one and the same stock—the Fifth Root-Race—and spring from one single progenitor, [...] who is said to have lived over 18,000,000 years ago, and also 850,000 years ago—at the time of the sinking of the last remnants of the great continent of Atlantis.[5]

Blavatsky's Fifth Root Race and Himmler's idea of the lost roots of the Aryan Race are very close friends, and it seems quite apparent that if not directly, at least indirectly, Himmler was influenced by Blavatsky's doctrines, which spoke of lost civilizations and a history of a sunken continent that was thousands of years old.

Dr. Isrun Engelhardt, the foremost authority on Schäfer, is adamant that the man's personal ambitions for the expedition were purely scientific. Beger is known to have been exposed to alternative history from his professors at university, and it is assumed that he indeed hoped to find evidence that, somewhere in Asia, he would find evidence of the existence of the Aryan race. In fact, in 1943, Beger worked at the Auschwitz concentration camp, looking into hundreds of Jews and prisoners from central Asia, measuring their skulls and bodies.

After Beger's work was completed, everyone involved was gassed, and their corpses delivered to an old friend of Beger to become part of a university anatomical collection.

In short, the expedition was a scientific success, but no evidence of the Aryan race or Shambhala was found. Today, despite hundreds of books on Shambhala, Agharta, and the like, no evidence at all exists that these civilizations exist. The main problem of these myths is that they are recent. Some might argue that this is merely because Asia has only been unlocked in recent times, but it is a matter of fact that there are no ancient, openly available texts that document the existence of lost civilizations such as Mu—unlike Atlantis, which was written about more than 2,000 years ago. Though the Asian cultures have true legends about Shambhala, these myths have always been adapted for Western consumption, as a result of which an original myth has been changed, sometimes beyond recognition. Recently, though, archaeology has been able to show that the legends of ancient connections between Europe and Asia were indeed based on fact.

White Masters in the Deserts of China?

In 1907, the Russian explorer Pyotr Kuzmich Koslov (1863–1935) was one of the first to reach Lhasa and meet the Dalai Lama. Afterward, he organized further expeditions and excavated Khara Khoto. Khara Khoto was a Tangut city founded in 1032 that had been ruined by the Ming Chinese in 1372. Koslov unearthed a tomb 50 feet below the ruins and found the body of a woman, apparently a queen, accompanied by various scepters, wrought in gold and other metals. Though Koslov took numerous photographs that were published in *American Weekly,* he was not allowed to disturb or remove anything from the tomb, which was sealed again. His last expedition to Mongolia and Tibet occurred from 1923 to 1926 and resulted in the discovery of Xiongnu royal burials at Noin-Ula.

When he learned about this discovery, James Churchward believed that the primary colony of Mu was the Great Uighur Empire and that Khara Khoto was its ancient capital, but that the civilization was at its height about 15,000 BC. Check any encyclopedia, and you will find that Churchward "borrowed" that name from the historical Uighur, who today live primarily in the Xinjiang Uyghur Autonomous Region of China.

Later, French author Robert Charroux wrote about his theory that the Gobi Desert had Magi that surpassed even those that were resident in Tibet. Stories say that these cities had ocean ports, and Edgar Cayce even argued that elevators would one day be discovered in a lost city here. Others have seen this region as the homeland of those ancient UFOs, the vimanas.

But whereas it is the Gobi Desert that might still hold some secrets, it is the Taklamakan Desert that has provided us with revelations. The Taklamakan Desert is a large sandy desert, part of the Tarim Basin, a region roughly between Tibet and Mongolia, in western China, and crossed at its northern and southern edge by the Silk Road. Conditions are so harsh that travelers avoided the desert as much as possible, but in millennia gone by, the region was populated and habitable.

In recent decades, however, the desert has once again become an oasis—for archaeologists and anomalists, as it is here that hundreds of Caucasoid mummies have been found. The most notable mummies are the tall, red-haired Cherchen Man (dated to c. 1000 BC), the Hami Mummy (c. 1400–800 BC), and the Witches of Subeshi (fourth or third century BC), who received their name because of the tall pointed hats they wore. However, the oldest mummy of all is the Loulan Beauty (1800 BC).

Though not the oldest, one of the most famous mummies of the Taklamakan Desert is that of Cherchen Man. This European's body was placed in a poplar-wood box, lowered into a narrow shaft grave, and left for eternity. It was the climatic circumstances that make this region so inhospitable today that preserved these corpses throughout the millennia, turning them into mummies.

Cherchen Man is 6 feet tall, was around 50 years old at the time of his death, had reddish brown hair, a long nose, full lips, and a ginger beard. He was buried in a red twill tunic and tartan leggings, and his body is far better preserved than the notorious Egyptian mummies everyone stumbles across everywhere. Most interestingly, Cherchen Man too was buried with no less than 10 hats, one that looks Roman, another that looks like a beret, a cap, and even a conical "witch" hat—which is therefore something of a common feature of several of these mummies. His body dates back to 1000 BC, and DNA analysis has shown that he was a Celt.

Next to him were found the mummies of three women and a baby. One of the women is dressed in a red gown, wearing tall boots, with her hair brushed and braided. She has a red yarn through her ear lobes and—like the man—has several tattoos on her face. All mummies were painted with a yellow substance, believed to help in the preservation of the body. The baby, probably three to four months old, is wrapped in brown blankets, tied with blue and red cord, with a blue stone placed on each eye.

The oldest of the mummies is the 4,000-year-old Loulan Beauty, a mummy that was discovered in 1980 in the ancient Chinese garrison town that was discovered by Hedin on March 28, 1900. The town was located near the Lop Nor marshes, on the northeastern edge of the Lop Desert. Hedin was able to recover many manuscripts, which stated that the culture was wiped out by a large seismic occurrence, which drastically changed the climate of the area and turned it into a desert, as it remains today. That was several millennia after the Loulan Beauty lived. This female mummy has long, fair hair. She was 45 when she died and was buried with a basket of food, containing domesticated wheat, combs, and a feather. No doubt, these nourishments were for the afterlife.

At 1800 BC, the Beauty is the oldest mummy found in the Tarim Basin, but she is not the lone European to have lived here in those days: The cemetery at Yanbulaq contained no less than 29 mummies, which date from 1800 BC to 500 BC, 21 of which are Caucasoid. Best preserved of all the corpses is Yingpan Man, who is also known as the Handsome Man, a 2-meter-tall, 2,000-year-old Caucasian mummy that was discovered in 1995. His face was blond and bearded, and was covered with a gold foil death mask, which is a Greek tradition; he also wore elaborate golden-embroidered red and maroon wool garments with images of fighting Greeks or Romans. His head rests on a pillow in the shape of a crowing cockerel.

Elsewhere in the Tarim Basin, hundreds of other mummies have been found, all of which are known to have been of European origin. Some of the mummies are thought to have possibly been sacrificial victims. A young woman was found partially dismembered, her eyes gouged out. A baby boy had apparently been buried alive. The question is whether the latter was sacrificial, or whether he was "merely" buried with his dead mother.

However intriguing the local setting might be, the interest in these mummies exists largely because they are out-of-place remains. Not only is there DNA evidence that shows that these people originated from Europe, but analyses such as the weave of the cloth have also shown that it was identical to those found on the bodies of salt miners in Austria, dating from 1300 BC. The wooden combs buried in Asia are also identical to those found in Celtic countries. So are the stone structures on top of their burial sites—similar to the dolmens of western Europe. In short, Europeans in the second millennium BC may not only have gone to America; they are known to have come to the Far East.

Despite such certainties, archaeologists and historians have been unable to fill in the "soft evidence"—which are nevertheless the most important questions: How did they go to China, and why did they go to China?

That we know about these European visitors to China at all is largely thanks to the work of Dr. Victor Mair, a professor of Chinese studies at the University of Pennsylvania. His fascination began when he toured the Urumchi Museum, where some of these mummies are on display. He then invited Dr. Elizabeth W. Barber of Occidental College (California) to visit the mummies and give her expert opinion on the weaving that was on display.

"From around 1800 BC, the earliest mummies in the Tarim Basin were exclusively Caucausoid, or Europoid," says Mair.[6] East Asian migrants arrived in the eastern portions of the Tarim Basin about 3,000 years ago, whereas the Uighur peoples arrived after the collapse of the Orkon Uighur Kingdom, based in modern-day Mongolia, around the year 842. In short, Mair leaves little doubt that we are confronted with a lost civilization, existing of a group of European settlers in a region millennia before the history of this region started to be written.

The important question is whether we are in the same bailiwick as Churchward, who saw this region as being of central importance. That answer, it seems, is negative. Mair believes that early Europeans headed in all directions, some traveling west, into western Europe, but others heading east, eventually ending up in Xinjiang.

His opinions tally with those of textile expert Barber, who in her book *The Mummies of Urumchi* examined the tartan-style cloth and concluded that the garments can be traced back to Anatolia and the Caucasus, the steppe area north of the Black Sea. She argues this group of people divided, starting in the Caucasus and then splitting, one group going west and another east—contrary to Mair's opinion.

So what do we know about these people? We know that they were horsemen and herders, using chariots, and may have invented the stirrup. We know that they had arrived in this region by 1800 BC. We know that around 1200 BC, the Indo-Europeans were joined by another wave of immigrants, from what is now Iran (the so-called Saka branch). In fact, the Saka nomads had high-pointed hats (like the ones found next to Cherchen Man) as displayed on the Persepolis reliefs in southern Iran. A bronze statue found in the Altai Mountains from the fifth century BC wore a similar hat. Most important are the facts that the statue had Caucasoid features and showed similarities in dress to Cherchen Man. Apart from hard DNA evidence, there is much other incontrovertible evidence that makes this European presence in China a hard fact. The discovery of these mummies indeed rewrote history—whether some like that or not.

The current conclusion drawn about these mummies and the waves of settlements is therefore that it was only until several centuries BC that the eastward movement of the Western race to Xinjiang was more rapid than the western movement of Mongoloid people and that the region became "Chinese." When T.D. Forsyth reported on his 1875 mission to the region, he stated that these people were still tall, fair-faced, with light eyes and sandy whiskers and hair. He added that they "only require to be put into coat and trousers to pass, so far as outward appearance goes, for the fairest Englishman."[7] Two millennia before, Pliny the Elder in "Taprobane" wrote about the Seres, which were described to the Roman Emperor Claudius by an embassy from Taprobane (Ceylon). He said that they "exceeded the ordinary human height, had flaxen hair, and blue eyes," a description that comes close to those people living in the Tarim Basin. Pliny the Elder also said they had an "uncouth sort of noise by way of talking, having no language of their own for the purpose of communicating their thoughts."[8]

Though no Tocharian texts were found in relation to the Tarim Mummies, it is now largely accepted that these European emigrants spoke a language known as Tocharian (the Chinese called them Yuezhi), which has proven to be close to the languages of western Europe. Today's Uighur are therefore known to be more than half Caucasian, and travelers through the region remain often stunned as to how European the locals look.

If one were to find a Bronze Age seafarer in America, it would obviously create worldwide controversy. The discovery of Europeans on Chinese soil has also had major political implications. The region is rife with separatist movements, and the government fears that promoting a truly unique archaeological find might result in serious social and political unrest. That is one of the main raisons why the Terracotta Warriors are far more famous than the Tarim Mummies.

Social unrest is the greatest between the Uighur and the Han Chinese. In their drive to lay claim to the region, the Loulan Beauty was even raised to the status of racial icon by the Uighur, who call her "mother of the nation"—without little supporting evidence. Chinese historian Ji Xianlin, writing a preface to *Ancient Corpses of Xinjiang* by Wang Binghua, says that China "supported and admired"[9] research by foreign experts into the mummies—that is, Mair and Barber. "However, within China a small group of ethnic separatists have taken advantage of this opportunity to stir up trouble and are acting like buffoons. Some of them have even styled themselves the descendants of these ancient 'white people' with the aim of dividing the motherland. But these perverse acts will not succeed," Ji wrote.[10]

In comparing the DNA of the mummies to that of modern-day Uighur, Mair's team found some genetic similarities with the mummies, but no direct links. The Han Chinese, meanwhile, consider themselves to be occupiers of the center of the world. Everyone else were savages, so the discovery of Europeans on their territory—the remains furthermore older than anything the Han Chinese could point at in the archaeological record—meant that some mental gymnastics had to be performed to preserve their cherished self-opinion. The fact of the matter is that neither the Uighur nor the Han Chinese seem to be directly related to these ancient settlers—and that both are but modern additions to a region that was populated millennia earlier. In short, the discoveries have made it hard on both groups to continue to ratify their claim to the region.

In fact, what the discoveries suggests is that both immigrants and modern local Chinese are a mixture of races. "While it is clear that the early inhabitants of the Tarim Basin were primarily Caucasoids," Mair has written, "it is equally clear that they did not all belong to a single homogeneous group. Rather, they represent a variety of peoples who seem to have connections with many far-flung parts of the Eurasian land mass for more than two millennia."[11] He adds: "Modern DNA and ancient DNA show that Uighurs, Kazaks, Kyrgyzs, the peoples of central Asia are all mixed Caucasian and East Asian. The modern and ancient DNA tell the same story."[12] It underlines, once again, that so many cultures, whether ancient or modern, are genetically a mixture of so many races, contrary to so many political ideas of pure genes.

What brought these Europeans here? It is known that the southern Taklamakan Desert was an area where China's Silk Road once flourished and prosperous cities were built. In Khotan, two large rivers were channeled, creating an oasis that grew wheat, rice, corn, cotton, grapes, peaches, and melons, while sheep were grazing. Life must have been good in those days, and that these Europeans had everything they cherished. However, because of gradual climate change, many such cities were abandoned and subsequently eaten by the dunes.

The Silk Road was an ancient caravan route that connected China to the West. The European mummies in this part of the world might suggest that this trade route is indeed older than previously thought—very much like transoceanic contact might be several millennia older than Columbus's first voyage to America.

The Silk Road was not just a conduit for silk; many other products were transported and traded, and the routes were not merely traveled by merchants, but anyone wanting to go East—or West. The routes should therefore be seen as the ancient highway" between China and the Mediterranean Sea.

Trading between the East and West occurred from the dawn of civilization—if not before. Between 6000 BC and 4000 BC, people in the Sahara were already importing domesticated animals from Asia. By 3000 BC, lapis lazuli—the only known source of which was Badakshan, in northeastern Afghanistan—was found in Egypt. Most specifically, the supply of Tarim Basin jade to China from ancient times is well established. Nephrite jade from mines in the region of Yarkand and Khotan—not too far from the lapis lazuli mines of Badakshan—was found in China. Xinru Liu writes: "It is well known that ancient Chinese rulers had a strong attachment to jade. All of the jade items excavated from the tomb of Fuhao of the Shang dynasty, more than 750 pieces, were from Khotan in modern Xinjiang. As early as the mid-first millennium [BC] the Yuezhi engaged in the jade trade, of which the major consumers were the rulers of agricultural China."[13] When we know that Europe had expert miners, maybe these people came to this region because of their mining skills, not to mine copper or tin, but to mine jade, and add yet another mineral and item on the ever-growing list of materials that were traded thousands of years ago, across vast sections of, if not the entire world.

The Tarim Mummies have destroyed the idea that the West and the East developed independently and that they only relatively recently made contact. The discovery of these mummies has driven the final nail in this coffin—almost literally. Science, it is clear, has shown a straightforward link between these mummies and Celtic inhabitants of Europe. The question, however, is whether Europeans went east—or a Caucasoid group of people, perhaps native to the Tarim Basin, went to Europe.

Turning the path of travel in the opposite direction would offer some confirmation for the speculation that this region was indeed a "homeland" to our early ancestors and that they spread to other regions—specifically Europe—from here out.

With so little known about Bronze Age Celts both in Europe and Asia, no firm conclusions can be drawn either way—and perhaps never will. However, the Book of Manu (also known as the Laws of Manu), one of the supplementary arms of the Vedas, states that the "Uighers had settlements on the northern and eastern shores of the Caspian Sea" and the 19th-century German anthropologist Max Muller argued that the first Caucasians were a small company from the mountains of Central Asia. These conclusions are obviously old, but should they therefore be erroneous? Written more than a century before the Tarim Mummies were discovered, they actually did speak of the presence of Caucasians in China. If they got that right, is it possible they got other things right, too?

One final question that therefore needs to be added to the long list of questions about these mummies is in which direction the Caucasians traveled. Could the Caucasian mummies of the Taklamakan Desert be native, rather than European visitors? Only the future, and future discoveries, is likely to tell. It is at least an undeniable fact that there was contact between Bronze Age Europeans and China, along the Silk Road. The evidence is for all to see in the Urumchi Museum.

THE ELYSIAN FIELDS

In the 1930s, French police officer Xavier Guichard published his life-study into the place named Eleusis. There is such a city in both Greece and Egypt. The Greek city is the most famous, as it is the home of the Elysian mysteries. In mythology, we also have the Elysian fields, which are intimately connected to the afterlife. Guichard published his findings in a book called *Eleusis Alesia*, a study on the origins of

European civilization. Published in 1936, it had a print run of 500 copies, of which several were lost. In 1997, I asked a French friend whether he was able to locate a copy of this book. He found one in Lyons, the second largest library in France. My friend was able to tell me that no one had loaned out the book for the past 20 years!

These are the conclusions that Guichard reached: All places that were called Alesia (or a name closely related) had been given this name in prehistoric times. Not a single place had been given such a name in more recent times. He believed that the name derived from an Indo-European root, meaning "a meeting point to where people traveled." The majority of these sites could be found in France, where there were more than 400, but the name occurred as far away as Greece and Egypt, but also in Poland and Spain. Guichard was unable to find such names in Britain, which suggested to him that these cities might go back to the time of the last Ice Age, when Britain was covered with thick sheets of ice.

Guichard made it an issue to visit most sites figuring in his research in person. He discovered that they had two characteristic features: They were on hills overlooking rivers, and they were built around a man-made well of salt or mineral water. He also believed that all the sites lay on lines radiating like the spokes of a wheel from the town of Alaise, in eastern France.

This is an echo of what Mestdagh discovered regarding Sens and how 64 roads left this city, radiating in all directions. Guichard believed that in the case of Alaise, 24 lines, equally spaced radiating lines, plus four lines based on the sunrise/sunset at the two equinoxes and the summer and winter solstices, emanated from it. This was a total of 28 lines, which could have a lunar connection. Intriguingly, a play of numbers, starting from 28 (which is 2 times 14), gives numbers like 56, 64, and 72, all of them featuring prominently in sites such as Stonehenge, the megalithic civilization and other mythology. Of course, we can do a lot with numbers (which is, after all, what they were designed for in the first place), but it is interesting that certain key numbers keep coming back. In particular, these numbers always have direct astronomical significance.

Guichard never explored whether the lines were just lines someone in ancient times had drawn on an ancient map, or whether there was actually a system of roads underlying it. As four lines were sightlines connected with the sun, it is likely that these were in fact real roads. If so, this would make Alaise the older brother—or father—of the road system that was—likely—later built from Sens. And if this was a system of roads, then people traveled on it, at least on those sections that were on land. It also means that France was home to a prehistoric civilization, likely at the time of the Ice Age or pre-dating it, which should not come as a surprise by now. If Guichard's system of lines were roads, it also explains why these people were so highly mobile and why even the Far East was within their reach. Of course, even if Guichard's lines were not roads, then prehistoric Europe had other means of transportation, both over land and sea, for we know that this continent was one large exchange of goods, held together by the copper and tin trade for the production of bronze, which was the prehistoric equivalent of today's oil industry.

With Guichard's findings, we are back to c. 10,000 BC, when Göbekli Tepe was constructed, when Atlantis was ruling sections of Europe, and when civilization was already in existence, precisely as it is said in the ancient accounts.

Going beyond the 10,000 BC mark is far more difficult. At this moment in time, archaeological remains become sporadic—maybe, indeed, because the centers of civilization of those times are now located under sea level. We know that there were cave paintings in Europe, but how far does the history of civilization truly stretch?

Lост Civilizаtiоn оf thе Ѕtоnе Аgе

Large-scale prehistoric mines and quarries have been known to be excavated, at least in southern Africa, namely Southern Mozambique and Swaziland, 100,000 years ago. Others, dating to 45,000–35,000 years ago, have also been found. More than a million kilos of ore is known to have been extracted from the largest sites. At another site, half a million stone-digging tools were found. For Michael Cremo, these are bit recent examples of civilization, as he is convinced we have been here for millions of years.

Few will want to go that far with Cremo, but English anthropologist Richard Rudgley speaks of a lost civilization of the Stone Age, tens of thousands of years old, based on the anomalous pieces of evidence that lie scattered in various museums. Rudgley argues that "the prehistory of mankind is no mere prelude to history, rather history is a colorful and eventful afterword to the Stone Age."[14] He argues that Stone Age explorers discovered all of the world's major land masses, were able to count and measure, performed medical operations, including amputations and cranial surgery, and experimented with lichen and moss fuels, noting that prehistoric life expectancy was better than it is for contemporary third-world populations, while warfare was less prevalent than today.

Rudgley also dispels certain wide-held beliefs. For example, the adoption of farming is still generally seen as a clear sign of civilization. Yet the adoption of farming caused a decline in body stature, body size, and life expectancy, as well as the development of a new host of diseases and disorders, including leprosy. More recent, cancer, obesity and diabetes have been added to this list. It appears that prehistory was indeed some type of golden age in which man lived longer and with far less illnesses and diseases!

The Stone Age was far more advanced than we thought it was, but Science has one hang-up that it cannot get over: writing. The apparent absence of writing in those times has meant that Science treats everything before the invention of writing with disdain, no matter how much scientific accomplishments a civilization had. Even though our ancestors may not have been writing, they were definitely talking. In fact, the further one pushes back in history, the less languages there are; Rudgley labels this the quest for the Mother Tongue. Academics have proposed various types of classification and seldom are able to agree on the conclusions they draw, but what can be summarized is that some of our ancestors' language goes back tens of thousands of years. And it has to be, for how else could our ancestors organize themselves for such specific tasks as mining, 100,000 years ago? Take a look at modern mining. This involved at least basic understandings of science, social organization, and project management, which would have involved far more "civilization" than we are wont to bestow upon our ancestors so many tens of thousands of years ago. When the archaeological record further indicates that our ancestors were able to perform surgeries, again history is not as we often think it is.

Our ancestors were far more advanced than that. However reluctant Science is to go there, our ancestors were clearly expert astronomers. The megalithic monuments were expertly aligned to stellar phenomena, and cave paintings are known to have contained at least an understanding of the periods of the moon and certain constellations. At Lascaux, France, one depiction is of six large dots above an Auroch (a bull). In ancient times, the constellation of the Pleiades was represented above the shoulder or back of Taurus, the Bull. Though the Pleiades are known as the Seven Sisters, because the constellation is made up of seven stars, this seventh star is actually only visible with binoculars—which the artists of Lascaux may not have possessed, making this a constellation of six, rather than seven stars. If not a coincidence, our ancestors were depicting the constellations on the walls of this Paleolithic cave.

These cave paintings were principally responsible for the belief that our ancestors lived in caves. Caves were not for living, but instead were seen as the first—natural—cathedrals.

THE STONE AGE CATHEDRALS

Interestingly, the cave paintings were discovered in the deepest nooks of caves. What made our ancestors make these drawings in these inaccessible places, where there was little chance of these paintings serving any social function? The question as to why our ancestors painted these drawings is furthermore riddled with preconceptions. In 1865, Sir Edward Tylor argued that there was a correspondence between magic and prehistoric art. Other experts, such as Breuil, interpreted these as hunting magic, where the depictions were made for their magical power over the animal that would be killed. In the end, such an interpretation discovered to be too naïve: An overview revealed that only 15 percent of depictions were of animals that played any role whatsoever in the hunt.

To repeat the question: What is it that persuaded our ancestors to penetrate the innermost darkness of a cave and paint? Among those who have tried to answer this question is David Lewis-Williams, who felt that the status quo on the subject matter was inadequate. For some reasons, our ancestors were attracted to those darkest regions of the underworld, which was carefully explored and became a workshop to express the earliest expressions of art. Still, it was not art; it was religious art: The art had a purpose. Lewis-Williams is convinced that the caves became the cathedrals of the Stone Age, with the paintings depicting the core of their religious beliefs.

In the first decades of the 20th century, several researchers had cataloged the prehistoric caves, specifically in France and Spain. Each researcher tried to build a theory that might explain what he had discovered, but it seemed that each subsequent discovery invalidated the previous theory. One such theory was that the series of paintings found in the caves were part of a pattern, whereby certain depictions were only found in certain parts of the cave system (for example, near the entrance or in the deepest reaches). However, this theory was proven inadequate, resulting in the common understanding that it was very difficult, if not impossible, to make sense of what our ancestors had been doing. In short, it was felt that the art work, however brilliant for our primitive ancestors, had been nothing more than random paintings in caves—without any further logic.

Lewis-Williams thought differently. He felt that a pattern did exist. He also felt that the paintings were a distinguishing factor between our ancestors—modern man—and its "nephews," such as Neanderthal man. According to Lewis-Williams, Neanderthal man, despite his close proximity, did not possess an imagination in the sense that we do. He also identified that what was depicted were images of the mind: visions—in other words, what the mind observed when it was in another "reality." Our ancestors—or at least some of them— must have experienced altered states of consciousness. This must have greatly intrigued them, as it continues to the present day. In prehistoric times, Lewis-Williams argues, those visions would be the foundation for the creation of our religion, beginning with the belief in an "Otherworld" beyond our normal, physical senses. In this respect, the caves were the first cathedrals of humanity's proto-religion. This, of course, means that on top of Stone Age man's accomplishment was the exploration of other realities and the creation of religion.

These otherworldly explorers created the paintings using the natural contours of the rock and "exteriorized" what their visions had allowed them to see. Lewis-Williams is a firm believer that the artwork of the caves are depictions of what our ancestors witnessed in their visions: enigmatic lines, strange patterns, followed by animals. They form a logical sequence of what people today still see in their own hallucinogenic experiences. Such patterns are known from anthropological studies of shamanic cultures, which equally often used hallucinogenic substances to enter the Otherworld.

He further argues that many paintings seem to rise out of the rock. The paintings transform the natural shape of the rock, in the same way that our observation would be transformed under the influence of hallucinogenic substances. The act of painting was therefore bringing the visions of the Otherworld into this reality: creating the Otherworld here, in the deepest reaches of the Underworld.

Many anthropologists have identified that the shaman, in his voyage to the Otherworld, is either transformed in or aided by an animal, often totemic in nature. This animal acts as his spirit guide, or his power animal. Animals were often chosen for a particular quality, such as the ability of flight for birds, and it is this reason, not hunting magic why animals were often depicted on the walls of these caves.

The walls of the caves were a portal into another dimension. The Otherworld was located behind, or inside, the rocks. The figures painted on these walls had escaped that reality—bridged the divide, like the shamans. These were the mediators between our reality and our needs and the Otherworld, the home of the gods who had been identified as responsible for the creation of this world. The cave was therefore the first temple, where sacred space was created to allow contact with the divine. It was in its innermost recesses, in the belly of Mother Earth, that the Otherworld was closest—and where the darkness of the cave created a silence and solitude everyday reality did not offer.

Remarkably, 18,000 years ago, these cave paintings display a high level of scientific achievement, specifically in the science of acoustics. American researcher Steven Waller sampled a selection of cave sites in France and found that echoes normally vibrate at an average level of 3 decibels. Rock-art panels of hoofed animals, though, he noted, reflected sound at 23–31 decibels, and panels depicting feline creatures were far lower, at 1–7 decibels. Unpainted surfaces tended to be totally flay, showing that the placement of these animals was not at all coincidental, but defined by the acoustical qualities of the site in which they were found. "Modern humans, who understand sound reflection, tend to trivialize echoes, and this may be the reason why the motivation for rock art has remained so long an enigma. The discovery that echoes of percussive noises resemble to a remarkable degree the sounds of galloping hoofed animals provides a crucial link between the context and the content of the art."[15]

Confronted with these cave paintings, we are specifically staring at the birth of the physical representation of a belief in "another" world, which would evolve into a dedicated cult—and in the end organized religion. It would lead to the building of the Egyptian pyramids, artificial tombs trying to reflect natural caves, and the Book of the Dead being the written account of the shamanic visions experienced in the Otherworld.

Our ancestors, it seems ingested the food of the gods to establish this contact. This food was, on numerous occasions, magic mushrooms, though archaeology has compiled an extensive range of hallucinogenic substances that our ancestors used.

The oldest depictions of hallucinogenic mushrooms are 7,000 to 9,000 years old and are rock engravings in Tassilli. Here is a sequence of people that are dancing. Each dancer holds a mushroom-shaped object in his right hand. Two parallel lines radiate from this object, toward the central area of the dancer.

Greek civilization had the Temple of Demeter, the Goddess of the Earth, at Eleusis, the place-name that so greatly intrigued Xavier Guichard. Philosophers such as Aristotle, Plato, and Sophocles partook in its rituals, the Elysian Mysteries, the contents of which have never been written down, even they continued to exist until well into the Christian era.

253

These men were among the thousands of pilgrims who made the voyage between Athens and Eleusis, to partake in the yearly ceremonies. Once they were at Eleusis, from a hidden, central room in the temple complex, a substance derived from mushrooms was given to each participant. They remained in the temple for the duration of one night, but left in the morning forever changed. The divine potion had brought them to another reality, where some may indeed have come face to face with an otherworldly intelligence. Our Ancient Greeks were but a recent example in a long tradition, stretching back tens of thousands of years in the past, of people who had taken the food of the gods and came away convinced that there was more to life than we could see with our naked eyes.

In my opinion, it is this belief—or understanding—that reality was more than we experienced that was the true motor that propelled civilization—not farming, nor writing. Look at Ancient Egypt, and we see the temples and pyramids that survived, not the palaces of the Pharaoh, which were often not even made from stone. Look at the cave paintings of Lascaux, and realize it must have taken someone months to create these. Göbekli Tepe, too, was a temple, not a residence. Wherever you see physical evidence of civilization—or the best evidence of civilization—in the form of buildings, you will see that those buildings were normally connected with religion. The history of civilization is indeed largely distilled from the religious monuments are ancestors made. It is because our ancestors felt that those monuments were the most important, for whereas our existence here on Earth was but a temporary thing, that they believed that the soul and the divine were eternal.

Chapter 7

CREATING HEAVEN ON EARTH

FINDING CENTERS

In the eighth century, the Venerable Bede identified Lichfield Cathedral as the center of England. If he was trying to make a geographically significant statement, he was off target. In 1941, Sir Charles Arden-Close, director-general of the Ordnance Survey, identified the center of the British Isles as being on Watling Street, 4 miles east-southest of Atherstone, close to the railway bridge, between the villages of Higham-on-the-Hill and Caldecote. He acknowledged two sites that traditionally were said to mark the center of England: a cross at Meriden, in Warwickshire, and an ancient tree, the Lillington Oak, at Leamington. Neither of them are the center, though both have put in claims.

English writer John Michell in *At the Centre of the World* puts forward a series of examples that shows that our ancestors, thousands of years ago, were able to identify the center of islands, whether small or large—like Britain. Most of his studies were executed in western Europe, and he found that this knowledge of knowing the center preceded the Romans. Therefore it was at least in existence in Celtic times, but may stretch even further back, to megalithic times.

Whereas finding the center of small islands like Shetland or the Orkneys is quite straightforward, in the case of the British mainland or even England, that is not the case, as it involves distances of several hundreds of miles. Somehow our ancestors were able to do so, yet somehow all the attempts in the last few centuries to do so were less accurate than the work of our ancient ancestors.

Michell noted that at Meriden, an old stone cross is said to have marked the site that claimed to be the center of England, though he noted that early topographical writers did not make any mention of it. He discovered that the first reference to Meriden as the center was written in 1876 by J. Tom Burgess, who also mentioned the rival center at Leamington.

The cross at Meriden has been moved, and its original site is not exactly known. Meriden supposedly means "miry valley," but anyone will notice the close resemblance to meridian, the longitudinal lines linked with mapping time zones on the Earth. However, before the 13th century, the site was known as Alspath, suggesting Meriden is indeed more closely linked with "miry valley" than a meridian.

The other listed contender is the Midland Oak at Lillington, on the western outskirts of Leamington. Its iron railings were removed during the Second World War, which unfortunately led to the oak's death. In 1982, a new oak was planted.

However, like Meriden, Midland Oak is not the center of England. Though Arden-Close acknowledges only two contenders for this title, there are far more—and better—candidates. Nigel Pennick saw Royston, with the crossing of Icknield Way and Ermine Street, as the perfect geomantic center. This crossing was marked by the King Stone, sitting on top of the enigmatic Royston Cave, which contains a series of remarkable inscriptions whose origins remain unexplained. If ever these were centers of anything, it was of regions, not England.

The same applies to the case of Oxford, though its claim comes with a powerful legend. In the *Mabinogion,* it is said that the Celtic king Lludd was instructed to measure the length and breadth of England in order to determine its center. At that spot, he would find two fighting dragons that were responsible for the evils afflicting the nation. When he went on this quest, he found the two creatures fighting at what is now Oxford.

Others have used geography to define the center, including John Walbridge, who has identified Arbury Hill, Northamptonshire, as the English omphalos. On Arbury Hill, at 225 meters the highest point in Northamptonshire, the territories of three Celtic tribes converged, and it is the part of England most distant from the sea. Though interesting, in the end, it is clear that it has too little to become a genuine candidate.

Walbridge did underline certain conditions this sacred center had to meet. Michell stated: "In all traditional systems of religion this image [of the center] has provided the dominant symbol. The doctrine associated with it describes the universe as a divinely born creation, never the same, never at rest, but with a still, unvarying center which, like the core of a magnetic field, governs everything around it."[1] He added: "In every traditional society, [the center] is provided by a rock or pillar within the national sanctuary which is known to be the generation center of mankind and the spot where the pole of the universe penetrates the earth."[2]

This central rock was the omphalos, the sacred rock marking the sacred center. Perhaps the best known example is the omphalos of Delphi, whose position was defined by Zeus releasing two doves (some legends argue for eagles) from the east and west end of the world. The two birds met at Delphi, which therefore was the center of the world. The concept of birds cannot merely be found in Delphi, but also at

Heliopolis, in Egypt. Professor of ancient history Livio Stecchini stated that "usually on top of Sokar, as on top of any omphalos, there are portrayed two birds facing each other; in ancient iconography these two birds, usually doves, are a standard symbol for the stretching of meridians and parallels."[3]

Doves, or pigeons, were therefore specifically linked with oracle centers, of which Delphi was one. These kinds of birds were used by seafarers to discover whether or not they were close to land, and we now know that these ancient seafarers went much further than commonly appreciated. The "trick" can also be found in the Bible, where Noah released a dove to find out whether or not the Flood waters had subsided, as well as in its inspiration, the Epic of Gilgamesh. Finally, there is the mythical bird, the phoenix, linked with Heliopolis, resting on the benben stone, the primordial hill.

The omphalos stone at Delphi lay in the most important part of the temple of Apollo, near the Adyton, the seat of the Pythia. It was here that men were brought, to be shown visions of the Otherworld. It seems quite apparent that the proximity of the stone was not coincidental, as the stone marked the gateway to the Otherworld.

In Caesar's *Gallic Wars*, he relates that the center of the Celtic world was Chartres, now famous for its Gothic cathedral, which contains one of the surviving medieval labyrinths. Chartres was the Celtic place of assembly and was the center of Gaul, the Celtic realm, equidistant from its western and eastern extremities—the tip of Brittany and the mouth of the Rhine—which means that the Celts were able to map vast distances.

To define the center of England, though, we need to start with the "main axis" of Britain: the line between Duncansby Head, the most northeasterly part of the Scottish mainland, and St. Catherine's Point, on the Isle of Wight. Interestingly, it crosses the coast of

Southern Scotland at the point where the former of Scottish county of Haddingtonshire (now East Lothian) joins Berwickshire; this was once the most northern point of England and it is probably not a coincidence that the division of those two nations was precisely here.

Equidistant from that point and the opposite extremity at Land's End, the point on the main axis that is at the center of this isosceles triangle, is the center of England.

All ancient nations searched for the center: the Greeks, the Celts, the Romans. Meriden is c. 12 miles from Venonae, which the Roman surveyors identified as the center of England and where they placed the crossing point of two of their great roads, Watling Street and Fosse Way. When we compare the location arrived at by Arden-Close with modern means, with the location identified by the Romans, we are talking about a difference of a few miles. It underlines the geographical knowledge and expertise the Romans possessed, whereby they somehow were able to arrive at the same conclusions without the availability of any modern maps.

Venonae is now known as High Cross, an isolated point on the Warwickshire-Leicestershire border where four parishes meet. A visit to the place will last merely a few minutes: The A5, or Watling Street, is a two-way road that turns one-way at this crossroad so that people can more easily get off it. Once off, you have a crossing of two minor roads: the main one that takes you to Claybrooke Magna, and another one, Bumble Bee Lane. The once-Roman main road Fosse Street is now nothing more than a track, and on maps is listed as "Leicestershire Round."

High Cross sits on top of a rise in the landscape and is therefore indeed an omphalos. Burgess said that 57 church towers can be identified from this location. Dr. William Stukeley described High Cross as "the centre, as well as the highest ground in England; for from hence rivers run every way."[4] He might have been right about the center, but it definitely was not the highest ground from a geographical perspective.

High Cross is a crossing on high ground, but the name comes from a monument that was erected on orders of the Justices of Warwickshire in 1711, at a cost of £400 (U.S. $600): a tall cross. It had an inscription, which on one side read: "The noblemen and gentry, ornaments of the neighboring counties of Warwick and Leicester, at the instances of the Right Honourable Basil Earl of Denbeigh, have caused this pillar to be erected in grateful as well as perpetual remembrance of Peace at last restored by her Majesty Queen Anne, in the year of our Lord, 1712." It continued on the other side: "If, traveller, you search for the footsteps of the ancient Romans, here you may behold them. For here their most celebrated ways, crossing one another, extend to the utmost boundaries of Britain; here the Vennones kept their quarters; and at the distance of one mile from hence, Claudius, a certain commander of a cohort, seems to have had a camp, towards the street, and towards the foss a tomb." The "high cross" is now gone, but Stukeley left us with a drawing of the monument.

Whereas Chartres continues to rise at the center of the Gallic world, in Britain, far less is visible of this once-sacred center. Equally lost today is the importance of Fosse Way, while the other Roman highway, Watling Street, is "only" the A5, not a super-highway. Nearby is, nevertheless, still the connection of the M6 with the M1, the modern arteries of automobile England.

Venonae (sometimes referenced as Venonis) was therefore the settlement at the center of Britain. It is mentioned in the *Antonine Itinerary,* a document of the late second century AD. The document lists all Roman routes across the empire, 15 of which are within Britain nad three of which pass through this settlement: Iter II was the route from Hadrian's Wall to Richborough in Kent; Iter VI, the route from London to Lincoln; and Iter VIII, the route from York to London.

Though little visible remains, archaeological excavations of Venonae have occurred, and hence the settlement is known to have stretched at least half a kilometer to the southeast. Excavations on the south side of Watling Street have revealed post holes, hearths, gullies, and slots of timber buildings, but so far no complete building plan has been uncovered. Though centrally located, it appears it was important only for that reason. In fact, it is only mentioned once, as late as the second century AD, and the archaeological evidence—pottery—recovered on site dates only as far back as Flavian (c. AD 69–96). As such, though a center of Britain, it was from a commercial or demographic perspective almost insignificant.

One wonders how far advanced Roman geography was that they quite accurately identified this area as the center of England—and constructed their network of roads so that precisely here, two main routes would cross. But, as mentioned, however much the Romans might have known and given to the Brits, this knowledge did not begin with the Romans. It appears that the Celts were already aware of the centricity of this region, and their sacred center was not High Cross, but a hill nearby.

The Celtic omphalos was Croft Hill, 128 meters high, a few miles southwest of Leicester, and 5 miles from High Cross. It is known that the hill was used as a beacon in ancient times and that from its summit several kings of England surveyed their kingdom. Writing about this solitary hill in 1879, local historian T.L. Walker was convinced that this hill was the omphalos of Celtic Britain. British alternative researcher/ writer Paul Devereux agreed.

Most omphali are stand-alone hills, and Croft Hill definitely stands out. Furthermore, Croft Hill is quite conical and, most specifically, is made of granite, two characteristics that would have greatly pleased our ancestors, for omphali were often conical hills. It was a rock in the right shape, of the right material, in the right place.

Today, most of Croft Hill's interior has actually been carved out, which becomes truly visible when one stands on its summit and sees the massive canyon wall the quarrying has created. Noting that in ancient mythology the center of the world was said to be a midway station between Heaven and Hell, someone has definitely been taking this too literally and is making his way to Hell.

Croft Hill was an important gathering place. It underwrites the claim that this sacred center was recognized as such by many, and we should recognize it as such. At Croft, in AD 836, King Wiglaf of Mercia held council, which was attended by dignitaries that included the Archbishop of Canterbury and other bishops. The site was also used as an open-air court, as well as the site of an annual fair.

Both Venonae and Croft Hill are close to the "real" geographical center of England, which underlines that in Celtic times, perhaps as much as 3,000 years ago, if not longer, our ancestors possessed advanced knowledge about the geography of the island on which they lived.

John Michell stated that Caesar noted that the druids were skilled in astronomy and astrology, but also geodesy and land measurement. He added: "Despite Caesar's hint, accurate surveying is not generally attributed to the ancient priesthoods."[5] He went on to argue that it should nevertheless be seen as an ancient skill. In recent decades, we have credited the druids and their predecessor with an advanced understanding of astronomy. But astronomy was also connected to land measurement, according to the doctrine of "as above, so below." Having mastered knowledge of the lay of the land is something we have not yet endowed upon our ancestors.

How they acquired that knowledge is an excellent question, with no known answer. In a culture and a time where navel-gazing has almost become an art form, we should abandon our complacent self-absorption and try to answer how our ancestors could identify a real navel of an enormous island and get it so right. When we do, we will once again becoming truly centered.

The center of the world was a site out of which the nation radiated. This is precisely what we see in Sens and Alaise. We know that Sens was the geographic center of the original or copied Atlantis, but the question is what Alaise was the center of—something older and larger still, for its location was more inland, to the east.

Historians are often at a loss to explain why certain sites were abandoned as capitals in prehistoric times to be replaced by others. Among the myriad possibilities, one should be added: Because the borders of the land had changed, a center had to be defined. This explains why from megalithic to Celtic times, the center of the world moved from Sens to Chartres.

This knowledge was global; the town of Cusco was the navel of the entire Inca culture; *Cusco* means "navel." The Jesuit Father Bernabe Cobo, in his book *The History of the New World* (1653), wrote about the so-called ceques in Cusco. These were lines on which wak'as (shrines) were placed and that were venerated by local people. Ceques were sacred pathways, and Cobo described how the ceques radiated outward from the Temple of the Sun, the very center of the Inca capital. The ceques radiated out between two lines at right angles, which divided the city into four and extended out into the Inca Empire. Each ceque was in the care of a family. Wak'as mostly took the form of stones, springs, hills, or stones on hills.

Both ceques and wak'as reveal the global nature of how our ancestors divided the world; this universal approach makes it clear that this knowledge and methodology of doing things went back to the most ancient of times.

As in Gaul, so in Ireland

Ireland was never conquered by the Romans, which means that Celtic traditions survived longer. Ireland has remembered where its sacred navel was and remains: Uisneach. The sacred division of the island was done in four, the meridian dividing the two halves, then the horizontal cut dividing those parts again. As such, the five provinces were created: Ulster, Leinster, Munster, Connacht, and Meath, the latter around the center at Uisneach. The name *Meath* is derived from the Latin word *media* ("middle"), emphasizing the importance of centrality.

Nemhedh is credited with lighting the first fire at Uisneach. He pushed the Formorians, the legendary giants with one eye, one arm, and one leg, to the coastal fringes. Legend also has it that the followers of Nemhedh eventually dispersed across Europe and were succeeded by the Fir Bolg, who are said to have come to Uisneach, and from there they divided the country.

Each province was ruled by one of five brothers responsible for prosperity, order, and justice for all. It is recorded that each provincial king, when attending these assemblies, had to wear a hero's ring of red gold, which he left behind on his chair as a tribute for the High King. To quote Carry Meeghan: "This formed the basis of sacral kingship, a concept that survives to this day on some of the islands and in certain remote parts of the country."[6] Sacred kingship, of course, was once the norm throughout the world.

Apart from Nemedh, the center is also linked with Lugh, who came here to rescue his mother's people from the heavy taxes demanded from them by the Formorians. After their defeat, Lugh ruled from Uisneach, and it is said he died here also. This brings the concept home that the king ruled from the sacred hill, in the center of his land, Ireland. It also shows the tradition of the king (identified with the sun) marrying the land, often identified with the goddess.

As it forms the sacred center, we could presume that Uisneach would be a majestic or at least intriguing mountain. That is not the case. Uisneach is a 181-meters-high limestone outcrop west of Mullingar. Like so many other omphali, it is more the position and the shape than its height that sets these hills apart.

Archaeological digs have revealed that huge fires were burned there from Neolithic times onward. The near-circular sanctuary, 55 meters in diameters, was defined by a ditch 120 centimeters deep and 1 meter wide at the base. These two concentric beacon rings around the central Uisneach fire point have been identified as a fire eye, which has been discovered on several megalithic depictions, such as the Hill of the Hag at Loughcrew. The Old Irish word *súil* means both "eye" and "sun," and it seems fire connected both.

These ritual fires were then relayed to other hills, and so onward, until all of Ireland was "lit." Beacon fires could indeed be seen from there to more than a quarter of Ireland, and in most directions the hills upon the horizons could relay the message of the beacon as far as the seacoast. John Totland, as recently as 1740, recalled such chains of fires, "which being every one [...] in sight of some other, could not but afford a glorious show over a whole nation."[7] According to Totland, a pair of fires was lit at each site, "one on the cairn," "another on the ground," together evoking the rising sun: "I remember one of those Carns on Fawn-hill [...] known by no other name but that of Bealteine, and facing another such Carn on the top of Inch-hill,"[8] in his native region of the Inishowen peninsula.

Once the fire was lit, other rituals occurred. Tradition has it that at Beltane, cattle were driven through two fires, to preserve them from future accidents. It is this tradition, which survived in many places, from which the expression *a baptism by fire* comes: Literally, cattle, as well as people, were baptized by fire, to protect them from harm. That the tradition is not just medieval folklore but dates from ancient times was substantiated by excavations at Uisneach, where carcasses of animals that had been burned were found on the site; they were sacrifices to the gods.

These were the rituals of the fire god. What about the Mother Goddess whom he married? Uisneach is believed to have been the burial place of a goddess, Eriu, or Erin. She is the goddess who gave her name to the island: Eire, Ireland. The rocks were her bones, the earth her flesh, and the rivers her veins. Legend has it that this Mother Goddess was buried underneath the Cat Stone, on the southwestern slope. The stone is named as such because it is said to resemble a cat. However, its Irish name is *Ail na Mirenn,* or Stone of Divisions, underlining its central location; from here, the "body of the Mother Goddess," Eriu, was divided.

One of the centers of the provinces of Ireland was at Cruachain, the residence of the kings of Connaught, the O'Connor Don. The central feature is the Mound or Rath of Cruachain. She seems to be a local version of Erin and was named after the goddess Crochen Croderg. She was born of the sun goddess Etain (a local version of Lugh?), dropping from her apron as she passed over. When she fell, she went into the ground through the Oweynagat, the Cave of the Cats. Oweynnagat is a natural fissure, about 120 feet deep into the limestone, on the side of one of the earthworks that are part of Cruachain. Apparently, there was once an inscription in the cave, dating from the early Christian era, and written in Ogham, which read: "Stone of Fraech, son of Medbh (Maedbh)."

The cave has a small entrance—easily missed. We should see it as the "vulva" of the Mother Goddess, through which we enter her womb—the underworld. It should thus not come as a surprise that her female organs are aligned to the sun. Her entrance is aligned with the rising sun at midsummer, shining into the cave. *Croderg* itself means "blood red," the color of the setting sun, but also no doubt expressing the menstrual blood, with the sun penetrating into the cave no doubt symbolizing fertilization of the womb by the solar light. It should thus not come as a surprise to learn that this deity had a daughter, the infamous Maebh, who would become the queen of Connaught and whose palace was said to be mound of Rathcroghan—from which the kings ruled. The cave itself is said to be her burial place.

The usage of Oweynnagat is on par with the way our ancestors 20,000 years earlier were using the caves of Lascaux: sacred bellies of Mother Earth, in which contact with the divine was sought. It should be remembered that each conical hill was also the center of the world, from which one could reach the otherworlds, whether that was known as Heaven or Hell.

In his notes on Ireland, dating from AD 82, historian Ptolemy of Alexandria fixes the position of the capital cities of each of the five Irish kingdoms by giving longitude and latitude figures for each of them. Tara is not included, which suggests that, at that time, Uisneach was still the sacred center. In c. AD 400, Tara was the site where St. Patrick entered into a power struggle with the Celtic elite by lighting a rival Spring Equinox ritual fire on the Hill of Slane, as direct competition to the ritual fire lit from Tara, which was supposed to be the first light to be lit.

The word *Tara* simply means "hill." Legend says it contains the tomb of Tea, the queen of the ancestors, in yet another display of the kings marrying the Mother Goddess—in other words, the land. The best known feature of the site is the Mound of the Hostages, the name having nothing to do with any archaeological evidence found there, but the result of 19th-century naming conventions. Its special status is confirmed through various excavations, which have found over a hundred bodies, making it the most "popular" mound in Ireland. It would suggest that certain privileged people were buried in the presence of the tomb of the goddess.

The mound is the oldest monument on site, dating from about 3000 BC and has a short subterranean passage, into which the sun shines on November 8th and February 8th, dates identified as the beginning of winter and spring. The phenomenon works by placing a sill stone at the entrance, aligned to the horizon, so that a beam of light will enter the passage, striking the backstone, where there are carvings with circles and arcs. These must, once again, symbolize a unique interplay between solar deity and the fertility of the mother. We note that the period between the two days roughly coincides with the length of a human pregnancy (nine months).

It is at Tara that the role of sacred kingship has been best preserved. The new king had to seek acceptance from the gods. For this, a sacred stone, the Lia Fail, or Stone of Destiny, had to cry out, showing the divinities had accepted the new ruler. The sacred stone was said to have been brought to Ireland by the Tuatha De Danaan.

The stone is a somewhat ordinary, phallic standing stone, but there is a tradition that links it with the Stone of Destiny that the Scottish kings used in their coronation ceremonies and that therefore might also have ancient Egyptian origins, as the legend states. Before we go there, though, Ireland is able to clearly demonstrate how sacred kingship and marrying the land went hand in hand, and how the land was divided in a very holographic manner.

As in Ireland, So in Egypt

The Temple of Jerusalem was built in the center of the world, and it was to house the Ark of the Covenant. The temple represented the cosmology. The floor, which rose in a series of terraces, was the earth or primeval hill, from which grew lotus or papyrus plants, represented by columns. The roof was the vault of the sky, with depictions of stars and winged sun disks on the ceiling. The entrance section, a wide gate or pylon, represented the mountains behind which the sun rose.

Jerusalem as a center of the world kept its sacredness well into medieval times—if not into our present era. It was the sacred quest of the Crusades to liberate it from the Muslims. Jubilees 8 and Ezekiel specifically identify Jerusalem as the navel of the Earth—where the umbilical cord connects the child with the mother. This rock was called in Hebrew Ebhen Shetiyyah, the Stone of Foundation, and was the first solid thing to be created, placed by God amid the as-yet-boundless fluid of the primeval waters. Legend has it that just as the body of an embryo is built up in its mother's womb from its navel, so God built up the earth concentrically around this stone, the Navel of the Earth. Just as the body of the embryo receives its nourishment from the navel, so the whole Earth, too, receives the waters that nourish it from this Navel.

The center of the human body, halfway up and halfway down its front, is the navel. For this reason, and because it was once attached by the umbilical cord to our maternal source of life and nourishment, the navel provides an image of the notional world center, the spot on the Earth's surface through which runs the universal pole.

For Islam, this concept is situated at Mecca with the Ka'aba, its foundation stone. The sacred stone was said to have been brought to Earth by an angel to record the deeds of the faithful, to be examined hereafter on the Day of Judgment. The stone was the sole object from the pagan temple that the prophet Muhammad kept when he converted the shrine at Mecca into an Islamic temple.

Stecchini argued that he had found a central meridian for Ancient Egypt. The establishment of this meridian bisected the Nile Delta (at 31 degrees 14 minutes East) and allegedly pre-dated the building of the Great Pyramid. Stecchini built upon observations from Napoleon's savants, who observed when they arrived in Egypt in 1798, that the Great Pyramid was situated at the exact apex of the Nile Delta such that an arc centered on the Great Pyramid defined the extent of the Delta, perfectly enclosing its outer perimeter. The northern promontory of the Delta is due north of the pyramid. Since, others have observed that the Great Pyramid sits in the exact center of Earth's land mass. That is, its east-west axis corresponds to the longest land parallel across the Earth, passing through Africa, Asia, and America. Similarly, the longest land meridian on Earth, through Asia, Africa, Europa, and Antarctica, also passes through the pyramid. Statistically, the possibility that this is a coincidence is one in three billion.

In 1882, Robert T. Ballard pointed out that the placement of the Great Pyramid would have allowed the residents of the Nile Delta to easily re-survey their fields every year after the annual flood, using only a plumb-line, by sighting on the apex of the Great Pyramid. He further demonstrated that the combination of the three Giza pyramids would have improved this operation and provided more information than a single pyramid by itself could have.

Stecchini pointed out that the original name that was used by the ancient Egyptians for their country was To-Mera, "the Land that was Measured." The Egyptians were extremely concerned with determining exact boundaries and areas of land surface. The annual inundation of the Nile erased all boundary lines between fields. Herodotus, Plato, Diodorus, Strabo, Clemens of Alexandria, Iamblichus, and others ascribe the origin of geometry to changes that annually took place from the inundation, and to the consequent necessity of adjusting the claims of each person respecting the limits of the lands. These Greek authors were uniform that the ancient Egyptians were far more scientifically advanced than we often give them credit for.

The Egyptian center where the omphalos stone was kept was Heliopolis, but it was not the only town with a benben stone, as the Egyptian sacred stones were called. When Thebes rose to fame, it had its own foundation stone, kept in the Temple of Amun. After the 18th Dynasty, Thebes became known literally as the Heliopolis of the South and became the "center" of Egypt.

It was the controversial Pharaoh Akhenaten who was to establish a third, new center for Egypt: Akhetaten, between Heliopolis and Thebes. Each ancient center was precisely 172 miles from the new capital. The equidistance of the two places is similar to the story of the two doves of Zeus. It was Akhenaten's attempt to balance the power of the old with that of the new, with something of his own—a New Era. As such, he promoted the role of a minor characteristic of the sun, the Aten, the visible aspect of the sun god Ra, to chief deity.

The story of the creation of the new capital is interesting, for it shows us how ancient Egyptians went about these things. First, a site was selected, equidistant between Heliopolis and Thebes, which means that, as did the Celts, the Ancient Egyptians knew far more about the Earth's geography than we officially give them credit. Apparently, the site chosen was revealed by Aten himself, according to inscription on the stela. One of the people intrigued by this new town was Stecchini: "Akhenaten wanted to prove that Thebes could not properly claim to be the geodesic center of Egypt and that he had chosen (in Amarna) the geodesic center conforming to an absolutely rigorous interpretation of maat, the cosmic order of which the dimensions of Egypt were an embodiment."[9]

The new city was then laid out and 14 boundary stelae were erected. These were round-topped stones carved out of solid rock. Each bore a relief and a hieroglyphic inscription that proclaimed the king's commitment to Re-Harakthy-Aten. So here we have the prime functions of town layout: careful selection of a site, the setting of the

271

town's boundary, and only then did the building work begin. The same was present in the building of the Great Pyramid: selection of the site, orientation of the building to the cardinal points, and only then could the construction begin.

The benben or foundation stones themselves were often compared to an egg, as the egg is yet another symbol of creation. The story of an egg is also present in Egypt, where it is linked with Kematef, the primordial snake. Kematef was said to have been the self-begotten, or the creator of his own egg. The serpent was therefore seen as the creator of the nucleus, the omphalos, taking on the role of the creator god Atum of Heliopolis. In the Theban creation myth, the serpent personifies the soul of the primeval island. The coils of Kematef were seen as the stepped terraces that wound their way around the primeval hill. Hence, a spiral path was believed to ascend the primeval hill, the path of the serpent. The presence of a serpent on the mound of creation—paradise—might therefore throw new light on the Christian creation story of the Garden of Eden!

But there is another conclusion, however suggestive, to draw: Was the sacred benben stone of Akhetaten taken to Ireland? This is definitely what the story of Scota implied. Though there is no evidence for this other than legendary, our journey has shown that there is a consistent framework between all of these places, which shows that our ancestors saw the Earth and the land as sacred, and used the stars and geodesy to conform to its sacred nature. They adhered to the notion that a king could only rule over his country if it was properly aligned. For them, that was the true nature of civilization: that the terrestrial realm was properly organized in accordance with the heavens, so that the people could live good lives. For our ancestors, this could only occur by bringing down the divine order to Earth, and the chief executor of this task was the king, who did so from the center of his kingdom. It was his task to make Heaven upon Earth, which was in part a highly technical task, involving finding the center of his kingdom, a task the historical records reveal many nations were able to accomplish with an extraordinary accuracy, revealing yet another lost knowledge and science our ancestors possessed, several of thousands of years ago.

Muscovite historian Nikolai Goncharov marked all the centers of earliest human culture on a globe. As he did so, he began to see a geometric pattern emerge. It was only after Goncharov met Vyacheslav Morozov, a construction engineer, and Valery Makarov, a specialist in electronics, that he was able to extend his research into this. In the end, their findings were published in 1973 in *Khimiya i Zhizn'* (*Chemistry and Life*), the popular science journal of the USSR Academy of Sciences under the title "Is the Earth a Large Crystal?"

They theorized that the earth projected from within itself two geometric grids. The initial form of this grid had 12 pentagonal slabs, a shape known as a dodecahedron, examples of which have actually been found in several ancient cultures. The second grid was formed by 20 equilateral trangins, creating an icosahedron. Superimposing the two grids on the surface of the Earth resulted in mapping an energy structure that was linked with the earth's tectonic plates. The lines tracing out the dual grid coincided with zones of active risings and depressions on the ocean floors, core faults, and mid-oceanic ridges. On the edges of the polygons were regions of seismic and volcanic activity, and magnetic anomalies were found at the vertices of the polygons. Finally, the nodes of the grid were centers of great changes in atmospheric pressure, and hurricanes frequently formed in those areas. Most importantly, though, the scientists noted that to line the system up on the surface of the Earth so that all the factors could be correlated, the point they located as "position one" was that of the Great Pyramid of Giza. Knowing that this pyramid indeed sits in the middle of the Earth's land mass, that should not come as a surprise.

Does it come as any surprise that the dodecahedron was also high on the list of Plato? Plato's *Timaeus* associates the four platonic solids with the four classical elements, adding that "there is a fifth figure (which is made out of 12 pentagons), the dodecahedron—this God used as a model for the twelvefold division of the Zodiac."[10] The zodiac is of course one of the central tenants of astronomy, another key preoccupation of our ancestors, and to find that Plato may have preserved an ancient knowledge that the stars and the Earth were intimately linked should not come as a surprise. Our ancestors were all about "as above, so below," and, based on the extraordinary level of care and detail that went into choosing the position of sacred centers around the world, this was part of a phenomenal framework—one we are only beginning to rediscover.

Conclusion

It has sometimes been my rallying cry toward scientists to come out of their armchairs and go into the field. Alas, when they do so, as is in evidence at Glozel, it is worse than if they had remained behind their desks. Instead, my new motto is that we need to abandon the notion that writing marks the beginning of civilization. It is simply not true and all too convenient for Science. Too much of our human past is not considered as important currently because it sits within "prehistory." Thousands of years of civilization, most chartered by archaeologists, going back to 10,000 years BC, simply do not receive the attention they deserve.

The title of this book is *The Lost Civilization Enigma,* but one of the enigmas is why Science so steadfastly refuses to incorporate some of the found civilizations in what we know about these cultures. So much of this book is not truly lost; it is excluded. On purpose. By a consensus view embedded within the walls of academia, this has grown like a cancer, seen by everyone outside that scientific bowl, but both unnoticed and often reinforced as benign and good by the academics themselves.

Instead, civilization should be redefined as humanity's discovery that there was more to this reality than meets the eye—the birth of encountering the divine and incorporating it within everyday's existence.

J.W. Dunne stated that "there can be no reasonable doubt that the idea of a soul must have first arisen in the mind of primitive man as the result of observation of his dreams. Ignorant as he was, he could have come to no other conclusion but that, in dreams, he left his sleeping body in one universe and went wandering off into another."[1] This I feel, was one of humanity's greatest discoveries. It was the start of humanity's greatest quest, but one that Science has abandoned, several centuries ago.

In the 21st century, there is a major discrepancy between science and religion. Specifically, they study fields that are mutually exclusive: the world of hard, physical matters, and the world of consciousness. Little if no scientific research occurs on the subject of dreaming, and there is generally no scientific research that seriously wants to explore otherworldly realities. The little research that does occur is largely within the bailiwick of the near-death experience (NDE), and this is often executed by doctors whose patients' experiences convinced them that something happened at the threshold of death that was far more complex than Science believes.

Two eminent doctors, Peter Fenwick and Sam Parnia, investigated the experiences of 63 cardiac arrest victims at Southampton General Hospital (Southampton, UK). They concluded that

> these people were having these experiences when we wouldn't expect them to happen, when the brain shouldn't be able to sustain lucid processes or allow them to form memories that would last [...] Essentially, it comes back to the question of whether the mind or consciousness is produced from the brain. If we can prove that the mind is produced by the brain, I don't think there is anything after we die because essentially we are conscious beings. If, on the contrary, the brain

is like an intermediary which manifests the mind, like a television will act as an intermediary to manifest waves in the air into a picture or a sound, we can show that the mind is still there after the brain is dead. And that is what I think these near-death experiences indicate.[2]

The presence of consciousness as a vital ingredient to the universe, separate from the body, is what quantum physics has been trying to make humanity aware of for several decades. Near-death experiences have been around since the beginning of humanity; we can safely assume this, as death has been around since the dawn of humanity. Raymond A. Moody, PhD, MD, considered to be the father of NDEs, wrote *Life after Life* on the subject. He reported that the people who have experienced NDEs state that the experience has dramatically changed their lives. They have become a new being, and often material pursuits are traded in for more spiritual goals. A majority of them have a positive experience: They go through a black tunnel (gate) to enter into brilliant white light. There, they might see deceased family (ancestors), light beings, God, and so on. As late as Ancient Greece, there was an entire industry—like the Elysian Mysteries—in which people were given "controlled" NDEs—chemically induced experiences on par with the accidental nature of NDEs.

This quest did not begin in Greece, though. If anything, it ended there. It was happening in the Tassili and it was happening in the megalithic monuments of western Europe. No doubt, it was happening in caves like Lascaux, 20,000 years ago. In fact, there is evidence to suggest it was happening 450,000 years ago.

Europe's oldest human skull was found in the little French town of Tautavel. Our oldest European ancestor was buried in a cave. Nearby human remains, dated younger but still tens of thousands of years ago, all show evidence of burial. Specifically, these people were placed in caves, which were seen as the womb of the earth and a place where our ancestors would be able to access an Afterlife. As a species, we have been convinced of the reality of an Afterlife for hundreds of thousands of years.

These are explorations of a reality that exists beyond the threshold of what we see and experience in our everyday reality. In my opinion, the pursuit of civilization was precisely to bring some of that otherworldly reality into this one. The common denominator of all civilizations is not writing, as Science would so happily prefer it, but an expression of our ancestors that there was another reality, a belief they expressed in a number of ways: cave paintings, rock art, temple complexes, statues, and, indeed, religious texts. That is what propelled civilization—not writing. If anything, writing was but one step in the process of recording all of this information, which at some point in our past exceeded our ancestors' capacity to keep it all memorized. That's when writing became important.

Michael Talbot, in *The Holographic Universe,* states that NDEs often describe going through a "passageway to the land of the dead."[3] He argues that the similarities between the near-death experience and the Egyptian Book of the Dead are more than coincidence. The Book of the Dead is precisely what it says: a book for the dead on what to do when dead.

Several Egyptologists have spoken about the age of the Book of the Dead and how it was not a product of Ancient Egypt, but was much older. Gaston Maspero stated, in the 19th century, that "The Pyramid Texts carry us so far into the past that I have no way to date them but to say that they were already old five millennia before our era. As extraordinary as that figure may seem [...] those texts already existed before the First Dynasty, and it is up to us, in order to understand them, to place ourselves in the consciousness of those who wrote them down over seven millennia ago."[4]

Science is playing games here. The First Dynasty is seen as the dawn of the Egyptian civilization. The Egyptians considered the Book of the Dead one of their greatest accomplishments, as it documented the journey of the soul in the Afterworld—and there was nothing more important to them in life than accomplishing this journey in death. Maspero states those texts existed before the First Dynasty. So why is the dawn of Egyptian civilization still anchored in that First Dynasty by Science?

If the dawn of civilization were extended backward, many lost civilizations would bubble to the surface. We would learn that the path of civilization is not a nice, straight line leading all the way to the present. It would reveal ups and downs, especially when we look at it on a global scale. We would realize that the Industrial Revolution was not the first time that the world as a whole began to work together. There was a transoceanic and pan-European economy in 3000 BC. Man conquered the Amazon centuries ago, only for the jungle to reclaim its ground. When you pretend that Greek history only began in the eighth century BC, when you ridicule Plato when he speaks about Atlantis, when you attack the likes of Sam Osmanagic with a vengeance that has to be seen to be believed, when you hide the carbon-dating results of the Great Pyramid, you can pretend civilization was linear. But if Science purely did what textbooks say science should do, a completely different picture would emerge—one that shows us that civilization is older, more complex, and overall more interesting than how it is presented now. Overall, it would teach us one important lesson:

We were not the first.

Appendix

A World of Lost Civilizations

North America
Isle Royal, Michigan

Isle Royal is part of the Great Lakes, in the northwest of Lake Superior (Michigan). It is the focal point of a region in which, as early as 3000 BC, major copper mining activities occurred. Archaeology has been unable to identify where the copper was used in North America. The likeliest explanation is that it was exported to Europe, where it was pivotal in the European Bronze Age. Copper mining around Isle Royal stopped at the same time the European Bronze Age ended.

Burrows Cave, Illinois

Somewhere in Illinois, Russell Burrows discovered a cave containing ancient burials. Burrows never revealed the exact location of the site and even may have dynamited its entrance, after years of controversy when he announced his find. The cave allegedly contains human remains in golden sarcophagi, which some have identified as Egyptian nobles from Roman times.

Bimini Crystal, Bahamas

The waters of the coast of Bimini are linked with the saga of Atlantis following the discovery of the so-called Bimini Road in 1968. This 0.5-mile-long stretch of limestone blocks, now underwater, is seen by some as evidence that this land was once above water. Nearby, a crystal ball was allegedly found by Dr. Ray Brown during a dive in 1970. The so-called Bimini Crystal was apparently the central feature of a large crystal construction that Brown found underwater. Since, no further confirmation of the underwater structure has been made, though the crystal exists.

South America

Machu Picchu, Peru

In 1911, while searching for the city of Vilcabamba, the last Inca refuge during the Spanish Conquest of the Inca Empire, Hiram Bingham discovered the lost city of Machu Picchu. Considered one of the most beautiful archaeological sites in the world, the hilltop town built by a 15th-century Inca ruler remained undiscovered for hundreds of years, even though its location was not specifically remote.

Akakor, Brazil/Bolivia/Peru

Journalist Karl Brugger described the existence of an underground civilization Akakor, somewhere in Brazil/Bolivia/Peru. Brugger's information came from self-proclaimed Brazilian Indian chieftain Tatunca Nara. Though Tantunca Nara was subsequently exposed as a fraud, elements of the story were used in *Indiana Jones and the Kingdom of the Crystal Skull,* where the civilization was referred to as Akator. In recent years, however, the Amazon has been identified as the venue for several lost civilizations, which were described by early explorers but subsequently disappeared, their populations killed by the diseases these European explorers brought with them.

Caral, Peru

Caral, in northern Peru, is the site of several pyramids that date back to c. 3200 BC, making them for the scientific community the oldest pyramids ever found, not just in America, but worldwide. Caral was discovered in 1948, but it took another half century before its "hills" were identified as genuine pyramids, thus rewriting the history of Peru, if not the entire world.

Ica Stones, Peru

Dr. Javier Cabrera collected a series of stone artifacts, showing various anomalous depictions, including men using telescopes and humans interacting with dinosaurs. The collection was brought to Cabrera by locals, and some of the stones are known to have been modern fabrications. Some 4,000 objects, however, could be genuine, though even Cabrera's greatest supporters believe the final truth may never be known following the death of Dr. Cabrera.

El Dorado, Ecuador/Peru/Bolivia

The Spanish Conquistadors were told of a tribal chief who covered himself in gold dust, to become El Dorado. Soon, El Dorado transformed into a place, a Lost City of Gold, and many went in pursuit of the wealth and fame that would come to its discoverer. Among these explorers were Francisco Orellana and Gonzalo Pizarro, who departed from Quito in 1541 toward the Amazon Basin. Though he failed to find El Dorado, Orellana did become the first person known to navigate the Amazon River all the way to its mouth.

Paititi, Peru/Bolivia/Brazil

Paititi is a legendary Inca lost city, said to have been the last refuge of the Inca rulers, as well as the retreat center of Inkarri, the founder of the Inca capital, Cusco. Said to be east of the Andes, Paititi is normally situated in the rainforests of southeast Peru, northern Bolivia, or southwest Brazil. Dozens of expeditions have been launched in search of it, starting in 1925 with Percy Harrison Fawcett, who disappeared while looking for it.

Europe

Glozel, France

Located near Vichy, the tiny hamlet of Glozel became the center of international controversy when local farmer Emile Fradin discovered a series of enigmatic engraved stones in 1924. Original claims suggested the artifacts were thousands of years old and would rewrite early European history. Since, the stones have been known to date from various periods, but the site has remained the center of extraordinary controversy.

Visoko, Bosnia-Herzegovina

Since 2005, the small town of Visoko, near the Bosnian capital of Sarajevo, is the focus of the largest archaeological excavation in the world, following the discovery of a series of pyramids. The Pyramid of the Sun and the Moon are the tallest pyramids in the world and likely to be the oldest. The site sits in the heart of a civilization known as Old Europe, which was present in the Balkan from c. 6000 BC to c. 3500 BC. Until their discovery, this civilization was thought not to have built such giant structures.

Hyperborea

Hyperborea was a mythical Greek location, above the "North Winds." For millennia, it was thought to be fictional. Details in various Greek texts allowed archaeo-astronomers to identify the site of its main temple with Callanish, a megalithic stone circle on the Scottish Hebridean Isle of Lewis. It underlines that the Ancient Greeks were intimately familiar with the geography of northern Europe, far beyond their own shores.

Thera/Santorini, Greece

The volcanic island of Thera/Santorini was the site of a major eruption in c. 1500 c. A number of prehistoric towns on the island were subsequently buried under volcanic ash. They were only rediscovered during archaeological excavations in 1967. The eruption is thought to have contributed to the demise of the Minoan Civilization, located on the island of Crete, south of Santorini. Some have identified Santorini with the lost island of Atlantis, but there is no hard evidence to warrant this conclusion.

Sens/Alesia, France

The French towns of Sens and Alesia are both the center of a road network that dates back to prehistoric times. The road network around Sens was discovered by Belgian historian Marcel Mestdagh and linked with the lost civilization of Atlantis, as the structures conform to the dimensions given by Greek historian Plato for this lost civilization. The road network around Alesia was identified by police officer Xavier Guichard, who saw a pan-European network of sites named Alesia (or variations) and roads that seemed to predate the end of the last Ice Age, c. 10,000 BC.

Asia

Troy

For millennia, the site of Troy, the site described in a mythical battle in Homer's *Iliad,* was seen as a fictional setting. In 1868, Heinrich Schliemann dug at the Turkish site of Hisarlik, discovering a prehistoric settlement that he identified with Troy. Though now accepted by archaeology as the site of Troy, there are various details in Homer's account that suggest a northern European setting is more likely. The Baltic region and the area around Cambridge, England, are currently strong contenders for the site of ancient Troy.

Göbekli Tepe, Turkey

Discovered in 1994, the site of Göbekli Tepe, just outside the town of Şanlıurfa, is now the oldest religious site in the world, dated to c. 9,500 BC. It is one of a series of temple complexes, all roughly identical in age, in this region of southeastern Turkey. Their discovery has pushed back the date of civilization in Eurasia by several thousands of years.

Xi'an, China

For most of the 20th century, the existence of pyramids near the Chinese city of Xi'an was rumored, but no formal verification of their presence could be attained. In 1994, German tour operator Hartwig Hausdorf was able to take a series of photographs during visits to the site, confirming their existence. Since, China has opened its country to tourists, and thousands have been able to visit these structures that were built by the earliest Chinese emperors. Some are said to have been buried with vast treasures, which was validated when the Terracotta Army was found nearby. Many of the pyramids themselves, however, still await further archaeological excavation.

Shambhala

Shambhala is a mythical kingdom hidden somewhere in Inner Asia. It is seen as a Buddhist Pure Land, a kingdom where the inhabitants have attained great magical powers. Its location is unknown, but thought to be somewhere in or near Tibet. Various ancient Tibetan Buddhist texts and traditions mention it, and as a result several expeditions have been launched in search of it, especially by Westerners in the early part of the 20th century, when Tibet's borders were closed to foreigners. Some of these explorers were the first to reach the Tibetan capital of Lhasa.

Africa
Hall of Records, Egypt
The Hall of Records is said to be located near the Sphinx and Great Pyramid in Cairo. American visionary Edgar Cayce described the existence of this secret underground location, stating that, when found (which was to occur before the turn of the 21st century), it would contain records of Atlantis. Recent discoveries have shown there is a vast underground network near and under the pyramid complex, though whether this is related to Cayce's prophecy remains speculation.

Tassili n'Ajjer, Algeria
The Tassili n'Ajjer is a mountain range in the Algerian section of the Sahara Desert, known for its extensive examples of prehistoric rock art. The engravings and depictions, dating from c. 10,000 BC to 1200 BC, show a scenery and climate vastly different from the current harsh desert conditions. The area was once lush with vegetation and even had lakes, all teeming with life. When the conditions changed, the people moved elsewhere and may have been at the origin of the Egyptian civilization.

Undefined
Mu
Mu, sometimes known as Lemuria, is a mythical civilization in Asia, most often placed in the Indian Ocean. The first person to write about Mu was 19th-century traveler Augustus

LePlongeon, who claimed Mu was at the origins of the Egyptian and Mesoamerican civilization, which he claimed were created by refugees from Mu. Though LePlongeon located Mu in the Atlantic Ocean, in the early 20th century traveler James Churchward moved it to the Pacific, claiming to have found evidence for its existence in a series of secret documents in Indian temple libraries. Almost a century later, there is no evidence to suggest that the story of Mu has any historical foundation.

Atlantis

Plato's account of Atlantis, a continent that disappeared c. 12,000 years ago, continues to be seen as purely fictional by most archaeologists and scientists, even though Plato and other Greek contemporary authors underlined its historical origins. Located outside the Pillars of Hercules (that is, Gibraltar), the legendary lost civilization has been placed all over Europe and America, but remains elusive. Its most likely position is somewhere in the Atlantic Ocean, whose sea level was lower during the last Ice Age.

NOTES

Chapter 1

1. Gerard, *Glozel*, p. 18.
2. Ibid., p. 42.
3. Ibid., p. 18.
4. Ibid., p. 31.
5. Cordier, *The Travels,* p. 333.
6. Cathie, *The Bridge,* p. 113.
7. Page 45 of the reported book.
8. Cathie, *The Bridge,* p. 113.
9. Ibid, p. 117.
10. Private communication between Hartwig Hausdorf and the author, 1995.
11. Ibid.
12. Anthony Harding. Speech at the European Association of Archaeologists conference, September 2008, University of Malta.
13. "Aliens."
14. According to my notes taken during the ICBP 2008 Conference in Sarajevo, where Oleg Kharoshkin spoke.
15. Osmanagic, *About,* p. 15.
16. "Bosnian."

17. Marija Gimbutas wrote in *The Goddesses and Gods of Old Europe,* p. 131.

18. "Conclusions."

19. Cremo and Thompson, *Forbidden*, p. xxxi.

20. Ibid., p. 750.

21. *Antiquity, Volume 67,* p. 904.

22. *Atlantis Rising Magazine, No. 30,* November–December 2001, p. 20.

23. *Antiquity,* p. 238.

24. *The Forbidden Archaeologist,* Chapter 4, quoted at *www. forbiddenarcheologist.com/chapter.htm.*

Chapter 2

1. Finley, "Simon," p. 106.

2. Strabo, *Geography,* Book 13, chapter 1, section 27.

3. Finley, "Simon," p. 171.

4. Colvin, *Geographical,* p. 3.

5. Piggott, *Ancient,* p. 126.

6. *Odyssey,* x, 190–192.

7. Butler, *The Iliad*, 2007, p. 294.

8. Schulz, *Callanish,* p. 11.

9. Armit, *The Archaeology,* p. 82.

10. Ibid., p. 14.

11. Kelley, Milone, and Aveni, *Exploring,* p. 184.

12. Burl, "Memories."

13. Ibid.

14. McKerracher, "Was Arthur?"

15. *Proceedings.*

16. Ellis, *Scota,* p. 1.

17. Marshall, *Europe's,* pp. 3–4.

18. Ibid., p. 4.

19. Lhote, *The Search.*

20. Ibid.
21. Ibid. (This is from the color photo section of the book, which has no page numbers.)
22. Ibid.
23. "Maltese."
24. Knox, "Do These?"
25. Curry, "Göbekli?"
26. "Civilization."

Chapter 3
1. *Olney Daily Mail,* July 27, 1984.
2. Flavin, "Falling."
3. Ibid.
4. *The Chronicle,* p. 12.
5. Ibid, p. 13.
6. Ibid, p. 60.
7. Ibid, p. 13
8. Back cover.
9. Mann, *1491,* p. 4.
10. "The Road."
11. Mann, *1491,* p. 207
12. Ibid., p. 205.
13. Saxena, "The Mother."
14. Cabrera, *The Message,* p. 14.
15. Ibid., p. 47.
16. Ibid., p. 27.
17. *The Mysterious Origins of Man,* NBC TV, February 1996.
18. Cabrera, *The Message,* p. 45.
19. Ibid., p. 46
20. Ibid., p. 46
21. Von Däniken, *Arrival,* p. 64.
22. Burgaleta, *José.*

23. Sierra, "First," page 4.

24. Ibid.

25. Ibid.

26. Ibid, page 6.

27. Wilkins, *Secret,* p. 232.

28. Private correspondence between Maria del Carmen and the author.

29. Hearn, "Ancient."

Chapter 4

1. Gill, "Atlantis."

2. Plato, *Timaeus,* 24a.

3. Annas, *Plato,* p. 42.

4. Bauval, *Secret,* p. 195. Also see www.robertbauval.co.uk/articles/ articles/sc_chapt9.html.

5. Private correspondence with the author. The source asked for his name to be withheld.

6. Ibid.

7. Ibid.

8. See the Website of the American Research Center in Egypt at *www.arce.org/main/about/historyandmission.*

9. Ibid.

10. Ibid.

11. Hawass, "Keeping."

12. Hawass, "The Story."

13. Ibid.

14. Hancock, "Information."

15. Hawass, "Keeping."

16. Hawass, "Sphinx."

17. "Egypt."

18. Abdelhadi, "Egypt."

19. Ibid.

20. Hancock, "Information."

21. Ibid.

22. Ibid.

23. Picknett and Prince, *The Stargate,* p. 77.

24. Bauval, "Egyptology."

25. Ibid.

26. From the private blog *politicalarchaeology.wordpress.com/page/3/.*

27. Ibid.

28. Ibid.

29. "Egyptian Flare."

30. Milson, Peter (ed.), "Age of the Sphinx" (transcript of program transmitted on 27 November 1994), Broadcasting Support Services, London, 1994, p. 20.

31. Bauval, *Secret,* p. 198.

32. Hancock, "Information."

33. Bauval, *Secret,* p. 194.

34. Thom, *Megalithic,* p. 43.

35. Rolleston, *Myths,* p. 48.

36. *Bulletin de la Société d'Anthropologie,* Vol 4, Issue 4, p. 38.

37. Settegast, *Plato,* p. 9.

38. Ibid.

39. Ibid, pp. 69–70.

Chapter 5

1. "The Museum."

2. Ibid.

3. Ibid.

4. De Solla Price, "2,000."

5. Ibid.

6. Cic. Nat de. 2.34-35.

7. De Solla Price, "2,000."

8. Chatelain, *Our Cosmic,* p. 98.

9. Ibid, p. 99.
10. De Solla Price, "An Ancient."
11. Freeth, et al., "Decoding."
12. Ibid.
13. "Antikythera."
14. *Scientific American,* June 1959, pp.60–67.
15. The endorsement can be found on the cover of Robert Temple's *The Crystal Sun.*
16. Temple, *The Crystal,* p. 8.
17. Ibid., p. 12.
18. *Journal of the Optical Society of America, Vol. 35, Number 5,* May 1945, p. 357.
19. Temple, *The Crystal,* p. 124.
20. Ibid., p. 173.
21. "The Bimini Wall" (first aired February 1980), part of the series *In Search Of.*
22. Little, "Dr. Ray."
23. Private correspondence between Arthur Fanning and the author.
24. Little, "Dr. Ray."
25. See my book *The Ancient Alien Question* for a detailed discussion of why these skulls are ancient.

Chapter 6
1. Ritter, "Die Goldene."
2. Ibid.
3. Ibid.
4. Private correspondence between Jack Churchward and the author.
5. Blavatsky, *The Secret,* p. 249.
6. Coonan, "A Meeting."
7. Forsyth, *Report,* p. 61.
8. "Taproane," Chapter XXIV.

9. Xianlin et al, *Ancient,* p. xi.

10. Ibid.

11. Wilford, "Mummies."

12. Ibid.

13. Liu,"Migration."

14. Rudgley, *The Lost,* front flap.

15. Quoted in Devereux, *Stone Age,* p. 115.

Chapter 7

1. Michell, *At the Centre,* p. 8.

2. Ibid., p. 11.

3. Collins, *Gods,* p. 167.

4. Britton, *The Beauties,* p. 463.

5. Michell, *At the Centre,* p. 14.

6. Meehan, "The Traveller's."

7. Dames, *Mythic,* pp. 206–208.

8. Ibid.

9. Tompkins, *Secrets,* p. 343.

10. Plato, *Timaeus.*

Conclusion

1. Dunne, *An Experiment,* p. 9.

2. Petre, "Soul-Searching."

3. Talbot, *The Holographic,* p. 247.

4. Maspero, *Etudes,* p. 236.

Bibliography

Abdelhadi, Magdi. "Egypt Antituities Official Held." BBC News Website, September 17, 2007. *news.bbc.co.uk/2/hi/middle_east/6999298.stm*.

Adovasio J.M., with Jake Page. *The First Americans: In Pursuit of Archaeology's Greatest Mystery.* New York: Random House, 2002.

"Aliens to Science." The Archaeological Park Website, April 3, 2008. *piramidasunca.ba/en/index.php/aliens-to-science-and-the-professors-of-archaeology-and-geology-opposition.html*.

Allen, Richard Hinckley. *Star-Names and Their Meanings.* London: G.E. Stechert, 1899.

Annas, J. *Plato: A Very Short Introduction* Oxford University Press, 2003.

"Antikythera Mechanism." World-Mysteries.com Website. *www.world-mysteries.com/sar_4.htm*.

Appleby, Nigel. *Hall of the Gods. The Quest to Discovery the Knowledge of the Ancients.* London: William Heinemann, 1998.

Armit, Ian. *The Archaeology of Skye and the Western Isles.* Edinburgh: Edinburgh University Press, 1996.

Bauval, Robert. *Secret Chamber: The Quest for the Hall of Records.* London: Century Books, 1999.

———. "Egyptology and Anti-Semitism." Robert Bauval's Website. *www.robertbauval.co.uk/ articles/articles/hawass1.html*.

——. *The Egypt Code.* London: Century, 2006.

Bauval, Robert, and Adrian Gilbert. *The Orion Mystery: Unlocking the Secrets of the Pyramids.* London: William Heinemann, 1994.

Blashford-Snell, John, and Richard Snailham. *Kota Mama*: *Retracing the Lost Trade Routes of Ancient South American Peoples.* London: Headline, 2000.

Blavatsky, H.P. *The Secret Doctrine: The Synthesis of Science, Religion, and Philosophy.* Theosophical University Press Online Website. *www.theosociety.org/pasadena/sd/sd-hp.htm.*

"Bosnian Pyramids, Part II, No Photos Please!" Archaeologica.org Website. *archaeologica.boardbot.com/viewtopic.php?p=8728&sid =17981648b7a83a4b73d8f67e4c93c6e2#p8728.*

Britton, John. *The Beauties of England and Wales, Volume 9,* 1807.

Broad, William J. *The Oracle: The Lost Secrets and Hidden Message of Ancient Delphi.* New York: Penguin, 2006.

Brophy, Thomas G. *The Origin Map: Discovery of a Prehistoric, Megalithic, Astrophysical Map and Sculpture of the Universe.* Lincoln, Neb.: Writers Club Press, 2002.

Budge, E.A. Wallis. *The Egyptian Heaven and Hell.* Chicago, Ill.: Open Court, 1925.

——. *Osiris and the Egyptian Resurrection.* New York: Dover Books, 1973.

——. *The Gods of the Egyptians, or Studies in Egyptian Mythology.* London: Methuen and Co., 1904.

Burgaleta, Claudio M. *José de Acosta, S.J., 1540–1600: His life and Thought.* Chicago, Ill.: Jesuit Way, 1999.

Burl, Aubrey. "Memories of Callanish (column)." *British Archaeology,* February 2002. Retrieved February 8, 2010. *www.britarch.ac.uk/ ba/ba63/column2.shtml.*

Burrows, Russell, and Fred Rydholm. *The Mystery Cave of Many Faces: A History of Burrows Cave.* Marquette, Mich.: Superior Heartland, 1992.

Butler, Samuel. *The Iliad.* New York: Dover Publications, 1999.

Buttler, Alan. *The Bronze Age Computer Disc.* London: Quantum, 1999.

Byron de Prorok, Count. *In Quest of Lost World. Journey to Alveria, Ethiopia, Yucatan and Beyond.* Kempton, Ill.: Adventures Unlimited Press, 2002.

Castleden, Roney. *Atlantis Destroyed.* London: Routledge, 1998.

Cathie. Bruce L. *The Energy Grid: Harmonic 695: The Pulse of the Universe.* Tehachapi, Calif.: America West Publishers, 1990.

———. *The Bridge to Infinity.* Kempton, Ill.: Adventures Unlimited Press, 1997.

Chatelain, Maurice. *Our Cosmic Ancestors.* Sedona, Ariz.: Temple Golden Publications, 1988.

Childress, David Hatcher. *Lost Cities of China, Central Asia & India.* Stelle, Ill.: Adventures Unlimited Press, 1985.

———. *Lost Cities and Ancient Mysteries of South America.* Stelle, Ill.: Adventures Unlimited Press, 1986.

———. *Lost Cities and Ancient Mysteries of Africa and Arabia.* Kempton, Ill.: Adventures Unlimited Press, 1990.

———. *Lost Cities of North & Central America.* Stelle, Ill.: Adventures Unlimited Press, 1992.

———. *Ancient Tonga & The Lost City of Mu'a.* Kempton, Ill.: Adventures Unlimited Press, 1996.

———. *Lost Cities of Atlantis, Ancient Europe and the Mediterranean.* Kempton, Ill.: Adventures Unlimited Press, 1996.

———. *Technology of the Gods: The Incredible Sciences of the Ancients.* Kempton, Ill.: Adventures Unlimited Press, 2000.

The Chronicle of Anakor by Karl Brugger. Stangrist.com: Adventures into the Unknown! Website. *www.stangrist.com/Akakor.pdf.*

Cabrera, Javier. *The Message of the Engraved Stones of Ica.* Self-published, 1976.

"Civilization Collapse." Blog of Joshua Paul. *civilizationcollapse. blogspot.co.uk/2009/03/Göbekli-tepe.html.*

Clark, R.T. Rundle. *Myth and Symbol in Ancient Egypt.* London: Thames & Hudson, 1959.

Collins, Andrew. *From the Ashes of Angels: The Forbidden Legacy of a Fallen Race.* London: Michael Joseph, 1996.

———. *Gods of Eden: Egypt's Lost Legacy and the Genesis of Civilisation.* London: Headline, 1998.

———. *Gateway to Atlantis: The Search for the Source of Lost Civilisation.* London: Headline, 2000.

"Conclusions of the First Internationals Scientific Conference About the Bosnian Pyramids." Internationals Scientific Conference Bosnian Valley of the Pyramids Website. *www.icbp.ba/2008/.*

Colvin, Verplanck. *Geographical and Mathematical Discussion of Plutarch's Account of Ancient Voyages to the New World.* New York: Albany Institute of History and Art, C. Van Benthuysen & Sons, 1893.

Coonan, Clifford. "A Meeting of Civilisations: The Mystery of China's Celtic Mummies." *The Independent,* March 5, 2012. Available on-line at *lewrockwell.com/spl4/china-celtic-mummies.html.*

Cordier, Henri. *The Travels of Marco Polo.* Toronto, Ontario: Courier Dover Publications, 1993.

Cremo, Michael, and Richard L. Thompson. *Forbidden Archaeology: The Hidden History of the Human Race.* San Diego, Calif.: Bhaktivedanta Institute, 1993.

Cruttenden, Walter. *Lost Star of Myth and Time.* Pittsburgh, Pa.: St. Lynn's Press, 2006.

Cunliffe, Barry. *Facing the Ocean: The Atlantic and its People.* Oxford, UK: Oxford University Press, 2001.

Curry, Andrew. "Göbekli Tepe: The World's First Tmeple?" *Smithsonian* magazine, November 2008. *www.smithsonianmag. com/history-archaeology/gobekli-tepe.html.*

Dames, Michael. *Mythic Ireland.* London: Thames & Hudson, 1992.

De Jonge, Reinoud M., and Jay Stuart Wakefield. *How the Sun God Reach America. c.2500 BC: A Guide to Megalithic Sites.* Kirkland, Wash.: MCS Inc., 2002.

De Solla Price, Derek J. "2,000 Year Old Greek Computer Calculated Motions of Stats and Planets." Freedom Network—williambova. net Website. *uts.cc.utexas.edu/~wbova/fn/history/2000_6_01.htm.* From the June 1959 issue of *Scientific American* (pp. 60–67); updated September 28, 1998 by Rupert Russell.

———. "An Ancient Greek Computer." Hellenica Website. *www. mlahanas.de/Greeks/SCAMKythera.htm.* From the June 1959 issue of *Scientific American* (pp. 60–67).

Devereux, Paul. *Re-Visioning the Earth: A Guide to Opening the Healing Channels Between Mind and Nature.* New York: Fireside, 1996.

———. *The Long Trip: A Prehistory of Psychedelia.* New York: Penguin/ Arkana, 1997.

———. *Stone Age Soundtracks: The Acoustic Archaeology of Ancient Sites.* London: Vega, 2001.

Dunbavin, Paul. *The Atlantis Researches: The Earth's Rotation in Mythology and Prehistory.* Long Eaton, UK: Third Millennium Publishing, 1995.

Dunne, J.W. *An Experiment with Time.* Hampton Roads Publishing Company, 2001.

"Egypt Politics & Security." Menas Associates Website, September 10, 2008. *www.menas.co.uk/pubsamples/Egypt%20Politics%20 and%20Security%20-%2009.10.08.pdf.*

"Egyptian Flare, Sedona Connection." Sedona Red Rock News Website, August 15, 2007. *www.redrocknews.com/ news/egyptian-flare-sedona-connection.html.*

Ellis, Ralph. *Scota: Egyptian Queen of the Scots.* Kempton, Ill.: Adventures Unlimited Press, 2006.

Erlingsson, Ulf. *Atlantis: From a Geographer's Perspective: Mapping the Fairy Land.* Miami Springs, Fla.: Lindorm Publishing, 2004.

Evans, Lorraine. *Kingdom of the Ark: The Startling Story of How the Ancient British Race Is Descended from the Pharaohs.* London: Simon & Schuster, 2000.

Faulkner, R.O. *The Ancient Egyptian Book of the Dead.* London: The British Museum Press, 2004.

Finley, Moses. "Simon Hornblower." *The World of Odysseus,* Folio Society, 2002.

Flavin, Richard. "Falling into Burrows' Cave." Flavin's Corner Website. *www.flavinscorner.com/falling.htm.*

Flem-Ath, Rand, and Rose Flem-Ath. *When The Sky Fell: In Search of Atlantis.* New York: St Martin's Press, 1995.

Forsyth, T.D., *Report of a Mission to Yarkund.* Calcutta, India: Foreign Department Press, 1875.

Freeth, T., et al. "Decoding the ancient Greek Astronomical Calculator Known as the Antikythera Mechanism. *Nature, volume 444,* November 30, 2006, pp. 587–91. Available at *www.nature.com/nature/journal/v444/n7119/abs/nature05357.html.*

Gerard, Alice. *Glozel: Bones of Contention.* New York: iUniverse, Inc. 2005.

Gerber, Pat. *Stone of Destiny.* Edinburgh: Canongate, 1997.

Gill, N.S. "Atlantis: Plato's Atlantis from the Timaeus." About.com Website, Ancient/Classical History section. *ancienthistory.about.com/od/lostcontinent/qt/072507Atlantis.htm.*

Gimbutas, Marija. *The Goddesses and Gods of Old Europe, 6500–3500 BC: Myths and Cult Images.* Berkeley, Calif.: California University Press, 1982.

Gooch, Stan. *Cities of Dreams: When Women Ruled the Earth.* London: Aulis Books, 1995.

Grann, David. *The Lost City of Z: A Legendary British Explorer's Deadly Quest to Uncover the Secrets of the Amazon.* New York: Simon & Schuster, 2009.

Hale, Christopher. *Himmler's Crusade: The True Story of the 1938 Nazi Expedition into Tibet.* London: Bantam Press, 2003.

Hancock, Graham. *Fingerprints of the Gods: A Quest for the Beginning and the End.* London: Heinemann, 1995.

———. *Underworld: Flooded Kingdoms of the Ice Age.* London: Michael Joseph, 2002.

Hancock, Graham. "Information on the Great Pyramid and Sphinx." Morgana's Observatory Website. *www.dreamscape.com/morgana/ hancock.htm.*

Hancock, Graham, and Robert Bauval. *Keepers of Genesis: A Quest for the Hidden Legacy of Mankind.* London: Heinemann, 1996.

Hapgood, Charles. *Maps of the Ancient Sea Kings: Evidence of Advanced Civilization in the Ice Age.* Kempton, Ill.: Adventures Unlimited Press, 1996.

Hausdorf, Hartwig. *Die Weisse Pyramide: Ausserirdische Spuren in Ostasien.* Munich, Germany: Langen Müller, 1994.

———. *Nicht von dieser Welt: Dinge, Die Es Nicht Geben Dürfte.* Munich, Germany: Herbig, 2008.

Hawass, Zahi. "Keeping the Great Sphinx's Paws Dry." Zahi Hawass's Website. *www.drhawass.com/blog/keeping-great-sphinx's-paws-dry.*

———. "Sphinx Scientific Update Report." Zahi Hawass's Website. *www.drhawass.com/blog/sphinx-scientific-update-report.*

———. "The Story of the Sphinx." *www.drhawass.com/blog/ story-sphinx.*

Hearn, Kelly. "Ancient 'Lost City' Discovered in Peru, Official Claims." National Geographic News Website, January 16, 2008. *news.nationalgeographic.com/news/2008/01/080116-lost-city.html.*

Hope, Orville L. *6000 Years of Seafaring.* Gastonia, N.C.: Self-published, 1983.

Hubbard, Harry. *Ancient Mediterranean Treasure in North America: Tomb Chronicles Part I.* Coosa, Ga.: Lazeria Music and Publishing, 2006.

James, Peter, and Nick Thorpe. *Ancient Mysteries.* New York: Ballantine Books, 1999.

Joseph, Frank. *The Lost Pyramids of Rock Lake: Wisconsin's Sunken Civilization.* St. Paul, Minn.: Galde Press, 1992.

——. *Atlantis in Wisconsin: New Revelations About Lost Sunken City.* St. Paul, Minn.: Galde Press, 1995.

——. *The Lost Treasure of King Juba: The Evidence of Afriancs in America Before Columbus.* Rochester, Vt.: Bear & Co., 2003.

Kelley, David H., Eugene F. Milone, and A.F. Aveni. *Exploring Ancient Skies: An Encyclopedic Survey of Archaeoastronomy.* New York: Springer, 2005.

Knox, Tom. "Do These Stones Mark the Site of the Garden of Eden?" Mail Online Website, March 5, 2009. *www.dailymail. co.uk/sciencetech/article-1157784/Do-mysterious-stones-mark-site-Garden-Eden.html.*

Langdon, Robert John. *Prehistoric Britain: The Stonehenge Enigma.* Epping, UK: ABC Publishing Group, 2010.

Lawton, Ian, and Chris Ogilvie-Herald. *Gizeh: The Truth. The People, Politics & History Behind the World's Most Famous Archaeological Site.* London: Virgin Books, 1999.

Lehner, Mark. *The Complete Pyramids.* London: Thames & Hudson, 1997.

Lewis-Williams, David. *The Mind in the Cave: Consciousness and the Origins of Art.* London: Thames & Hudson, 2002.

Lhote, Henri. *The Search for the Tassili Frescoes: The Rock Paintings of the Sahara.* London: Hutchinson, 1959.

Little, Greg. "Dr. Ray Brown's 'Atlantean' Crystal: What Is the Full Story?" *Alternate Perceptions Magazine, issue #155* December 2010. Available at the Alternate Perceptions Magazine Online Website *www.mysterious-america.net/brown'scrystal.html.*

Liu, Xinru (2001), "Migration and Settlement of the Yuezhi-Kushan. Interaction and Interdependence of Nomadic and Sedentary Societies," *Journal of World History 12 (2):* 261–292.

Maclellan, Alec. *The Lost World of Agharti: The Mystery of Vril Power.* London: Souvenir Press, 1996.

Mahan, Joseph B. *The Secret: America in World History Before Columbus.* Columbus, Ga.: Self-published, 1983.

———. *North American Sun Kings: Keepers of the Flame.* Columbus, Ga.: ISAC Press, 1992.

"Maltese Claims Extraordinary Discovery in Sahara Desert." The Malta Independent Online Website, December 23, 2007. *www. independent.com.mt/news.asp?newsitemid=62457.*

Mann, Charles C. *1491: New Revelations of the Americas Before Columbus.* New York: Vintage Books, 2005.

Marchant, Jo. *Decoding the Heavens: Solving the Mystery of the World's First Computer.* London: William Heinemann, 2008.

Marshall, Peter. *Europe's Lost Civilization: Uncovering the Mysteries of the Megaliths.* London: Headline, 2004.

Maspero, Gaston. *Etudes de Mythologie et d'Archeologie Egyptiennes, volume 2.* Paris: Lerouxm 1893.

McKenna, Terence. *Food of the Gods: The Search for the Original Tree of Knowledge.* New York: Bantam Books, 1993.

McKerracher, Archie. "Was Arthur a Scot?" *ftp.cirr.com/pub/ SCRIBE/History/Arthscot.Txt.*

Meehan, Cary. *The Traveller's Guide to Sacred Ireland.* Gothic Image Publications Website. *www.gothicimage.co.uk/books/ sacredireland1.html.*

Mehler, Stephen S. *The Land of Osiris: An Introduction to Khemitology.* Kempton, Ill.: Adventures Unlimited Press, 2001.

Menzies, Gavin. *1421: The Year China Discovered the World.* London: Bantam Press, 2002.

———. *1434: The Year a Magnificent Chinese Fleet Sailed to Italy and Ignited the Renaissance.* London: HarperCollins, 2008.

———. *The Lost Empire of Atlantis: History's Greatest Mystery Revealed.* London: Swordfish, 2011.

Mestdagh, Marcel. *De Vikingen bij Ons: Het Grote Leger (879–892) in België en Frankrijk.* Ghent, Belgium: Stichting Mens & Kultuur, 1989.

——. *Atlantis: Het Ile-de-Framce = het Atlantis van Plato*. Ghent, Belgium: Stichting Mens & Kultuur, 1990.

Michell, John. *The Dimensions of Paradise: The Proportions and Symbolic Numbers of Ancient Cosmology*. San Francisco, Calif.: Harper & Row, 1988.

——. *At the Centre of the World. Polar Symbolism Discovered in Celtic, Norse and Other Ritualized Landscapes*. London: Thames and Hudson, 1994.

Moffat, Alistair. *The Sea Kingdoms: The Story of Celtic Britain & Ireland*. London: HarperCollins, 2001.

——. *Before Scotland: The Story of Scotland Before History*. London: Thames & Hudson, 2005.

Morrison, Tony. *Pathways to the Gods: The Mystery of the Andes Lines*. ChicagoIll.: Academy Chicago Publishers, 1988.

"The Museum Gallery: The Antikythera Mechanism." The International Society for the Research and Preservation of Paranormal Artifacts Website. *www.lehigh.edu/~x010/ antikythera.html*.

Naydler, Jeremy. *Temple of the Cosmos: The Ancient Egyptian Experience of the Sacred*. Rochester, Vt.: Inner Traditions, 1996.

——. *Shamanic Wisdom in the Pyramid Texts. The Mystical Tradition of Ancient Egypt*. Rochester, Vt.: Inner Traditions, 2005.

Neugebauer, Otto, and Richard A. Parker. *Egyptian Astronomical Texts I: The Early Decans*. Providence, R.I.: Brown University Press, 1960.

Nur, Amos, with Dawn Burgess. *Apocalypse: Earthquakes, Archaeology, and the Wrath of God*. Princeton, N.J./Oxford, UK: Princeton University Press, 2008.

Oppenheimer, Stephen. *Eden in the East: The Drowned Continent of Southeast Asia*. London: Phoenix, 1999.

Osmanagic, Muris. *About the Cultural Layer of the Bosnian Pyramid*. Sarajevo: Private publication, 2008.

Petre, J. "Soul-searching Doctors Find Life After Death," *The Sunday Telegraph,* October 22, 2000.

Picknett, Lynn, and Clive Prince. *The Stargate Conspiracy: Revealing the Truth Behind Extraterrestrial Contact, Military Intelligence and the Mysteries of Ancient Egypt.* London: Little, Brown & Co, 1999.

Piggott, Stuart. *Ancient Europe.* Edinburgh: Edinburgh University Press, 1965.

Pinchbeck, Daniel. *2012: The Return of Quetzalcoatl.* New York: Jeremy Tarcher, 2006.

Pitts, Mike. *Hengeworld.* London: Arrow, 2001.

Plato, *Timaeus.* The Internet Classics Archive Website. *classics.mit. edu/Plato/timaeus.html.*

Poe, Richard. *Black Spark, White Fire. Did African Explorers Civilize Ancient Europe?* Rocklin, Calif.: Prima Publishing, 1997.

Proceedings of the Society of Antiquaries of Scotland, Volume 8, 1871, p. 80.

Pryor, Francis. *Seahenge: A Quest for Life and Death in Bronze Age Britain.* London: HarperCollins, 2002.

Radka, Lary Brian (ed). *The Electric Mirror on the Pharos Lighthouse and Other Ancient Lighting.* Parkersburg, W.V.: The Einhorn Press, 2006.

Rice, Michael. *Egypt's Making: The Origins of Ancient Egypt 5000–2000 BC.* London: Routledge, 1990.

Richer, Jean. *Sacred Geography of the Ancient Greeks: Astrological Symbolism in Art, Architecture, and Landscape.* Albany, N.Y.: State University of New York Press, 1994.

Ritter, Thomas. "Die Goldene Tempelbibliothek von Mu." Erlebnis Reisen Website, August 2010.

"The Road to Now." Human Journey Website. *www.humanjourney. us/1491.html.*

Rolleston, Thomas William. *Myths & Legends of the Celtic Race.* New York: Mundus Publishing, 1911.

Rudgley, Richard. *The Lost Civilizations of the Stone Age.* New York: The Free Press, 1999.

Rydholm, Fred. *Michigan Copper: The Untold Story.* Marquette, Mich.: Winter Cabin Books, 2006.

Salazar, Fernando, and Edgar Salazar. *Cusco and the Sacred Valley of the Incas.* Cusco, Peru: Tanpu, 2003.

Sarmast, Robert. *Discovery of Atlantis: The Startling Case for the Island of Cyprus.* San Rafael, Calif.: Origin Press, 2004.

Saxena, Shobhan. "The Mother of All Civilisations." *The Times of India* Website, December 16, 2007. *articles.timesofindia. indiatimes.com/2007-12-16/science/27988573_1_civilisation- pyramids-discovery.*

Schele, Linda, and David Friedel. *A Forest of Kings: The Untold Story of the Ancient Maya.* New York: William Morrow, 1990.

Schele, Linda, and Peter Mathews. *The Code of Kings: The Language of Seven Sacred Maya Temples and Tombs.* New York: Scribner, 1998.

Scherz, James P., and Russell E. Burrows. *Rock Art Pieces from Burrow's Cave. Vol I.* Madison, Wisc.: Ancient Earthworks Society, 1992.

Schmidt, Klaus. *Sie Baute die Ersten Tempel: Das Rätselhafte Heiligtum der Steinzeitjäger.* Munich: Deutscher Taschenbuch Verlag, 2006.

Schulz, Hellmut. *Callanish: A Guide to the Standing Stones and the Callanish Complex.* 1990.

Schwartz, Jeffrey H. *Sudden Origins. Fossils, Genes, and the Emergence of Species.* New York: John Wiley, 1999.

Sellers, Jane. *The Death of the Gods in Ancient Egypt: An Essay on Egyptian Religion and the Frame of Time.* London: Penguin, 1992.

Settegast, Mary. *Plato, Prehistorian: 10,000 to 5,000 BC: Myth, Religion, Archaeology.* Hudson, N.Y.: Lindisfarne Press, 1990.

Sierra, Javier. "First Report: Inca Gold." The Official Graham Hancock Website. *www.grahamhancock.com/forum/SierraJ1-p4. php.*

Strabo, *Geography.* New York: Forgotten Books, 2012.

Sullivan, William. *The Secret of the Incas: Myth, Astronomy, and the War Against Time.* New York: Crown Publishers, 1996.

Talbot, Michael. *The Holographic Universe: The Revolutionary Theory of Reality.* San Francisco, Calif.: Harper Perennial, 2011.

Temple, Robert. *The Sirius Mystery.* London: Sidgwick & Jackson, 1976.

——. *The Crystal Sun: Rediscovering a Lost Technology of the Ancient World.* London: Century, 2000.

——. *Egyptian Dawn.* London: Century, 2010.

Temple, Robert, with Olivia Temple. *The Sphinx Mystery: The Forgotten Origins of the Sanctuary of Anubis.* Rochester, Vt.: Inner Traditions, 2009.

Thom, Alexander. *Megalithic Sites in Britain.* Oxford: Oxford University Press, 1976.

Thompson, Gunnar. *Nu Sun: Asian-American Voyages 500 B.C.* Fresno, Calif.: Pioneer Publishing, 1989.

Thomson, Hugh. *The White Rock: An Exploration of the Inca Heartland.* London: Phoenix, 2001.

Tompkins, Peter. *Secrets of the Great Pyramid,* London: Allen Lane.

Vinci, Felice. *The Baltic Origins of Homer's Epic Tales: The Iliad, the Odyssey, and the Migration of Myth.* Rochester, Vt.: Inner Traditions, 2006.

Von Däniken, Erich. *Arrival of the Gods.* Element Books, 1998.

Von Dechend, Hertha, and Giorgio de Santillana. *Hamlet's Mill: An Essay Investigating the Origins of Human Knowledge and its Transmission Through Myth.* Boston, Mass.: Nonpareil, 1969.

Wilford, John Noble. "Mummies, Textiles Offer Evidence of Europeans in Far East." *New York Times,* May 7, 1996. Available at *www.nytimes.com/1996/05/07/science/mummies-textiles-offer-evidence-of-europeans-in-far-east.html?pagewanted=all&src=pm.*

Wilkens, Iman Jacob. *Where Troy Once Stood: The Mystery of Homer's Iliad and Odyssey Revealed.* Groningen, Netherlands: Gopher Publishers, 2005.

Wilkins, Harold. *Secret Cities of Old South America.* New York: Cosimo Classics, 2008.

Wilson, Colin. *From Atlantis to the Sphinx. Recovering the Lost Wisdom of the Ancient World.* London: Virgin Books, 1996.

Wood, Michael. *The Road to Delphi: The Life and Afterlife of Oracles.* London: Chatto & Windus, 2004.

Xianlin, Ji, et al. *The Ancient Corpses of Xinjiang: The Peoples of Ancient Xinjiang and Their Culture.* Beijing: CIP, 1999.

Yenne, Bill. *Cities of Gold: Legendary Kingdoms, Quixotic Quests, and the Search for Fantastic New World Wealth.* Yardley, Pa.: Westholme, 2011.

Zangger, Eberhard. *The Flood from Heaven: Deciphering the Atlantis Legend.* New York: William Morrow, 1992.

Zapp, Ivar and George Erikson. Atlantis in America. Navigators of the Ancient World. Kempton: Adventures Unlimited Press, 1998.

Zitman, Wim. Kosmische Slinger der Tijden. Hollandscheveld: De Ring, 1993.

——. Sterrenbeeld van Horus. Uniek kleitablet brengt bakermat van voorouders van de Egyptische beschaving in kaart. Baarn: Tirion, 2000.

Index

315

About the Author

Philip Coppens's publishing career began at the age of 23, when he edited the legacy of the late Belgian historian Marcel Mestdagh's research into European megaliths into a much-anticipated sequel. That same year, he also helped edit a controversial non-fiction thriller on the theft of Jan Van Eyck's *The Adoration of the Lamb*, which was made into a documentary both for Flemish television and the BBC.

One thing that sets Coppens apart from other writers, it is that he is often ahead of the trends. He wrote the first guide in more than four decades about Rosslyn Chapel—the only one to do so before *The Da Vinci Code* made that Scottish chapel world-famous in 2003. He also researched the origins of the Mitchell-Hedges Crystal Skull before the 2008 *Indiana Jones and the Kingdom of the Crystal Skull* movie, resulting in a series of controversial articles, which even came to the attention of *The Washington Post*.

Among others, he is the author of *The Stone Puzzle of Rosslyn Chapel* (2002); *The Canopus Revelation* (2004); *Land of the Gods* (2007); *The New Pyramid Age* (2007); and *Servants of the Grail* (2009). Most recently, he published an e-book, *2012: Science or Fiction?*, which aims to bring clarity as to what 2012 is truly all about, and is the first to have incorporated video, featuring an interview-style conversation with Philip.

Philip has also contributed to, or been acknowledged in, the following publications: *Pre-Atlantis* (Dutch title), coauthor with Marcel Mestdagh (1994); *The Templar Revelation,* by Lynn Picknett and Clive Prince (1997); *The Stargate Conspiracy,* by Lynn Picknett and Clive Prince (1999); *Saunière's Model and the Secret of Rennes-le-Château,* by André Douzet (2001); *EGYPT: "Image of Heaven"—Het Sterrenbeeld van Horus* (Dutch title), with Wim Zitman (2006; Dutch edition 2000); *The Dan Brown Companion,* by Simon Cox (2006); *Rosslyn Revealed,* by Alan Butler & John Ritchie (2006); *The Cygnus Mystery,* by Andrew Collins (2006); *An A to Z of King Arthur and the Holy Grail,* by Simon Cox & Mark Oxbrow (2007); *Darklore (Volumes I, II and III),* compiled and edited by Greg Taylor (2007–2009); *Unearthing Ancient America,* compiled and edited by Frank Joseph (2009); and *Exposed, Uncovered, & Declassified: Lost Civilizations & Secrets of the Past,* by Kirsten Dalley and Michael Pye, editors (2011).

Apart from books, Philip also devotes a lot of attention to essays and feature articles, which have appeared in magazines and anthologies on all continents. His articles have appeared in *Fortean Times, NEXUS, Hera, Fenix, Mysterien, New Dawn, Atlantis Rising, Ancient American, Paranoia Magazine,* and more, and has a large and dedicated following on the Internet. He holds the record as having most articles published in NEXUS, a magazine published in more than 10 languages, with newsstand distribution in Australia, Great Britain, the United States, Italy, France, and many other European countries.

Since 1995, he has lectured on the subject in the United States, Great Britain, France, Australia, Belgium, and the Netherlands. He has been extensively interviewed for radio and television, including Belgium's Kanaal 2 and VRT news, Voyager (RaiDue—Italy), and Edge Media TV (UK). He is also one of the key contributors and interviewees for The History Channel's most popular television series *Ancient Aliens,* for the fourth season running.

All of these books, articles, and appearances have made him a household name in the field of alternative science, where he holds a unique position, as he is considered to be a believer by the skeptics, and a skeptic by the believers—a testament to his investigative knack.

His Website is *www.philipcoppens.com.* He can be followed on Facebook at *www.facebook.com/coppensphilip* and on Twitter at *www.twitter.com/philipcoppens.*